To Dearest Dom,

The King of Acton!

Happy Birthday.

Lots of love,

Grant, Janet & Orla.

xxxxx

KINGS
OF THE KING'S
ROAD

KINGS
OF THE KING'S
ROAD

Clive Batty

VSP

Vision Sports Publishing
2 Coombe Gardens,
London, SW20 0QU

www.visionsp.co.uk

This First Edition Published by
Vision Sports Publishing in 2004

© Clive Batty 2004

ISBN 0-9546428-1-3

Editor: Jim Drewett
Design: David Hicks

Set in Village 9.5pt/13pt
Typeset by Palimpsest Book Production Limited, Polmont, Stirlingshire

Printed and bound in the UK by
Cromwell Press

A CIP catalogue record for this book is available from the British Library

CONTENTS

ACKNOWLEDGEMENTS

This book would not have been possible without the generous contributions of the Chelsea players who were more than willing to discuss every aspect of their careers at the club. Special thanks, then, are due to Tommy Baldwin, Alan Birchenall, John Boyle, John Dempsey, Tommy Docherty, Mickey Droy, Steve Finnieston, Ron Harris, Tony Hateley, Marvin Hinton, Alan Hudson and Peter Osgood.

Doug Hayward, Alvaro Maccioni, Terry O'Neill and Eric Swayne provided some great stories for the chapter on the King's Road, while Mark Colby, Tony Easter, Ron Hockings Andy Jackson, Jim Luck, Fred Roll and Ray Taylor made equally valuable contributions to the fans' chapter.

Thanks also to Matthew Hirtes, who lent me a number of reference books and pointed me in the direction of some useful websites. Despite being an ardent Manchester United fan, Dave Hicks did a superb job designing the cover and the lay-out. Jim Drewett, my editor/publisher at Vision Sports, was a constant source of (mostly excellent) ideas and encouragement. I would also like to thank his business partner Toby Trotman for giving his backing to this project.

Finally, thanks to my father, Robert, who took me to my first Chelsea match in 1971 shortly before my ninth birthday.

FOREWORD
BY ALAN HUDSON

I am delighted to add my memories to this terrific book. Playing in this magnificent Chelsea team was unbelievably exciting, and it's fantastic that Clive Batty has re-united us all on these pages so we can all re-live those great days.

I was just 17 when I broke into the Chelsea team in 1969. The youngest member of a wonderful side, full of talented individuals and colourful personalities. It took me a little while to settle in, and I didn't feel I'd really arrived until just before Christmas that year when we went up to Old Trafford and beat Manchester United – George Best, Bobby Charlton, Denis Law and all – by a couple of goals. After that anything seemed possible. And with the team we had, anything *was* possible.

Every player in the side contributed something special. When Charlie Cooke, that great entertainer, was on the ball I could just stand and watch, marvelling at his skill. Then, when Peter Osgood got the bit between his teeth and was really in the mood, nothing or nobody could stop him. His sidekick Hutch, the bravest of the brave, was like a walking time bomb, ready to explode into action at any time. McCreadie was another class act, simply breathtaking in his early years when no one had ever seen a full back whizzing up and down the pitch like that before. Eddie could also pick opponents off like a sniper in waiting. So could the rest of our defence. Ronnie 'Buller' Harris was one of those players who love seeing an opponent in pain while Webby just revelled in being a part of this band of rogues. Dempsey and Hinton were two unsung heroes who were both vastly under-rated, and the same was true of 'Nobby' Houseman – an educated player who took a lot of stick without batting an eyelid, and kept raking in those crosses for our deadly duo, Ossie and Hutch.

John Hollins, running all over the pitch, was the 'here, there and every-where' man of the team. Then there was Tommy 'the Sponge' Baldwin, a player who just loved shooting at the opponent's goal at every oppor-tunity. He'd run until he dropped for our band of brothers and, if there was any consolation in my missing that epic Cup Final against Leeds, it was that the Sponge took my shirt. But it still never really eased the blow! Last, but far from least, was 'the Cat'. How this slim, not especially tall man could leap above those giant centre forwards of the time almost defied logic. He was a class act and every Chelsea supporter will agree we would not have swapped him for any other keeper in the world!

So many gifted individuals, so many strong personalities. For managers Tommy Docherty and Dave Sexton putting the whole thing together must have been a bit like working on a jigsaw puzzle, an analogy I explore further in my new book, *The Tinker and Talisman*, an in-depth account of more recent developments at the Bridge and much more besides. Tommy and Dave had a tough job, and the players didn't always see eye-to-eye with them.

Perhaps that was because off the pitch we were like a bunch of desper-adoes riding into Dodge City looking for excitement. Pubs, afternoon drinking clubs and nightclubs were all part of our regular itinerary. We'd tie up our horses and the whole saloon would turn their heads. When Charlie and the Sponge were out it was a case of 'watch out' – that pair of pranksters were far more dangerous than anything Jeremy Beadle could come up with. As for me, the King's Road was my hunting ground and the boys used me as their scout, tipping them off about all the latest pubs, clubs, restaurants and clothes shops. The sixties were in full swing and the upbeat tempo of that very special period was reflected in our style of play – both on and off the pitch.

I can't write about those times without mentioning our wonderful supporters. Coming home on the train from away games we used to drink with the fans, and we did the same after home games in the pubs near the Bridge. In those days players would mix with their supporters almost as if they were part of the team – well, of course, they were!

Kings of the King's Road is a complete one-off: a brilliant recreation of some incredible times, told through the words of the players and the fans. Clive has done a superb job in bringing all the stories together and, over a pint or two on the King's Road, it's been a real pleasure chatting to him about a truly fabulous era.

INTRODUCTION

LONG LIVE THE KINGS

INTRODUCTION
LONG LIVE THE KINGS

helsea v Bruges, 24th March 1971. Stamford Bridge. European Cup Winners' Cup Quarter Final. Alan Hudson, his long hair almost reaching down to the white number 10 on the back of his royal blue shirt, dribbles the ball to the by-line at the Shed end. A Belgian defender, having spotted the danger, lunges in but it's too late. Hudson has already pulled the ball back to Peter Osgood, lurking unmarked near the penalty post. Osgood, dark frizzy sideburns covering most of his cheeks, steadies himself before smashing a left-footer into the back of the net. It takes a fraction of a second for the crowd to react, and then Stamford Bridge is engulfed by a tidal wave of noise. The place goes mad. Chelsea have come from two goals down to book a place in the semi-final. Later that evening Osgood, Hudson and the rest of the Chelsea team will relive the goal as, surrounded by jubilant fans, they sink a few celebratory pints in the Lord Palmerston pub, a short distance from the ground at the top of the King's Road. Who says the glory days are just arriving at Stamford Bridge?

In July 2004, shortly before Chelsea set out on a pre-season tour of America, club director Paul Smith was asked by a reporter from *The Times* to outline the "brand image" the Blues would be attempting to build in the States and elsewhere around the globe. Smith's response was curt. "It's not as if Chelsea came out of nowhere," he replied. "There's still something [at the club] reminiscent of the 'Swinging Sixties'"

It is perhaps ironic that Chelsea – a club powered by Roman Abramovich's millions, and generally considered to be drivingly ambitious and forward-looking – should seek to define itself by harking back to the past. Yet, for many older fans especially, Smith's comments made perfect sense. If anything, they rather understated the influence that the late sixties and early seventies continue to exert at the club.

The casual visitor to the Bridge will find few visible signs of this decades-old heritage – in stark contrast to Anfield or Elland Road, for instance, where statues of club legends Bill Shankly and Billy Bremner are monuments to past glories. At Chelsea, lounge bars named after former heroes Peter Osgood, Bobby Tambling and Roy Bentley are virtually the only reminders of the great triumphs of yesteryear.

Dig a little below the surface, however, and modern-day Chelsea's connections with the 'Swinging Sixties' – an era of change which, incidentally, most social commentators agree continued well into the 1970s, possibly even until the birth of punk in 1976 – become more apparent. Take two of the songs played in the pre-match build-up at every game at the Bridge, for instance. The club's 1972 League Cup Final theme tune *Blue is the Colour* is still the Chelsea anthem, more than 30 years after it made the top 10. Likewise, *The Liquidator* – a hit for Harry J and the Allstars way back in 1969 – remains a vital, not-to-be-missed, foot-stomping, hand-clapping three minute demonstration of support for the Blues fully 35 years after it reached the charts and was adopted as a battle-cry by the Shed. A straw poll of fans attending the Bridge, meanwhile, would almost certainly reveal the following: a) a disproportionate number of supporters are aged 40 or over; b) a similarly disproportionate number of fans who date their support for the club back to the 1970 FA Cup Final (or a little bit before – after all, no supporter cares to be lumbered with the 'glory hunter' tag); and c) the 1970s royal blue Chelsea kit, unsullied by sponsors' logos and featuring the original club badge, is most fans' all-time favourite Blues kit.

Cynics may dismiss all this as misty-eyed nostalgia, but there's no denying that the 1970s still resonate at Stamford Bridge. Most importantly, the flamboyant Chelsea team of the period gave the club a legacy of entertaining, attractive, attacking play – 'sexy football' if you like, a quarter of a century before Ruud Gullit coined the term – which lives on to this day. Playing with style, panache and a swaggering self-confidence which bordered on the arrogant, the Chelsea sides created by managers Tommy Docherty and Dave Sexton helped define the club's image for years to come. Even now, if you ask any football fan which words come to mind when they think of Chelsea the answer is likely to include the following: 'flashy', 'stylish', 'cocky', 'inconsistent'. All of which, with plenty of justification, was said about the seventies team.

Individually, the players possessed personality and character in abundance. In goal, Peter Bonetti was a breathtakingly acrobatic keeper who lived up to his famous nickname, 'the Cat'. In defence, skipper Ron 'Chopper' Harris' scything tackles made him a cult figure on the terraces, while fellow defender David Webb was the team's 'Mr Versatilty', filling virtually every position on the pitch, including goalkeeper, at one time or another. At the other end of the pitch Charlie Cooke and Alan Hudson, two midfielders blessed with exquisite technique and oodles of imagination, provided much of the side's hallmark flair and creativity. The focal point of the attack, charismatic centre forward Peter Osgood, 'The King of Stamford Bridge' to his adoring fans in the Shed, was a genuine superstar for whom the spectacular was the norm. With their fashionably long hair and bushy sideburns, their shirts hanging out and their socks rolled down, the Blues team of the seventies had a rock star image and, increasingly as the decade wore on, the rebellious attitude to match.

Although deadly serious about winning, the Chelsea lads also had a highly developed sense of fun which was wholly lacking in some of their stern-faced rivals. This was sometimes expressed in a well-rehearsed routine which invariably hoodwinked even the top referees of the day.

"Alan Hudson used to come out at half time and put the ball down to kick off, even if we'd already done so in the first half," Ian Hutchinson once revealed. "Huddy did that about ten times a season and usually got away with it. The odd time we would get caught. That summed up playing for Chelsea – taking the piss and having a laugh. Nevertheless, when the nitty-gritty came, we were up for it too."

Off the pitch, meanwhile, most of the team fully embraced the goodies – sexual freedom, fashionable clothes and groovy hairstyles – thrown up by the Swinging Sixties. From their base just off the King's Road, the cultural capital of London at the time, the Chelsea boys – especially those like Hudson, Baldwin and Cooke who lived up in town, rather than in the stockbrokers' belt in leafy Surrey – enjoyed a champagne lifestyle. They mixed with pop stars, actors and some of the most glamorous women of the age, including Raquel Welch, the dancers from Pan's People and, when George Best didn't get in there first, a Miss World or two. At the same time, they never lost contact with their fans, and were just as likely to be spotted downing a few post-match pints in a pub round the corner from the Bridge as dining at an exclusive King's Road eaterie.

"It was an absolutely fabulous era," says Alan Birchenall. "I don't care who you are or what the players earn today, anyone who was around in the sixties and seventies will say the same. I've got great football memories, but I've got even better memories from the life we lived. When I turn my toes up I probably won't remember a single match, but I'll remember everything around the game. The present day players think they've got it made, they think they invented having a good time, but it's simply not true."

Sometimes the quest for a good time landed the players in trouble – usually with the Bridge management, frequently with the football authorities and, occasionally, with the Metropolitan Police. The English game has always produced its fair share of rebels, mavericks and non-conformists but, perhaps, no team has ever boasted as many such characters as the Chelsea side of the late sixties and early seventies.

"If anybody had filmed what went on all this stuff about what the celebrities get up to in the jungle would be second-rate," says Alan Hudson, summing up his days as a member of the King's Road rat pack.

Well, the cameras may not have been there but that matters little when the main players have such vivid memories of one of the most colourful periods in Chelsea history.

CHAPTER ONE
BUILDING THE TEAM

CHAPTER ONE
BUILDING THE TEAM

In the autumn of 1961 Chelsea, not for the first time in the club's history, were in some disarray. Six years earlier, in 1955, thousands of fans had celebrated on the pitch at Stamford Bridge as the Blues had marked their 50th anniversary by winning the league championship for the first time. The intervening years, however, had been mediocre ones, redeemed only by the remarkable goalscoring feats of the young Jimmy Greaves.

Now, though, Greaves had gone – sold to AC Milan for £80,000 after a final prolific season at the Bridge in which he had scored 43 goals, including four in his last match for the club at home against Nottingham Forest. Gone, too, were nearly all the old championship-winning heroes: captain Roy Bentley, Eric 'The Rabbit' Parsons and future England manager Ron Greenwood. Indeed, just two regular members of the 1955 side remained: full-back Peter Sillett, whose Easter Saturday penalty against Wolves in front of 75,000 fans at the Bridge had virtually clinched the title; and fleet-footed winger Frank Blunstone, the youngest member of the class of '55 at just 21.

After a poor start to the 1961/62 season saw the Blues win just one of their first six matches, Chelsea chairman Joe Mears decided that manager Ted Drake, who had been in charge of the team since 1952, would benefit from the services of an assistant. Having made enquiries among his contacts in the game, Mears offered Arsenal's Tommy Docherty, a former Scottish international wing-half, the role of Chelsea player/coach.

"Mr Mears contacted the FA, and they suggested Jimmy Adamson, who was at Burnley, and myself," recalls Docherty. "Jimmy wanted to continue playing, but I was 33, and quite happy to get involved in coaching. At the interview Mr Mears said he knew nothing about football, and his directors even less – so I thought, 'Well, that'll do me'."

Docherty immediately made his playing debut for Chelsea, helping the Blues to a morale-boosting 6-1 win over Sheffield United, a match in which 19-year-old striker Bobby Tambling confirmed his potential as a possible successor to Greaves by scoring his first hat-trick for the club. The result, though, did not kick-start a recovery and Drake's mix of old stagers and inexperienced youngsters continued to flounder.

The life of a football manager has always been perilous but in those days poor results did not inevitably lead to the sack. Moreover, having steered the Blues to their greatest triumph, Drake could rely on the residual loyalty of most board members. All the same, the directors' patience was not infinite and, apart from understandable worries over the team's unimpressive form, there was a growing feeling among the board that Drake had become something of yesterday's man.

In the early 1960s football was moving into a new, more glamorous era. The abolition of the maximum wage was fundamental to this sea change in social perceptions of the game. Overnight top players, notably Fulham and England captain Johnny Haynes, were able to negotiate wage increases from £20 to £100 a week. At last, fortune as well as fame beckoned the successful. Drake, though, gave little impression of being the man to lead Chelsea into this exciting, if unknown, territory. His greatest achievements – winning the championship, his bold introduction of the teenage Jimmy Greaves and his successful campaign to replace the old 'Pensioners' tag with a new nickname, 'The Blues' – were all firmly in the past. Regarded as an aloof figure by many of the younger players, and presiding over a divided team with low morale, his stock was no longer high. Finally, in late September 1961, after a crushing 4-0 defeat at Blackpool, the Chelsea board decided to act.

"I was about to fly up with Ted Drake to Scotland, because we were interested in signing Celtic's Pat Crerand," remembers Tommy Docherty. "But before we left we were asked to wait until after the board had met. I was waiting outside the boardroom when Mr Battersby, the club secretary, came out and said, 'Ted Drake has gone.'

'What, to Scotland?' I said.

'No,' he said. 'He's gone.'

He'd resigned, or been sacked – whatever you want to call it. So the board asked me to take over as caretaker and I agreed."

Docherty's appointment was made permanent in January 1962 and the new manager's wages were doubled from £30 to £60 a week. An ebullient, energetic and dynamic figure with a gift for a sharp one-liner, 'the Doc' quickly set to work, tightening discipline, organising more rigorous and physically demanding training sessions, and swiftly assessing which players fitted into his new Chelsea vision. The ones who didn't, or didn't care for the new regime, were soon sent packing.

"The big problem at the club was that there were too many old players swinging the lead," says Docherty. "There was a real split between them and the youngsters coming through, who had won the FA Youth Cup two years running. Some of the established players – Ron Tindall, Reg Matthews, the Sillett brothers – even wanted the young ones to call them 'mister'. It was ridiculous. Anyway, I soon got rid of the dead wood and the players who weren't up to it."

Although the club was struggling, Docherty knew that Chelsea's future was potentially a bright one. For some years, the Blues' youth system had been renowned as one of the best in the country, rivalled only by Manchester United's. Drake's predecessor, Billy Birrell, deserved much of the credit as he had established the club's first junior scheme, called 'Tudor Rose', in 1947. Renamed Chelsea Youth two years later, under the direction of Dick Foss, a former Blues player, a stream of talented footballers emerged from the youth team's base at the Old Welsh Harp ground in Hendon. In the second half of the 1950s players such as Peter Brabrook, Les Allen, Ron Tindall and, of course, Jimmy Greaves were among those to come through the junior ranks to make a mark in the professional game. Ultimately, though, the so-called 'Drake's Ducklings', with the obvious exception of Greaves, had failed to fulfil their promise. Now another generation of highly-rated young players – some of whom had already been thrust into the first team by Drake – had been developed on the Hendon production line.

Among the players falling into this bracket was Peter Bonetti, an extraordinarily agile goalkeeper whose quick reflexes had earned him the nickname 'the Cat'. Unlike most other keepers at the time, Bonetti was not afraid to come off his line to collect crosses and would even advance beyond the penalty spot to claim corners and free-kicks. His biggest weakness was his kicking which lacked power, a deficiency he compensated for by throwing the ball out swiftly and accurately whenever possible.

Then aged just 18, Bonetti had taken the place of former England international Reg Matthews in the Chelsea team in April 1960, the same month in which he also helped the Blues win the FA Youth Cup. His first full season in the Chelsea side, 1960/61, had not been an easy one: playing behind a defence which was little more than a shambles, the Cat had only managed to keep one clean sheet in 36 league appearances. Nonetheless, this depressing statistic could not disguise his outstanding natural ability.

Chelsea's defence, which had conceded a club record 100 league goals in Drake's last full season at the club, was by far the weakest area of the team when Docherty arrived on the scene. True, the same could be said for many other clubs, yet even in an era of attacking formations which tended to encourage high scoring games Chelsea's back line was well known for its generosity. For some time under Drake a lack of defensive organisation had been apparent, regardless of which players he picked. If the Blues were to have any chance of avoiding the drop, Docherty needed to remedy this flaw – and fast.

One of his first decisions, then, was to fill the two full back positions with youth products Allan Harris and Ken Shellito. On the left, Harris was a steady if unspectacular performer, while on the opposite flank Ken Shellito was a pacy, technically accomplished player who liked to get forward. However, there was no short-term solution to the lack of an effective partnership in the centre of defence, a bugbear for a number of seasons. Docherty tried several players in this key area but, whatever the combination, the goals still flooded in – another 94 in the 'goals against' column by the end of the 1961/62 season.

There was better quality in midfield, where Terry Venables was already building a reputation as a sharp, quick passer with an eye for the killer ball. On the wings Blunstone and Bert Murray, yet another youth product, were pencilled in by Docherty as mainstays of his revamped side, particularly after long-serving right-winger Peter Brabrook moved on to West Ham in the summer of 1962. Up front, meanwhile, Tambling and fellow Chelsea homegrown Barry Bridges both possessed blistering pace and could be guaranteed to score their share of goals – 42 in total by the end of Docherty's first half season in charge.

The duo's goals, though, were not enough to prevent Chelsea finishing bottom of the table. Relegation, which had always appeared likely, was duly confirmed a couple of games from the end of the campaign and the Blues went down with Cardiff City. Despite this setback, Docherty was far from down-hearted and remained convinced that, once his rebuilding work was finished and the 'dead wood' had been completely rooted out, he would have the basis of a decent team.

While the Doc continued his sweeping purge, new players came in. Welsh international striker Graham Moore was signed from Cardiff and East Stirling left-back Eddie McCreadie, who had impressed when Docherty visited Stirling's Firs Park ground on a scouting mission for another player, was snapped up for a paltry £5,000. Strong, quick, skilful on the ball and a forceful tackler, McCreadie possessed all the attributes Docherty was looking for in a full back and would prove to be an inspired signing. In the dressing room, meanwhile, the new arrival's poor eyesight quickly gained him the nickname 'Clarence', after the cross-eyed lion in the hit TV series *Daktari*.

Back in the Second Division for the first time since 1930, Chelsea faced stiff competition for the two automatic promotion places. Middlesbrough, Newcastle and Sunderland, who had just missed out on promotion by one point, were all expected to mount a strong challenge from the north-east. Leeds, under new manager Don Revie, had only just escaped relegation to the Third Division the previous season but, like Chelsea, had an exceptional crop of youngsters coming through the ranks. Stoke, who still had wing maestro Stanley Matthews on their books at the age of 47, were also fancied to do well.

Realising that it would be a huge gamble to take on such powerful rivals with youthful promise alone, Docherty fortified his young side with three experienced pros: Blunstone, long-serving centre-half John Mortimore and, alongside him, Frank 'the Tank' Upton, a tough defender Ted Drake had signed from Derby shortly before his departure from the Bridge. Their role would partly be a paternal one, encouraging the younger players when form and confidence dipped.

Tactically, Docherty had been influenced by the Brazilian side which had won the 1962 World Cup using overlapping full-backs in an innovative 4-3-3 formation which the Chelsea manager was keen to copy. The Blues had the players to duplicate this newfangled attacking ploy, as Ken Shellito on the right and Eddie McCreadie on the opposite flank both possessed the pace, skill and stamina needed to make regular forward raids from deep. The rest of the team was also set up offensively, with Venables directing play from his position as the midfield lynchpin, Murray and Blunstone providing width and Tambling, Bridges and Moore forming a three-pronged spearhead.

Second Division defenders in 1962 weren't really designed to counter South American-style attacking manoeuvres; given the choice they preferred to battle, scrap and trade broken noses with a couple of heftily-built centre forwards. So, in this unsophisticated environment, Chelsea's fluid movement, quick-fire passing and supercharged counter-attacks had a surprise factor that proved irresistible. By Christmas the Blues were seven points clear of the chasing pack and still unbeaten at home. Among the teams to have left the Bridge empty-handed were Charlton (5–0), Cardiff (6–0) and Newcastle (4–2). The fans were impressed and so, too, were the critics.

"They possess the poise, speed, method and spirit of a side that could flower into a commanding force over the coming seasons," one reporter predicted after a 2–0 win over Norwich at the Bridge in November 1962. "No doubt there are two or three positions that need developing if they are to live on more than mere nodding terms with the Tottenhams, Evertons and Burnleys of this age . . . but it is the future that beckons. It could be rich and full indeed if Chelsea's young men fulfil their promise."

Throughout the first half of the season Barry Bridges and, especially, Bobby Tambling had been scoring goals at a Greaves-like rate, while Docherty's new look back four had rediscovered the art of defending, conceding an average of less than a goal per game. Nothing, it seemed, could stop Chelsea's promotion bandwagon. Except, perhaps, the weather. The winter of 1962/63 was one of the worst on record: temperatures plummeted to Siberian levels, thick snow covered the country from Cornwall to the Clyde and toboggan sales soared. Inevitably, football fell victim to the Arctic conditions with hundreds of matches being postponed.

By the time the Blues eventually resumed their league campaign in February 1963 the fizz had completely evaporated from the side. A run of five straight defeats saw Chelsea's lead eaten up and prompted Docherty to move into the transfer market for West Brom striker Derek Kevan and veteran schemer Tommy Harmer, a former Tottenham player. Neither, though, figured prominently in the initial stages of the run-in which saw the Blues' erratic form continue. Far from being favourites for promotion, Chelsea were now just one of a number of clubs, including Stoke, Sunderland, Leeds and Middlesborough, with aspirations of filling one of the top two places. Everything would depend on the Blues' last three games, at home to Stoke, away to Sunderland and at home to Portsmouth.

On May 11th, Chelsea's biggest crowd for three years, 66,199, squeezed into the Bridge for the visit of Stoke and their ancient winger Matthews.

Stan, soon to become Sir Stanley, might have been a pre-war relic but he was still capable of giving the Chelsea defence a torrid time. So, in a bid to nullify the winger's influence, Docherty instructed 18-year-old Ron Harris, playing in one of his first games for the Blues, to follow Matthews all over the pitch.

The brother of Allan and a talented all-round sportsman who had played schoolboy cricket for England, Ron had made his Chelsea debut the previous season and Docherty had been sufficiently impressed by the young defender to recall him for the promotion run-in. A specialist man-marker who stuck to his prey like a limpet, Ron was quickly making a name for himself as one of the toughest tacklers in the game.

The match against Stoke was pivotal in establishing this reputation. On a number of occasions Harris hacked down Matthews as he dinked his way down the wing. Even the home fans, upset by what they saw as the unnecessarily brutal treatment of a national institution, booed the youngster. Harris, though, remained unperturbed and would joke later that the reason why Matthews struggled to get up after being repeatedly felled was because he suffered from arthritis. Still, on this occasion, Matthews had the last laugh as his side's 1-0 win virtually guaranteed Stoke promotion

The defeat left Chelsea needing to win at Sunderland to retain their hopes of going up. A home win or draw, meanwhile, would see the Rokerites promoted at the Blues' expense. Essentially, the match was a cup final and the whole of Wearside wanted to see it. "We stayed in a hotel near the ground," remembers Docherty, "and the day before the match you could see people queuing up outside to get in the next day."

In what he would later describe as "the biggest gamble of my life", Docherty dropped Bridges and Moore and replaced them with a heavy-weight strike force of Kevan and Upton, who was more used to stopping goals than scoring them. If the plan was to batter the Sunderland defence into submission, it wasn't one which appeared to worry the home team.

"On the way into Roker that day, I met Brian Clough, who was out of the Sunderland side through injury," recalled Frank Upton. "He said, 'What are they playing you up front for – a joke?'" The joke, though, was on Sunderland as Chelsea hung on for a 1-0 win after a first half corner flicked off little Tommy Harmer's groin and bobbled over the line.

"We went up there with a side packed with defenders and people who could look after themselves," said Bobby Tambling later. "We knew it wasn't going to be pretty, but the result bore out the tactics. It was tremendously windy and Peter Bonetti couldn't reach the 18-yard line with his kicks. I think we played the whole of the second half pinned in our box, after Tommy Harmer scored probably the most important goal of his career."

In the dressing room afterwards there was much discussion about which part of Harmer's anatomy had got the vital touch. Was it his thigh, stomach . . . or somewhere else? Harmer ended the debate in unconventional manner, as Bert Murray related later: "He whipped his little dick out and was swinging it around, pointing to it and saying, 'It hit this, it hit this.'"

Buoyed by the crucial victory at Roker Park, Chelsea approached their final match against Portsmouth three days later in good spirits. A win would put the Blues level on points with Sunderland, who had finished their campaign, leaving the second promotion spot behind champions Stoke to be decided by goal average. Chelsea just had the edge in this department so a victory by any margin over Pompey would guarantee promotion.

Fielding the same team that had beaten Sunderland, the Blues tore into a Portsmouth side containing future Chelsea manager Bobby Campbell. To the joy of the home fans, Derek Kevan gave them a second minute lead and after that it became a rout. Three-nil up at half-time Chelsea went on to win 7–0 with Bobby Tambling hitting four of the goals to take his season's tally to 37. At the final whistle, hundreds of youths poured onto the pitch, thrilled that the promotion which had seemed a certainty before Christmas had finally been achieved.

In truth, Chelsea had limped over the line. A haul of 15 points from the last 18 matches was near-relegation form – even in those days of two points for a win – and didn't augur well for the coming season back in the big time. Not that Docherty was worried. "I was very confident we'd do well because the players could only get better," he says. "We had a young team – some of the boys were just 18 or 19 – but that year in the Second Division gave them all a bit more experience."

Nonetheless, the First Division would be a different matter altogether. A little over a year earlier the Blues' young team had struggled in the top flight and some fans, especially those of a more pessimistic disposition than the Chelsea manager, couldn't help wondering if history was about to repeat itself.

CHAPTER TWO

DOCHERTY'S DIAMONDS

CHAPTER TWO
DOCHERTY'S DIAMONDS

In the early 1960s clubs that had won promotion to the First Division, unlike their Premiership counterparts today, could look forward to rather more than a fight for survival. In season 1961/62, for instance, Alf Ramsey's Ipswich Town amazed everybody, including their own fans, by becoming league champions a year after winning the Second Division title. The following season Liverpool, after nearly a decade out of the top flight, had made a less spectacular but nonetheless worry-free return to the First Division finishing eighth. Doing 'an Ipswich' might be beyond them, but Tommy Docherty had every expectation that his youthful Chelsea side could perform at least as well as the Merseysiders.

In preparation for the forthcoming season, Docherty made few changes to the squad that had won promotion. In the summer of 1963 Derek Kevan, having played just seven games for the Blues, moved on to Manchester City for £40,000. Graham Moore followed soon afterwards, joining Manchester United. In the newspapers, meanwhile, there were rumours that the name Chelsea might be changed to 'Kensington FC' as the Royal Borough of Chelsea became the Royal Borough of Kensington – predictably, the stories turned out to be nothing more than 'silly season' gossip.

Suitably relieved, the fans looked forward to the new season with keen anticipation. Season tickets, priced at £6–£12, were much in demand, while the less affluent supporter only needed to stump up two shillings (10p) to get on the terraces. For fans who liked something to read on the tube or bus home, the Chelsea programme was available for a further sixpence (2p).

After beginning the season with two disappointing 0–0 draws against West Ham and Burnley, the Blues adapted quickly to life back in the First Division. The team certainly didn't look out of place in the top flight and, following a good run of form in November and December, remained tucked in behind title contenders Liverpool, Manchester United, Everton and Spurs.

Peter Bonetti, his confidence boosted by a dependable back line in front of him, was rapidly emerging as one of the best and most spectacular goalkeepers in the country, although the imperious Gordon Banks blocked his path to international honours with England. The back four of Ron Harris – now christened 'Chopper' by the fans, in tribute to his ferocious tackling – Mortimore, McCreadie and Shellito was solid and uncompromising, but also possessed attacking flair on the flanks. In midfield, Terry Venables revelled in his role as the team's conductor, threading astute passes forwards for the pacy Tambling and Bridges to race onto, while wingers Murray and Blunstone provided a stream of crosses and their fair share of goals.

Among the season's highlights were a 5–1 Boxing Day win at Blackpool and a 4–0 thumping of former champs Ipswich at the Bridge in February. Before the final match of the season at home to Everton, Chelsea fans were treated to a display by the Butlins' Young Ladies dancing troupe before settling back to watch a Bert Murray penalty give the Blues the points to secure fifth place, seven points behind champions Liverpool. "We were all quite happy with that after having just come up," says the Doc. "We had a great side, full of skill and speed."

The major disappointment of the campaign came in the FA Cup, the Blues surprisingly losing 2–1 at home to Second Division Huddersfield in the fourth round after having knocked out Tottenham in the third.

The summer of 1964 produced more changes in the side. Frank Blunstone was forced to retire after suffering an achilles tendon injury in training, although he stayed on at the club to coach the Chelsea juniors where future star Alan Hudson was one of his protégés. To fill the gap left by Blunstone's retirement, Docherty toyed with the idea of promoting Peter Houseman, an 18-year-old left-winger from Battersea who had made a handful of appearances the previous season. Deciding that Houseman was too raw, the Doc bought Aston Villa's tall, elegant striker George Graham for a mere £5,000, partnered him with Barry Bridges up front and moved the left-footed Tambling to the wing. Problem solved.

A second new face in the team was youth product John Hollins, a tireless box-to-box midfielder with a strong shot whose equally tireless chatting earned him the nickname 'Ena', after the *Coronation Street* gossip Ena Sharples. With Ken Shellito's appearances restricted by a chronic knee injury, in

September 1963 Docherty had splashed out £30,000 on Charlton's Marvin Hinton, a cultured, smooth-passing defender who was just as happy playing in the centre of defence as at right-back. And by the start of the 1964/65 season Hinton would be a regular in the team, while Shellito's ongoing injury problems made him an increasingly peripheral figure. "Marvin was a fantastic player; he was great at coming out with the ball and, because he hated having to run, he never made a bad pass," says Docherty.

A further change was to the team strip. The shirts, of course, remained blue but the colours of the old shorts (white) and socks (blue) were reversed, giving Chelsea a snazzy, modern look which suited the team's fast, upbeat, vibrant playing style. By now, too, the Blues had a second nickname, 'Docherty's Diamonds', which was born after the manager had been captured by the TV cameras high up in the East Stand shouting, "Come on, my little diamonds!" Following a series of pre-season friendlies against strong continental opposition, the Diamonds were ready to sparkle.

Chelsea got off to a scorching start – in fact, the best ever in the club's history in the top flight – winning seven and drawing three of their opening ten games. For the first time in a long while, the football world was having to take the Blues seriously. "Chelsea, now bubbling over with youth and vitality, no longer look the sort of team music hall comedians can joke about," commented Geoffrey Green in *The Times*.

A significant factor in the team's improvement was the promotion of Dave Sexton from assistant coach, a position he had held since February to 1962, to first-team coach in September 1964. Thoughtful, quietly spoken and with a football brain the size of a small planet, Sexton was the ideal man to complement the bubbly, irrepressible Docherty and the players responded well to their chalk-and-cheese partnership.

"Dave and the Doc were the perfect pair," said Bobby Tambling some years later. "Docherty was the greatest motivator of players I have ever known. He used to build us all up so that we felt ten feet tall. He would pick his moment to boost the confidence of an individual and we all got the treatment at some time or another. He would tell the boys from the press that so-and-so was a great player and when you read the things that were written about you, you started to believe you could play a bit. Dave, on the other hand, was more reserved. But his knowledge of the game was tremendous and he really knew how to bring the best out of each player by concentrating on their qualities. If you had skill, Dave would bring it out."

John Boyle, yet another teenager who made his debut in the 1964/65 season, was also hugely impressed by the Docherty-Sexton combination. "Tommy and Dave were very open to new ideas," he says. "Tommy was almost like a revolutionary figure in football – along came this wise-cracking Glaswegian, who was only about 35 at the time, and he thought the best thing he could do was to get rid of the old players. Luckily enough, all the young players were ready to come through to the first team. And he added a few astute signings. As a manager he was great. If he said, 'There's a wall, I want you to go through it', you'd only say 'How?' not 'Why?'

"He dramatically improved the work-rate. Suddenly there were people all over the field running hard. The athleticism was greatly improved. If you look back to videos of games in the fifties they are very pedestrian, but Tommy really worked on that. He wanted to play a high tempo game. He got midfield players who would put people under pressure rather than giving them time to play, full-backs who would get forward and strikers with loads of pace."

Ron Harris agrees. "Tommy transformed Chelsea Football Club," he says. "I think his attitude, wherever he's been, is that youngsters never cheat you. In the side at that time we only had a couple of older heads, people like John Mortimore, Frank Blunstone and occasionally Tommy Harmer. So he got rid of all the older fellows, and I think one of the reason loads of youngsters went to Chelsea was that even at 17 if Tommy thought you were good enough he'd give you a chance."

In a revealing interview with *The Times* during the 1964/65 season, Docherty outlined the key elements of the football philosophy he was seeking to instil in his young players. "Tactically, we aim at the man over in attack," he said, referring to his overlapping full-back ploy. "It is a kind of concertina movement. We demand mobility, and though only Venables, at the hub of things, is given free reign to improvise, we encourage the others to play by ear, not sticking to rigid positions. As they develop they are thinking more."

The high levels of fitness, skill and mental agility required by the players in this free-flowing playing system in turn demanded an intensive training regime. "The accent is on accuracy, high speed and endurance, a mixture of strength and finesse, with no player in practice games allowed more than two consecutive touches of the ball," the Doc continued. "Running off the ball, and playing the ball off quickly, are the basic things for us."

In the same interview, Docherty admitted that many of his best ideas had been copied or adapted from other teams. The ploy of using full backs as auxiliary wingers, for example, had stemmed from a fortnight Docherty had spent in Spain, watching Real Madrid's training methods.

"I picked up their tactic of players overlapping in attack. Only their forwards did it. I have extended it at Chelsea to the backs and half backs. We have picked up useful things, too, from West Ham United. Our free-kick play around the edge of the opposing penalty area – glancing the ball through the defensive 'wall' – we copied and adjusted from Burnley. Even the numbers on the players' shorts in our new all-blue strip was developed from a suggestion by one of our supporters."

Confident, brash and fearless, Docherty gave every impression that his young Chelsea team were on the verge of greatness. Only one thing, it seemed, could hold the Blues back. "Stamford Bridge is our biggest enemy," he said. "It lacks warmth and intimacy. The players themselves feel remote out there in the middle, detached and watched from a distance as if they were puppets – as if the audience was set too far back from the footlights."

Docherty had a point. At the time, Stamford Bridge was a very different stadium to the one that fans know today. Originally an arena for athletics events, the oval-shaped ground was unusual in having a greyhound track running round the pitch. Although this facility provided the club with extra income, it also pushed the fans back from the action on the pitch which, in turn, made the Bridge a much less intimidating venue for away teams than compact grounds like Anfield or Upton Park.

At the Fulham Road end, a roof had been erected in the 1930s to provide cover for bookmakers at evening greyhound meetings and 'the Shed', as it became known in the mid-sixties, quickly gained a reputation as the focal point for Chelsea's most enthusiastic fans. But they were still a long way from the pitch. The terracing at the North End was uncovered, although some fans could seek refuge from bad weather under the pre-war North Stand, a peculiar stilted structure in the north-east corner with seating for just 1,000. Next to the North Stand, the 5,000-capacity East Stand, which dated from the club's foundation in 1905, ran along the full length of the pitch. On the opposite side, meanwhile, the club was planning to build a stand on the massive West terracing. Eventually unveiled in January 1966, three-quarters of this new West Stand were traditional seats, while the front quarter was made up of unreserved concrete slabs known as 'the benches'. Taken as a whole, the ground was a strange mish-mash, reflecting the evolution of stadium design over the past 60 years.

Consequently the Bridge was no fortress, and the Blues crashed to their first defeat of the season at home to Manchester United at the end of September 1964, Denis Law and George Best grabbing the goals for the Reds. The 2–0 reverse was only a temporary setback, however, and Chelsea continued to challenge for the championship throughout the winter and spring.

In fact the Blues were fighting on three fronts as they made good progress in the two domestic cup competitions. In the FA Cup, Northampton were crushed 4–1 in the third round before a Bobby Tambling goal decided a London derby at West Ham in the fourth. Another derby in the fifth round, this time at home against Tottenham, was settled by Barry Bridges' first half goal. In the quarter-finals, Third Division Peterborough were hammered 5–1 at the Bridge, setting up an enticing semi-final with Liverpool.

As the Blues entered March, the League and FA Cup Double – previously only won by Preston, Aston Villa and Tottenham – was very much a possibility. But, optimistic fans wondered, could Chelsea make it an unprecedented Treble by winning the League Cup as well?

The brainchild of Football League secretary Alan Hardaker, the League Cup had been launched in 1960 with the intention of providing another source of revenue for cash-strapped lower division teams. Many big clubs, though, saw it as an unwanted addition to the fixture list and boycotted the competition. Having entered the League Cup in its first season, Chelsea had then joined the long list of non-competing clubs in the next two years.

In 1963/64 Chelsea had re-entered the competition with a weakened team and promptly gone out to Second Division Swindon at the first hurdle. The following year, Docherty maintained his policy of using the competition to blood promising youngsters. Peter Osgood, Joe Fascione and future Scottish international Jim McCalliog all made their debuts in the League Cup in 1964, while rarely called upon squad members such as Frank Upton, Allan Young and Ian Watson were also given run outs.

After disposing of Birmingham, Notts County, Swansea and Workington in front of crowds ranging from the small to the pitiful (fewer than 6,000 attended the home tie against the Swans), the semi-final draw pitted the Blues against Aston Villa. Villa were the first winners of the League Cup and one of the few First Division clubs to treat the competition completely seriously.

Anticipating a tough match in the first leg at Villa Park, Docherty recalled his first-choice players, although there was also a debut for young Scottish midfielder John Boyle. "It was a terrible pitch, covered in snow, mud and sand but it was wonderful to be playing," recalls 'Boylers'. "It was 2–2, then with five minutes to go, I got the ball about 30 yards out and whacked it into the corner of the net for the winning goal. Incredible." Boyle's goal in the 3–2 win proved decisive as a 1–1 draw in the second leg at Stamford Bridge put the Blues into the final against the holders of the competition, Leicester City.

A week after the return with Villa, Chelsea flew to Duisberg to play the West German national team in a friendly. The match had been arranged at the request of the West German manager Helmut Schoen as part of his team's preparations for the 1966 World Cup in England. Schoen had particular reasons for choosing Chelsea as warm up opponents, telling Docherty, "You play like a South American team. You don't play like an English team at all. Your full-backs come like wingers. We haven't seen this before in Europe."

Lining up against the Blues for the Germans were four players who would go on to play in the World Cup Final against England the following year: goalkeeper Hans Tilkowski, defender Horst-Dieter Hottges, striker Uwe Seeler and new midfield *wunderkind* Franz Beckenbauer.

"I think it was Franz Beckenbauer's first game for West Germany," says John Boyle, who was playing just his sixth match for Chelsea. "Uwe Seeler was coming back from an achilles injury and Helmet Schoen wanted him to have a game to test it out. So we got Ronnie Harris to mark him." How thoughtful.

Watched by 3,000 British troops in a crowd of 32,000, the Blues pointed the way forward for Bobby Moore, Geoff Hurst, Bobby Charlton and co, with Barry Bridges scoring the only goal of the game late on. No overlapping full-back was involved but the goal was still a typical example of Chelsea's attacking play at the time, Hollins lofting the ball forward for Bridges to burst clear of the German defence and shoot past Tilkowski. Schoen was gracious in defeat.

"Considering their average age is under 22, Chelsea are a marvellous team," he said. "They are the best English club side I have seen for a long time."

One German sports writer was equally enthusiastic about the Blues' performance. "Chelsea gave the national team a lesson with their cultured football and played like a top-class continental side as they fell back in defence with eight or nine men, or moved smartly forward with seven or eight."

There was no question either of the game being a kickaround friendly in which neither side was especially concerned about the result. "It was a real match," insists Boyle. "Obviously, when a club team plays a national team there's a huge incentive for the club side. I'm not saying we'd have beaten them every time, but we managed a win and for us it was incredible to play against all those famous names. It was a great boost for us."

It may have been after this game, or another similarly impressive Chelsea display, that Tommy Docherty congratulated one of his players in a rather unorthodox way. "I'll never forget the time when, after we'd put in a particularly good performance, he took all his clothes off and jumped in the bath with us," says Terry Venables. "He started messing around and then gave Marvin Hinton a love bite on his neck. On his neck! I mean can you imagine the amount of explaining Marvin had to do when he got home to his wife."

A month after their German adventure the Blues lined up against Leicester in the first leg of the League Cup Final. The match came at a bad time for Chelsea who had suffered their heaviest defeat of the season two days earlier, going down 4-0 at championship rivals Manchester United. Again, United's brilliant young winger George Best had got on the scoresheet and generally run the Blues' defence ragged.

There was more worrying news, too: leading scorer Barry Bridges had picked up a knock at Old Trafford and would miss the final. To the irritation of reserve team centre forward Peter Osgood, Docherty handed Bridges' number nine shirt to a surprising choice, left-back Eddie McCreadie.

The 20,690 fans who tore themselves away from *Coronation Street* to attend the match at the Bridge were bemused by McCreadie's change of position. Yes, Eddie was quick and skilful, but he was a defender and his goals record – two in more than 100 games for the club – hardly inspired confidence. On the other hand, one of those goals had been against Leicester earlier in the season in a 4-1 home victory. Could he do it again?

The answer was yes. With the scores tied at 2-2 after Bobby Tambling and a Terry Venables penalty had twice given the Blues the lead, McCreadie collected a throw from Peter Bonetti. Charging up the muddy field he outpaced the Leicester defence and, as Gordon Banks rushed off his line, poked the ball past the England goalkeeper and into the net for the winner. It was, said McCreadie later, "one of the best goals you've ever seen", although unfortunately the lack of interest in the League Cup meant there were no TV cameras present to record it for posterity.

For the return leg three weeks later the unlikely match winner was back in defence. So, pretty much, was the whole Chelsea team after Docherty instructed his players to get behind the ball and make it difficult for Leicester to score. The plan worked perfectly as the match ended o–o, giving the Blues their first piece of silverware for a decade. The home fans, though, were incensed by Chelsea's negative tactics and demonstrated their feelings with loud boos when skipper Terry Venables went up to collect the cup from Football League President Joe Richards.

"In the second leg we showed what we had learned against the various European teams we'd played in friendlies," says an unrepentant John Boyle. "Basically, we played for the o–o draw from the kick-off. It was great to win the cup, especially as it was so early in my career and because we'd only recently come up from the Second Division, but it wasn't the competition it became a few years later. Quite a few of the top teams were missing because they were involved in Europe." Chelsea, too, were bound for the continent the following season and would choose not to defend their trophy.

The League Cup was in the bag, but there would be no Treble. Between the first and second legs of the final Chelsea had lost 2–0 to Liverpool in the FA Cup semi-final at Villa Park. The Blues could feel slightly aggrieved as John Mortimore, playing one of his last games for the club before a summer move to QPR, headed what appeared to be a legitimate goal at o–o only for the referee to disallow it. That decision apart, Chelsea could have no complaints. Liverpool were there to be beaten, having played a tough European game in Rotterdam which went into extra-time just two days earlier. Unfortunately, Chelsea captain Terry Venables had unwittingly fired up the tired Reds, as former Liverpool hardman Tommy Smith later told the Chelsea programme.

"We were knackered and we were sitting in the dressing room before the game when [Bill] Shankly came in fuming and pinned this brochure to the wall. 'You won't believe it,' he told us, 'but those cocky lot think they're in the final already. Look! They've made up a mock-brochure for the final.' And they had. Terry Venables had done it to show off to his mates."

The bizarre 'Cup Final programme' proved to be the ultimate motiv-ational tool for the Liverpool manager. "Shanks was fuming and so were we," said Smith. "We went out there and your lot never stood a chance!"

At least the Blues exacted some revenge on Good Friday with a 4-0 thrashing of the Reds at the Bridge, keeping them in a three-way title race with Manchester United and Leeds. However, a dropped point the following day at home to West Brom and then a 2-0 defeat at Anfield on Easter Monday meant that Chelsea would have to win their last two fixtures - at Burnley the following Saturday and away to Blackpool two days later - to have any chance at all of lifting the championship.

Rather than returning to London after the Liverpool defeat, the Blues elected to stay in the north-west, choosing Blackpool as their base. It turned out to be an unfortunate choice as the resort went down in Chelsea history as the scene of the infamous 'Blackpool Incident'.

Accounts of the incident vary, but what is not in dispute is that eight Chelsea players - captain Terry Venables, Barry Bridges, George Graham, Eddie McCreadie, John Hollins, Bert Murray, Marvin Hinton and Joe Fascione - broke Tommy Docherty's curfew, slipping back into the hotel via the fire escape in the early hours of the morning. Tipped off by an eagle-eyed porter, the Doc had known for some time that half his squad were not in the hotel.

"We'd only just come back from the pictures when the night porter came to see me and said, 'They've all gone out again.' I said, 'No, it can't be, they've all just come in from the cinema.' But they weren't in their rooms and the porter was getting upset because it broke the fire regulations if guests went out without informing the hotel. So we waited until nearly 3am, and after they'd sneaked back in, I went into one of the rooms, and there was John Hollins pretending to be asleep. But when I pulled the cover back, he was still wearing his jacket and tie!"

The rest of the night owls were soon rounded up to be faced by an incandescent Docherty. "This sort of thing had happened before," he says, "and I'd turned a blind eye. But this time I had to make a decision, and I sent the eight of them home."

The players were shocked. It was a Wednesday night and the Blues weren't playing again until Saturday - it wasn't as if they had gone out on the razzle the evening before a match. And while they were a little bit tipsy, they certainly weren't reeling drunk.

"We'd just been out to a late-night drinking bar for a couple of drinks," says Marvin Hinton. "We weren't looking to get hammered, we were just a group of lads who fancied staying out a bit longer."

Docherty, though, could not be swayed. The gang of eight players, he insisted, would get the first train home to London and wouldn't play against Burnley. What's more, according to Hinton, the manager also told the group that none of them would ever play for Chelsea again. At the time Docherty made no mention of this ultimate sanction in his comments to the press. He was, though, more than willing to explain the reasons for his drastic decision.

"I feel this was the only way to do it," he told reporters. "I lay down the rules and if players break them they must take the consequences. The club is more important than individual players or league championships. How can you win the championship with disloyal players?"

By sending home the players Docherty had all but conceded defeat against Burnley and, consequently, thrown in the towel in the championship race. Effectively he had sacrificed the club's title ambitions for a point of principle: namely, his right as manager to set boundaries for the off-field conduct of his players. Some club bosses may have felt that, under the circumstances, the 'blind eye' Docherty referred to might have been given another run out. But Chelsea chairman Joe Mears, who enjoyed an excellent relationship with his manager, publicly backed the Doc's action, telling pressmen, "I am sure Tommy has done the right thing and will have the fullest support of the board."

Returning to London, the players had an unpleasant surprise waiting for them. News of the scandal had leaked out and the media was out in force to greet the disgraced 'Chelsea Eight'. "We couldn't believe it when we got to Euston and saw all the photographers, cameramen and reporters," recalls winger Bert Murray. "We had to cross a police cordon to get to our Chelsea van parked down the platform."

And Marvin Hinton remembers: "The story made the front pages the next day. I think we were treated unfairly; a large fine would have been more appropriate. It wasn't as if we had done anything terrible while we were out."

However, it didn't help the players' cause that one elderly guest was quoted as saying, "I was woken up by a great rumpus. Doors were banging and people stamping along the corridor. I thought we were being invaded."

Fired by a sense of injustice, the players released a joint statement to the press, intensifying the war of words with their manager. "We have done nothing to be ashamed of," it read. "We have not been the subject of any complaint from a member of the public or any member of the staff of an hotel in Blackpool. We have done nothing which we could not talk freely about. We admit to a breach of club discipline in that we were late back at the hotel and if necessary we can obtain proof of the way we spent every minute of the evening. We are shocked by the punishment, which we believe is out of all proportion."

The players were soon on their way back to the north-west, attending the Burnley match at the invitation of a TV station. "We met up with Docherty who brought us back to Blackpool," remembers Murray. "He was the one who apologised. He told us he wouldn't do anything like that again and that would be the end of the matter."

Although he didn't regret his actions, Docherty recognised that some sort of gesture of reconciliation was necessary to bring the episode – which, by now, had become so notorious it even had its own name, the 'Blackpool Incident' – to an end. He decided that a 'happy family' picture of himself with the eight miscreants back at the hotel would fit the bill nicely.

The photo that appeared in the following day's newspapers was designed to reassure fans that all was now well in the camp. A close study of the picture, however, reveals the underlying tensions that existed between manager and players. Docherty, staring into the camera, has his arms around the shoulders of George Graham and Marvin Hinton. Friendly enough, you might think, except the slightly manic grin on his face – think Jack Nicholson in *The Shining* – suggests he's about to bash the two players' heads together.

The players' expressions and body language, too, give away something of their true feelings. George Graham has turned his scowling face away from Docherty towards his mate Terry Venables on his right. Venners, his eyebrows arched quizzically and his hands stuffed in his pockets, looks thoroughly fed up. Barry Bridges, meanwhile, is chuckling away to himself as though the whole thing is a huge joke. To his left, Eddie McCreadie is yawning, his night on the tiles having apparently caught up with him. Only the two youngest players, John Hollins and Joe Fascione, wearing the glum expressions of naughty schoolboys summoned to see the headmaster, and Bert Murray, his eyes cast down, look remotely sheepish or remorseful.

The Blackpool Incident of April 1965 proved to be a pivotal moment for the Chelsea team of the mid-sixties. A little over a year later, four of the late-night revellers, all of them first-team regulars, would have been shipped out of the club. Docherty's smile, as the photo hinted, really was that of an assassin.

After a severely weakened Blues team, filled with reserves who had been hastily summoned from London to replace the 'Chelsea Eight', had been thrashed 6–2 at Burnley, Docherty restored six of the miscreants to the team for the game at Blackpool. The Blues lost that one as well, ending a season which had promised so much on another sour note.

While Chelsea fans should have been reflecting on an excellent season – silverware in the League Cup, an FA Cup semi-final and a creditable third place in the league behind Leeds and champions Manchester United – instead they were mulling over the consequences of the players' late-night shenanigans on the Golden Mile, which continued to excite much press comment. The fear for the fans was that the episode might create an irre-trievable rift between manager and players, a concern shared by former Tottenham captain and future Chelsea manager Danny Blanchflower.

"It was a brave-looking action at the climax of their championship challenge and it will please the partisans and hypocrites up and down the country," he wrote in a newspaper column, referring to Docherty's decision to send the eight players home. "But will it prove very wise in the end? I don't think so. It was not a public crime and Tommy was impulsive to make it public. I think there's no-one more sincere about the game and the club. But I feel he's been a bit rash as most young managers would be. I think his young team have been a bit rash, too, as young men often will. But young men have a way of remembering hard punches; they continue to think they were not fair."

Certainly, the relationship between Tommy Docherty and Terry Venables, who the Doc believed to be the ringleader of the Blackpool Incident, never recovered and continues to be spiky to this day. Yet, initially, the pair had got on well, with the Chelsea manager recognising Venables' leadership qualities by making him captain. "Not only could he play, but I liked the boy's inquisitive nature," says the Doc. "He had an old head on young shoulders, and I reckoned he would handle the extra responsibility."

Soon, though, Docherty felt Venables was, if anything, trying to take too much responsibility. "He was a very disruptive influence," he says. On the training pitch, we'd be working on something, and he'd say out loud: 'That won't work!' He was always criticising, though he'd come and see me later and apologise. It didn't undermine my authority, though, because I was too strong to let that happen. On the field, too, more and more of what went on was revolving around Terry and eventually he wanted to run the show."

"That's Docherty's assessment," Venables once retorted. "That's his truth. My recollection of it was that I would always ask questions and he encouraged that. I was deadly keen to learn and that was misconstrued by Docherty. He was a young manager and I was a young player. We had our differences of opinion. But it wasn't only me he fell out with. He was unpredictable, one of those guys who'd do something different to what he said he was going to do. He fell out with everybody. It'd get to the stage where you felt you didn't want to talk to him and then he'd have you laughing within a couple of minutes. He really was a hysterical bloke. Looking back, it was a clash of two strong personalities."

Providing an outside view of the relationship, Bobby Tambling says: "Terry was very tactically minded and I think they clashed in that area. And they clashed as comics because they were both comedians trying to be the funnyman in the dressing room, which Tommy shouldn't have been competing for anyway because he was the manager and above that. But, being so young, Tommy still felt like a player."

A psychologist might suggest that the two men – both of whom were confident to the point of cockiness and had a supreme belief in their own abilities – were competing for the role of 'Alpha male' in the Chelsea dressing room. If this was the case, who would come out on top? And what would be the implications for the club as a whole? The coming season would provide all the answers.

CHAPTER THREE

QUEST FOR THE CUP

CHAPTER THREE
QUEST FOR THE CUP

'If it ain't broke, don't fix it' is an adage that has served generations of craftsmen well down the years, but it's clearly not one that Tommy Docherty subscribed to. Having created a Chelsea team bursting with talent, enthusiasm and youthful promise the Doc might have been expected simply to sit back and enjoy the results of his handiwork. Instead, within a year of seeing his young Blues side come close to pulling off a remarkable Treble, Docherty had more or less dismantled the team and started afresh.

Although the Blackpool Incident had aroused his destructive urges, Docherty kept them in check for a while. There were no departures from the Bridge before the start of the 1965/66 season. The most significant arrival was Jimmy Andrews, a Scot who had played for three London clubs, as team coach, filling the gap left when Dave Sexton had taken the manager's job at Leyton Orient a few months previously.

One of Andrews' first tasks was to attempt to improve morale in the camp. The fallout from Blackpool hung over the club like a toxic cloud, which even a summer tour of Australia had failed to disperse. Bobby Tambling later remarked that the atmosphere on the trip Down Under was "like a morgue", a clear illustration of how far management/player relations had deteriorated. Still, there was plenty to look forward to. By virtue of finishing third in the League, the Blues had qualified for Europe for the first time since a brief foray in the Fairs Cup – the forerunner of the Uefa Cup – in 1958/59. To help prepare his team for this continental adventure, Docherty arranged a series of testing pre-season friendlies against strong German and Swedish opposition, including a re-match with the West German national side in Essen.

At half-time against Beckenbauer and co, the Blues appeared on course for another famous victory. Goals from Jim McCalliog, a teenage forward from Scotland who would soon be on his way to Sheffield Wednesday, and Barry Bridges gave them a 2-0 lead. In the second half, though, the Germans scored three times to win 3-2. For Peter Bonetti in the Chelsea goal the dramatic turnaround in fortunes provided a slightly eerie foretaste of things to come. Five years later the Cat would again be on the receiving end of a German recovery from two goals down – only this time the game was a somewhat more important affair: a World Cup quarter-final in Mexico which saw England blow their chances of retaining the Jules Rimet trophy.

Once it got under way, the 1965/66 season had the fans in a state of almost perpetual excitement. The Fairs Cup (see Chapter Nine, *The End of the Doc*) served up a heady mix of glamour, euphoria, violence and, with the final in Chelsea's sights, ultimate disappointment. Another long run in the FA Cup, meanwhile, prompted dreams of Wembley only for these to be shattered by a surprise 2-0 semi-final defeat at the hands of relegation-threatened Sheffield Wednesday. "We were big favourites," says Ron Harris of this setback, "everybody thought it would be a one-sided game but it was a quagmire of a pitch at Villa Park and we didn't perform."

Gallingly, one of the Wednesday goals was scored by McCalliog, just a few months after Docherty had decided he was surplus to requirements at the Bridge. The Doc had offloaded the Scot primarily because another young striker had come through the ranks to make the number nine shirt his own. Peter Osgood, the son of a Windsor builder and an occasional hod-carrier himself, had made an electrifying Chelsea debut aged just 17 the previous season, scoring two goals against Workington in the League Cup. Banner headlines the following morning hailed a new hero, but they were soon forgotten as Docherty consigned the young starlet to the reserves for the next nine months.

In October 1965, however, Docherty finally decided the time was right to unleash his exciting protégé, giving Osgood an extended run in the team at the expense of Barry Bridges. "Barry was an England centre-forward and a big idol at the time," recalls Ossie, "but Tommy said, 'I'm going to give you ten games no matter how you play.' To hear that gives you a lot of confidence to try things which may not always come off."

After a quiet settling-in period, during which some fans campaigned for the return of Bridges, Osgood won over the crowd with a series of dazzling displays. Tall, quick, beautifully balanced and an elegant, almost balletic, figure on the ball, Ossie possessed magnificent control, a deft touch and superb vision. While not a traditional English centre forward, he also had some of the attributes of that breed: strength in the air, physical presence and a powerful shot in both feet. Above all, though, it was his precocious ability to strike spectacular goals – perfectly-timed volleys, full-length diving headers, solo efforts that left a couple of defenders on their backsides – which had the fans excitedly chanting his name. For the press, too, Osgood's dramatic arrival on the London football scene was little short of a sensation.

After a 2–1 victory over Spurs at the Bridge on January 8th 1966, a match which saw the opening of the new West Stand, *The Times* described Osgood as 'a west London Hidegkuti' (a reference to the famous deep-lying Hungarian centre-forward who, along with Ferenc Puskas, had starred in the Magyars' legendary 6–3 win against England at Wembley in 1953).

"His artistic footwork and shooting power mark him as one who could yet lead England's attack for the World Cup," gushed *The Thunderer*, "provided he is not weighed down by the praise he deserves." In the event, England manager Sir Alf Ramsey named Osgood, along with Bridges, Bonetti, Hinton, Hollins and Venables in his original squad of 40 players, but only the Cat made the cut for the final 22. Two weeks after the Tottenham match, a mazy Osgood dribble from inside his own half to the edge of the Liverpool area in the Blues' third round FA Cup victory at Anfield had BBC commentator Kenneth Wolstenholme drooling on *Match of the Day*. "This boy Osgood . . . he really is good!" he cooed.

Later that month, Osgood scored a stunning solo goal at Burnley which he now nominates as the best of the 150 he notched for the club. Unfortunately, Wolstenholme and the BBC cameras weren't at Turf Moor to record the event but, happily, Ossie himself has a vivid recollection of his Lancastrian masterpiece.

"They had a corner, Peter Bonetti caught it, threw it out to me and I ran almost the length of the pitch, beat about five players, took the ball round their keeper and put it in the back of the net. I remember the whole ground applauding me as I went back to the centre circle, which was a fantastic feeling. I've been back to Burnley a few times since and people still come up to me to talk about that goal."

While great news for Chelsea fans, the rise of the teenage prodigy was not so welcome for England international Barry Bridges, who found himself occasionally consigned to the substitutes' bench. After a few weeks on the sidelines Bridges demanded a transfer, which Tommy Docherty turned down. Another player keen to move was Eddie McCreadie. After his successful cameo display as a striker in the 1965 League Cup Final the Scotsman had become convinced that he was the new Jimmy Greaves. "I'm a great centre forward," he told Docherty, "but you've been playing me out of position for three years."

The Doc said he'd alert other clubs to the availability of this new striking talent and, the following morning, informed McCreadie that a number of clubs were interested . . . headed by Mansfield Town. Surprisingly, Eddie seemed less keen to quit the Bridge after that.

With Osgood contributing seven league goals the Blues finished the season in fifth place, ten points behind champions Liverpool. Add in the pair of cup semi-final appearances and the season could be viewed from two distinct perspectives: reasonably satisfactory and full of promise for the future on the one hand or, on the other, somewhat disappointing.

Docherty took the latter view, being particularly annoyed by the Sheffield Wednesday FA Cup debacle. His reaction was typically impulsive, impetuous and extreme. Where another manager might have opted for a bit of tweaking with a screwdriver, Docherty took a sledgehammer to the team he had so painstakingly put together. Within a space of a few months the side was split apart, as Terry Venables moved to Spurs, George Graham joined Arsenal and Barry Bridges and Bert Murray left for Birmingham City. Peter Bonetti also looked set to depart, having put in a transfer request ahead of his involvement in England's World Cup campaign. If Chelsea fans were distraught by this sudden turn of events, so too were the players.

"It was so frustrating that Tommy Docherty lost his patience and that side was not allowed to fulfil its potential," Barry Bridges reflected years later. "We were a young team and team spirit was excellent. A lot of the players had played together all the way through from the youth team. We were inexperienced and we were getting better all the time. We played some great football as well. All off the cuff, the sort of thing only youngsters can get away with. Docherty overreacted to the Blackpool Incident when he sent us all home. We lost the last three games to cost us the championship and it all went wrong from there. Terry Venables has told me that it is his biggest disappointment in football what happened to that Chelsea team."

Peter Osgood may not have been that concerned about the departure of Bridges, his rival for the number nine shirt, but he was sorry to see Terry Venables leave the club. "Terry was brilliant. I loved him to death and I thought he was a fantastic footballer. I thought he was superb, one of the one best passers of the ball I've seen since Johnny Haynes. Johnny was the best passer of a ball I've seen in my life and Terry was his equal – that's how good a player Terry was. On top of that, he had a great engine on him, he could score goals and he was the leader of the pack. He was just a fantastic character to have around."

For Tommy Docherty, though, Venables and the others had been an irritant for some time. The rift created by the Blackpool Incident had not healed and, according to the Doc, his only option was to show the malcontents the door.

"Eddie McCreadie said to me, 'You've broken the team up.' But I told him, 'No, you lot broke it up, not me. If everyone had played the game, things could've been different.' Some of the lads started getting a bit stroppy after the Blackpool Incident and I decided to move them on. I don't regret doing that. Barry Bridges, for instance, wasn't a great player. He was quick and he scored goals, but he missed more than he scored. As for Venables, I should have sold him earlier than I did."

Having lost four components of his side, Docherty set about finding replacements. He had already strengthened the defence by buying West Ham full-back Joe Kirkup in March 1966. The following month he re-signed Ron Harris' brother, Allan, from Coventry for a second spell at the Bridge which would end in July 1967 when Harris joined QPR. Next, he moved to fill the gap in midfield left by the imminent departure of Terry Venables. The Doc's target was Charlie Cooke, a supremely gifted playmaker with Dundee. Cooke needed little persuading to move south and proved to be an instant hit with the Bridge crowd, who had always had a weak spot for an old-fashioned, ball-juggling entertainer.

"He was my best signing," enthuses Tommy. "What I loved about him was that when he came down to London he didn't say anything about money. He just said, 'Boss, isn't it great that I'm going to be playing for Chelsea?' And, of course, he was a marvellous player, far better than Terry Venables."

In truth, they were very different players who could not easily be compared. Venables was a team player, an organiser and a tremendous passer of the ball; Cooke, on the other hand, was a far more individualistic talent, a hypnotic dribbler who could send an opponent the wrong way with a snake-like swivel of his hips before accelerating away into the distance.

Meanwhile, Peter Bonetti's future at Chelsea remained uncertain. Relations between manager and player were hardly improved when Docherty refused to allow the Cat to report a week late for pre-season training after the goalkeeper had performed his understudy duties to Gordon Banks at the World Cup. Bonetti took a week off anyway, and Docherty responded to this latest flouting of his authority by promptly buying a new keeper, Millwall's Alex Stepney.

"The reason he got Alex was purely out of spite for me," Bonetti remarked later. "That's no disrespect to Alex because he was a brilliant keeper. Tommy and I were in dispute because I wanted to leave. He fined me and said Alex was going to play, so I put in another transfer request. There was speculation I was going to leave. But when the season started I was in the team and Tommy said he was going to play us in alternate games. Neither of us were going to put up with that; we both said the best keeper should be chosen on merit. But he sold Alex to Man United straight away so it didn't apply. Manchester United was my favourite club when I was a kid and I was just choked that it wasn't me going up there instead of him."

At the other end of the pitch, Docherty bolstered his striking options by signing Tommy Baldwin from Arsenal in exchange for George Graham in September 1966. "That was a great deal," the Doc says. "Tommy was the less established player so we also got around £50,000 from Arsenal as well." A wholehearted, unselfish performer who could be relied upon to harass defences for the full 90 minutes, Baldwin was also an intelligent, opportunistic striker who specialised in supplying the finishing touch at the near post. Having replaced the popular Graham, Baldwin might have worried about the reception he'd get from the crowd. The fans, though, couldn't resist such a transparent trier and the Gateshead-born forward proved to be an instant hit.

By this time the dust had settled after all the comings and goings and, somewhat surprisingly considering all the rumblings of discontent, the Blues had got off to a magnificent start to the 1966/67 season. An impressive opening day win at West Ham, where the Hammers' World Cup-winning trio of Bobby Moore, Geoff Hurst and Martin Peters had been paraded before an adoring East End crowd prior to kick-off, set the tone and helped to propel the Blues on a scintillating 10-match unbeaten run.

What's more, Chelsea were playing with a verve and panache which suggested a trophy of some sort was very much on the agenda. A 6–2 away thrashing of Aston Villa in September, a match in which Bobby Tambling scored five goals, only seemed to confirm the widespread view that Chelsea would be among the league title contenders. For new man Tommy Baldwin, who made a scoring debut in another emphatic away win three weeks later at Manchester City, the free-flowing style he discovered at Chelsea was a revelation after the tactical rigidity he had experienced at Highbury.

"It was a complete change," he says. "As an Arsenal player I was taught that you had to defend all the time – even as centre-forward I had to be running back and chasing. The accent was on defending. From being in the youth team they told us that if you got a 0–0 draw that was okay, you'd got a point. You had to keep a clean sheet – that was the emphasis all the time. It was very different at Chelsea. When Tommy Docherty signed me we had a team meeting before the game. All he said was, 'You've all met Tommy, haven't you? He's playing up front, so knock the ball up to him, he'll hang onto it and we'll play from there.'

"That was it. It was a real breath of fresh air. He didn't say anything like, 'Oh, this full back likes to bomb on so make sure you close him down.' He didn't worry about the other teams at all. Of course, he'd tell the defence about the opposition strikers and if they had a guy who was a bit quick or whatever, but with me he just said to concentrate on attacking. My game was always about running back and chasing so I still carried on doing that, but it was nice to be able to concentrate on scoring goals. Anyway, we went out and won that first game 4–1, which was a great start for me."

Baldwin had another reason to be happy as his bank balance showed an instant improvement after his move across London. "My wages jumped from £25 to £80 a week and I got a signing on fee," he says. "But the idea of just playing for Chelsea really appealed to me, because they had a young team full of good players."

Arguably the best of those young players was Osgood, who with six goals in those first ten games had maintained the form which had catapulted him into the nation's consciousness the previous season. But, just four days after helping the Blues to the top of the table after the win at Maine Road, the young striker's season came to an abrupt end when he broke his leg in a tackle with Blackpool's Emlyn Hughes – a devastating blow for both player and club. Chelsea's season – in the league, if not the FA Cup – never really recovered and a final placing of ninth was well below the heightened expectations of the early autumn.

Deprived of his talismanic centre forward, Docherty wasted little time in recruiting a replacement, signing Aston Villa striker Tony Hateley (the father of 1980s England centre forward Mark Hateley) for £100,000. A former schoolboy high jump champion, Hateley was rated as one of the best headers of the ball in the game. His ground skills, though, were altogether more prosaic and Chelsea fans soon became used to intricate passing moves coming to a sudden halt at the feet of the floundering forward.

"Tony was a lovely lad and a good pro, but we were a quick, skilful and very fit side and he didn't fit into our style of football," admits Docherty. "He was great in the air and we had very quick players down the wings who could put over good crosses, so I thought he'd give us another outlet. But he turned out to be a bad signing. Probably my worst."

Despite that blunt assessment, it's only fair to point out that Hateley played a central role that season in Chelsea's run to their first ever Wembley FA Cup Final (the only other final the Blues had reached, when they lost 3–0 to Sheffield United in 1915, had been played at Old Trafford). The route to the Twin Towers began with a 2–1 win at Huddersfield, where Bobby Tambling and left-winger Peter Houseman, enjoying his longest spell in the side since making his debut three years earlier, were on target. In the fourth round, the Blues were drawn away to lowly Brighton and took the opportunity to spend a relaxing week on the south coast in preparation for the game.

"We went down there on the Tuesday and met up with a local book-maker, George Gunn, who was a friend of Dave Sexton's," recalls John Boyle. "He took us to a club that night and then we went to the dog track on Wednesday evening where we had a meal and a drink. Then, on Thursday, we went to a casino. Tommy was with us the whole time, so there was no problem."

Maybe, though, the accent was just a little too much on fun rather than training, as the Blues survived an almighty scare at a packed Goldstone Ground, holding on for a 1–1 draw after Boyle was dismissed.

"It was really quite rare in those days to get sent off, it had to be a pretty bad foul even to get a booking," says Boylers. "They had a guy called Wally Gould and I got sent off for fouling him. I got changed immediately. I felt so upset about it I left the stadium and went for a walk along Brighton beach. I remember sitting by the sea, thinking, 'What have I done? If we lose it'll be my fault.' I thought I'd put us out of the FA Cup. Fortunately, we got the draw and Tommy Docherty was very good about it. He picked me for the replay four days later which we won 4–0. I felt a whole lot better after that."

The Blues repeated their Brighton sojourn before the fifth and sixth rounds, both won at home against the two Sheffield teams, United and Wednesday. The benefits of the bracing sea air and a change of scenery weren't the only factors in Docherty's *Groundhog Day* policy, according to Ron Harris.

"Tom was superstitious," he says, "so we had to do the same thing every round. We used to go down to Brighton and stay in the same hotel, the Dudley Hotel. We trained nearby at Worthing. He used to give us some money to go to a Chinese restaurant or go to a club to have a couple of drinks. It became our Cup routine."

In the semi-final draw Chelsea were paired with Leeds at Villa Park while Tottenham and Nottingham Forest were due to meet at Hillsborough in the other tie. The longstanding, and frequently tempestuous, rivalry between the Blues and the Yorkshiremen is often traced back to this match but, as John Boyle recalls, there had been a good number of ugly incidents in the clubs' previous meetings.

"One of the first matches I played for Chelsea was against Leeds at Elland Road in January 1965. The pitch was very icy, and the Leeds players had these leather studs which were screw-ins but also had nails in them. They'd actually clipped off half their studs and left the nails sticking out. Chelsea complained afterwards, and I think it was soon after that refs started inspecting studs.

"Then, about a year later back at Elland Road, I dived to head the ball and Billy Bremner booted me in the face, knocking me out. Harry Medhurst, our trainer, came on and gave me some smelling salts; the game restarted, and I was looking around, thinking 'Um, nice lights.' I could just about make out Ossie screaming, 'Get 'im off!' Even when I got to hospital I didn't have a clue where I was!"

Boyle describes Leeds as "cynical bullies", a description which seems generous given the treatment meted out to him in the semi-final by the Yorkshire side's goalkeeper, Welsh international Gary Sprake. "I was chasing a long ball," he says, "Sprake came out to catch it and kicked me in the face. I had a thick lip and bloody nose, but we won the game, so it didn't matter. Anyway, a couple of years later we were up in a club in Leeds after playing at Elland Road, and Sprake was there, so Ossie went over and said, 'You took a right liberty when you kicked John in the face!' Gary looked at me and said, 'John, I promise you, I only meant to kick you in the chest!'"

Boyle downplays the incident, but according to Tommy Baldwin and other witnesses, the injury he sustained in the semi-final was one of the goriest they have ever seen on a football field. "It was a terrible sight," says Baldwin, "there was blood dripping all down his face and onto his shirt. But great credit to John Boyle, who played on regardless. At half-time we were absolutely furious about the incident."

Ironically, Sprake needed treatment himself in the second half after an accidental collision with Tony Hateley knocked out a couple of his teeth. And Hateley made an even more telling contribution later in the game, scoring the all-important goal which took Chelsea to Wembley. "Charlie Cooke picked the ball up on the halfway line, beat about five players and slung a great ball in," he remembers. "I just powered it in past Gary Sprake from around the penalty spot. I remember Ossie, who still had his leg in plaster, jumping out of the dug out and hopping on the pitch."

If a header from 12 yards sounds impressive, then think again. Ron Harris, who admittedly would have been some way back from the crucial action, reckons Hateley scored from double that distance. "Honestly, I've never seen anybody head a goal so far or so hard," he says. "It was well outside the penalty area."

The champagne was out on the train home, with even teetotaller Hateley joining in the wild celebrations. No doubt some of the toasts were to referee Ken Burns who had controversially disallowed a trademark Peter Lorimer piledriver free-kick because he hadn't blown his whistle. The Blues, though, could convincingly argue that they deserved that spot of luck, after the misfortune of losing in the semi-final in both 1965 and 1966.

It didn't take long, however, for the champers to go flat. At a time when the players should have been solely focused on the final against Tottenham, the victors in the other semi-final, much of their energy in the build up to Wembley was taken up by a heated dispute with the club over bonuses and the allocation of Cup Final tickets.

"In our contracts we were on £250 for reaching the final and £500 for winning the Cup," explains Tommy Baldwin. "But, obviously, players talk to each other and we found out that the Tottenham team were on £1,000 for getting to Wembley and £2,000 for winning the game. Initially, the Spurs players had been on similar bonuses to us but the club had increased the money as a reward. Chelsea, though, just wouldn't budge.

"Another problem we had was with the distribution of Cup Final tickets. Under FA rules we only got 13 tickets each. Why 13, I don't know. But you can imagine that if you get to the Cup Final with all your family, relations and friends to consider, 13 tickets doesn't go anywhere. Again Tottenham were doing better than us. I know the club gave them about 100 tickets each. So that didn't help."

Indeed, gripes about players' tickets had been a feature of the Cup run with the squad holding protest meetings over what they claimed was an insufficient allocation before both the fourth round tie at Brighton and the semi-final with Leeds.

"The whole thing was a bit of a shambles, to be honest," adds John Boyle. "Whatever the FA said, the unwritten rule was that each player would get 100 tickets from his club for the Cup Final. They used to keep 20 or 30 and the rest went to touts. Stan Flashman was the big name but there were a few other well-known touts as well. For the married guys, especially, the extra money was a bonus because it wasn't listed on their pay slip and so the wives didn't know about it. It was money in your pocket. Usually Marvin Hinton, who was one of the married players, would collect all our tickets and do the business for us.

"Anyway, before the Cup Final Tommy Docherty read the riot act to us. 'If anybody is thinking of selling their tickets, I can tell them they're going to be in serious trouble,' he warned us. Then, a few minutes later, the groundsman came in with a brown paper bag for Tommy. 'Here's your bag, Tommy,' he muttered. As he passed it to him, somebody caught a peep inside and there was a load of cash there. We thought 'he's only gone and sold his tickets!'"

Tommy Docherty, though, strongly denies that he sold any of his tickets above their face value. "As manager I received 100 tickets from the club for the Cup Final and I had to pay for them myself," he says. "It's ridiculous to say I sold them to touts. The tickets went to family and friends. When you have an allocation like that you have to write down the names and address of every person you give a ticket to, which you wouldn't be able to do if a tout bought them off you. The only 'deal' I made was to swap four tickets for four seats at Wimbledon.

"In those days players signed a contract every year and the bonuses would be included. Whatever the players say, the contract could not be altered during the season without permission from the Football League – Alan Hardaker, the Football League secretary, was a stickler for that. So I doubt very much that Tottenham adjusted their bonuses. As for the dispute about the tickets, they wanted a bigger allocation so they could sell them and make a few quid. In fairness, they were only on about £50 a week then, but all the same how could they justify doing that to the supporters who ended up having to pay well over the odds for a ticket?"

The players' ticket allocation was eventually increased to 20, still way below the unofficial norm. The dispute over bonuses, though, took longer to be settled and, incredibly, was still a matter of bitter debate on the morning of the Cup Final.

"We had a meeting at the hotel in Hendon, and seven players including myself said to Tommy Docherty that if we didn't get a better offer we weren't going to play," says Tommy Baldwin. "In the end they doubled the original offer to £500 for making the final and £1,000 if we won it. But that was still half what Tottenham were on."

The strike threat may have been little more than a bargaining chip but, all the same, the whole episode was hardly the best preparation for the final, the first ever between two London clubs. Dubbed, inevitably, 'the Cockney Cup Final' by the popular press the match was a hard one to call. Tottenham had finished the season in third place behind champions Manchester United and Nottingham Forest and were the form team, having put together a long unbeaten run. Chelsea, by contrast, arrived at Wembley with no momentum at all, after having lost five of their last seven league games.

On the other hand, the Blues could point to a good record against Spurs in their head-to-head meetings that season: a 3–0 win at the Bridge in October and a 1–1 draw at White Hart Lane in March – a match in which 16-year-old Ian 'Chico' Hamilton set a double record as both Chelsea's youngest ever player and youngest goalscorer.

In his Cup Final preview in *The Times*, Geoffrey Green alerted readers to "a strong feeling in my boots that Chelsea will win the Cup at last." His hunch seemed to be based more on an appreciation of the Blues' fluid style of play than anything else. "Chelsea are fashioned in the modern idiom," Green wrote. "They do not boast accepted wing players: numbers on players' backs are for mere identification in the programme and bear no relationship to old-fashioned positions on the field; full backs and wing halves overlap as the pattern unfolds playing, as it were, positional leapfrog."

If the Chelsea game plan was to confuse the opposition with unlikely players popping up in unexpected places, it didn't work. Tottenham, with Terry Venables prominent in midfield, took control of the game through goals by Jimmy Robertson and Frank Saul, and although Bobby Tambling replied late on it was the scantest of consolations for the Blues. As with so many Cup Finals, the game was a flop as a spectacle, primarily because Chelsea had under-performed so badly.

"No doubts about it, we were completely outplayed," admitted John Hollins some years later. "I was nervous. I think we all were. Nerves can destroy a team. They drain you, and when the time comes to raise your game, you can't because you're exhausted."

Other players also blame nerves for the disappointing showing but Marvin Hinton has a different slant on the main reason for the defeat. "Tommy Docherty changed the system," he says. "I'd been playing sweeper all season, and he put me in as marker. I had to mark Alan Gilzean, who was a good touch player and quite slippery. I was awful, I admit it. The argument about tickets and bonuses didn't help either."

"Players are always great tacticians after the game," responds the Doc. "I don't remember him complaining before the match. In any case, Marvin hadn't been playing as a sweeper. He played just like Bobby Moore, off the centre half. But it's true we didn't play well in the final. Neither did Tottenham – it was a dreadful game. I always think the best cup finals are between a northern team and a southern team."

A few days after the Cup Final Chelsea set off on a three-week tour of America, Canada and Bermuda. The trip was meant to be little more than an end-of-season jolly, and seemed to provide the perfect opportunity for the players to put the heartbreak of Wembley behind them. Life at Chelsea, though, was rarely so uncomplicated and for Tommy Docherty and his players events on the tour were to have far-reaching and dramatic consequences.

CHAPTER FOUR

KINGS OF THE KING'S ROAD

CHAPTER FOUR
KINGS OF THE KING'S ROAD

By any objective standard, Stamford Bridge can justifiably claim to be the capital's premier football venue. As former chairman Ken Bates was fond of pointing out, its location – "ten minutes by taxi to Harrod's" – is unrivalled, particularly for the well-heeled supporter who enjoys a spot of up-market post-match shopping. Almost entirely redeveloped in the last decade (only the East Stand dates back to before the mid-90s), with seating for 42,000 fans, the ground itself features a host of first-rate facilities, including two hotels, a health club, a night club and numerous bars and restaurants.

The Fulham Road, running past the front entrances to the ground, also provides hungry fans with a wide variety of dining opportunities ranging from hot dogs to sushi, as well as an ultra-convenient underground station and, in Fulham Town Hall, a focal point for exuberant cup-winning celebrations. Backing onto the East Stand, meanwhile, beyond the railway line, Brompton cemetery, with its ornate gravestones and elaborate tombs, makes for a tranquil and relaxing approach to the ground for fans arriving from Earl's Court tube station. A little further away, but still within walking distance, the route over Battersea Bridge, offering splendid views of the Thames up to Vauxhall and the hugely expensive Victorian townhouses along Cheyne Walk, is popular with fans living south of the river.

Above all, though, it's the nearby King's Road, one of the most famous streets in the whole of London, which has always given an extra buzz to any trip to the Bridge. Designed by Charles II as a royalty-only thoroughfare providing a short cut to Hampton Court, the King's Road finally opened to the public in 1830. More than a century later the street's fame spread worldwide as it became an informal stage set for the 'Swinging Sixties'.

Although still featuring on many tourists' 'must see' list, today the King's Road is not what it was: high rents have forced the smaller, quirkier shops out and the familiar big chains – Boots, Starbucks, various mobile-phone retailers and Rymans to name but a few – have moved in. Most depressingly of all, a branch of the Abbey National building society now stands on the site of the Markham Arms, a favourite haunt of the Chelsea players during the 1960s and 1970s, while the Chelsea Drugstore bar, once celebrated by the Rolling Stones on their classic track *You Can't Always Get What You Want*, became a part of the ever-expanding McDonald's empire many years ago. All the same, a few landmark sites have survived the culling process including the flower-festooned Chelsea Potter pub, cowboy-boot retailers R Soles and Pucci Pizza, a long-established Italian restaurant where model Sophie Dahl used to work as a waitress, serving cheap but tasty pizzas to the likes of Jack Nicholson and George Best.

Happily, for the players at the time, the heyday of the King's Road coin-cided with the emergence of Chelsea as London's most glamorous team in the mid-sixties. "There was so much going on then," says Alan Hudson, who was born just around the corner from the Bridge. "When I got in the first team it was the real Swinging Sixties. The King's Road was incredible. There were a lot of nice girls walking around, and the pubs were great as well. The Palmerston was the main pub where the players would go, and boxers went there too. Further down the King's Road you had the Trafalgar which was Tommy Baldwin's favourite pub. The Markham was the main pub that I used to go to because my favourite restaurant, Alexander's, was next door down in the basement."

Alexander's was owned by Alexander Plunkett-Green, who was married to the fashion designer Mary Quant. The couple were well-connected and the restaurant attracted an A-list clientele, ranging from pop and film stars to royalty. "Adam Faith was a regular in Alexander's," recalls Huddy. "Marc Bolan had a place over the road from the restaurant, so he would use it. Everybody went there. Apart from Annabel's in Berkeley Square it was the place where you could walk by and see all sorts of famous faces, even kings and princes. As you walked in the door there was a round table called the Royal Table, and when there was no royalty in that was where the Chelsea boys sat.

"I didn't discover the place to begin with – that was down to my brother, John, who was on Chelsea's books at one time. He used to clean the windows there – not that they had many. So, I was the one who introduced Alexander's to all the lads and it became very popular with everybody. We'd go in there after training for lunch – especially on a Friday, after we'd been training at Stamford Bridge. Then we'd go on to a drinking club, because pubs weren't open in the afternoons in those days."

Despite claiming that "it's a bit of a myth that I was part of the King's Road gang", Windsor-based Peter Osgood was also a regular diner at Alexander's. "It was definitely the 'in' place," he says. "You'd get Conners – Sean Connery – in there and Princess Anne and so on. Sir Richard Attenborough would go down there with his actor mates. We knew who they were and they knew we were the Chelsea boys. They were brilliant to us; we'd leave them alone and they'd leave us alone but if they wanted to come over and say 'Hello' that was fine, too. It was smashing. We got introduced to quite a few people down there. I didn't speak to Princess Anne, she was royalty, after all. We'd have loved it if she had come across to said 'Hello' but you can't approach, can you?" Surely, though, the onus was on Princess Anne to pay her respects to Ossie – after all, he was 'King of the Bridge'.

Another popular spot with the players was Alvaro's restaurant, which opened in April 1966 virtually next door to Alexander's at 124 King's Road and opposite Royal Avenue – the street where James Bond had his London address in the Ian Fleming books. "There were just a couple of other Italian restaurants in the area at the time," remembers owner Alvaro Maccioni. "When I bought the site off the man who owned it the place was the Magic Carpet Inn, a traditional old English-type bistro. He shook my hand when we completed the deal and said, 'I wish you all the luck in the world, because as far as I'm concerned the King's Road is finished.' Maybe his type of King's Road was finished, but it was the beginning of the new fashionable one.

"It took off immediately. It was as though people were just waiting for us to open. To begin with I didn't know any of the Chelsea players, but within one week of the restaurant being open we had Sammy Davis Junior and Princess Margaret come in on the same night. Princess Margaret said she would love to meet Sammy Davis Jnr so I went over to him and had a word, and then they had a chat. The following day it was all over the papers, not just the *Evening Standard* but the nationals."

Alvaro's was so successful that a year later, in 1967, Signor Maccioni opened a nightclub in the King's Road called the Aretusa which soon became a favourite with the players. "When we opened the Aretusa club

I sent invitations to Peter Osgood and Peter Bonetti," says Alvaro, "because they were the only two I knew well from Alvaro's. From then onwards we met them all. The restaurant in the club was booked a month ahead in advance, and we didn't let anyone in off the street even if we were empty as it was a strictly members only club. In those days you had to be strict about the membership because otherwise you could have lost your licence as we were allowed to serve alcohol outside normal pub hours. But, as a member, you could drink from 11am to three o'clock the following morning."

In this era of strict licensing laws, the Aretusa's liberal policy made it an especially appealing venue to the heavy drinkers among the squad. "There were days when they were in there a long time," Alvaro says. "But, having said that, I don't remember them overdoing it. Of course they had a drink. They used to come in the evening, they used to come in the afternoon. It was open all day long and it was the place to come in the sixties and seventies for Chelsea players. We had lots of pretty girls coming too, which was another attraction – many models, film and TV people, the Rolling Stones, David Bailey, all the James Bond crowd, Michael Caine and so on. The club attracted a very creative crowd." Another frequent visitor was the hard-drinking actor Richard Harris, who would occasionally challenge Tommy Baldwin to a drunken bout of arm wrestling.

"During the day the Rolling Stones and Beatles often used to come to try out their new records before they released them," continues Alvaro. "We had one of the best sound systems in any discotheque and they wanted to hear how their records sounded in that environment. Often they would leave the record behind afterwards so I've got a big collection of records with a label on only one side. At the time I didn't realise how valuable they would become. It was only a few years ago when I saw something on the internet about rare records that I realised they would be worth something. So I went back in the loft to search them out."

It wasn't only players from Chelsea who came to the club. Despite playing for Manchester United, George Best, the most famous and most talented footballer of the era, was a regular. "He had his own chair at the bar," remembers Alvaro. "He used to come in most nights, often with a different woman. It was a shame he didn't play for Chelsea, but he still spent lots of time in London. I couldn't understand how he did it. I remember once he was still at the club at 2am and the next evening United were playing AC Milan in the European Cup in Manchester. He'd had a few drinks but he wasn't in a bad way; in fact, I never saw him in a bad way, he could hold a drink so well you could never tell if he was drunk or sober. Anyway, George gave me a pass to go and watch the game, I left him in the club and went home.

"The following day I arrived at Old Trafford and I only had this pass, not a proper ticket. I needed to meet George at a particular door where he'd let me in. I was thinking, 'I'm sure he won't be playing, not after last night . . .' But I got to the door and there he was. And when the game started he was brilliant and scored two goals. I couldn't believe it, it really was unbelievable."

Alvaro sold his club and restaurant in 1972. Three years later he opened another eaterie, La Familigia, just off the top of the King's Road in Langton Street. "Carlo Cudicini uses us as his canteen," jokes Alvaro, a loyal Chelsea fan who has graduated over the years from the Shed to a box in Di Matteo's hospitality suite. Roman Abramovich, Claudio Ranieri and Ken Bates have also been spotted in the restaurant, which is so popular on matchdays customers need to book months in advance to be sure of getting a table.

In the 1960s the King's Road, along with Carnaby Street, was prime clothes-shopping territory for the fab, groovy and 'with-it' young. Signalling their own fabness, grooviness and 'with-it-ness', simple clothes shops became boutiques – part of a wider trend which saw restaurants turn into bistros, dancehalls reinvent themselves as discotheques, and even plain old barbers' re-emerge as salons. For High Street shoppers everywhere 'O' level French had never seemed so useful.

Mary Quant had opened Britain's first ever boutique, Bazaar, on the King's Road in 1955. Selling skinny rib sweaters, plastic raincoats, colourful tights and, later, Quant's own ground-breaking creations such as the mini, micro-mini and hot pants, the store was a huge success and was soon joined by similar outlets along the length of the King's Road. Among the more famous names were Take Six, Topgear, the hippy store I Was Lord Kitchener's Valet and Let It Rock, which was opened by Vivienne Westwood and Malcolm McLaren in 1971, and later became the legendary punk shop, Sex.

Being a local lad, Alan Hudson was especially in tune with the fast changing fashion scene and, although younger than the other players, he was considered something of a style guru. "Ossie asked me to take him down the King's Road a couple of times," he says. "He didn't know how to dress because he came from Windsor. I took him along to some top-notch places like Just Man and Take Six there and we bought a load of gear. Personally, I was having suits made up for about £200 a pop. I also used to like the shirts and the ties in the same colour, especially the floral ones."

A valued adviser on fashion matters, Huddy's clothes sense, shoulder-length hair and popularity with young female fans also made him a target for the modelling agencies. "I did a bit of modelling, but only for fun," he says. "I did a thing for a shampoo company and there was ads all over the underground with my picture on them. I also did some modelling for Limited Edition shirts. They didn't pay me, but I got to keep the shirts."

As the Sixties progressed, fashions became more bizarre or 'far out' in hippy-speak. The Chelsea boys had broadly adopted the sharp-suited 'mod' look in the mid-sixties, but although their hair grew longer as the seventies approached, kaftans, bandannas and tie-dye T-shirts did not become a part of the typical player's wardrobe.

"We didn't get into wacky clothes," says John Boyle, "partly because we always had to wear a suit when we travelled away. We used to get our suits from Soho. Terry Venables and George Graham had a few friends in the business and we used to go with them to get fitted up. You'd pick your own material, take it down and they would do you a suit. We never did much shopping on the King's Road because we were mostly pretty conservative. It was more about being smart and smooth than being flamboyant.

"To begin with we all had short hair – it got a lot hairier later. The Beatles were a big influence on us because they grew their hair long in the late sixties. Before that we didn't like long hair at all. I can remember coming back from a game in Barcelona in 1966 we bumped into the singer Crispin St Peter at the airport. There were a few comments about 'long-haired pop stars' because he had a ponytail and very few men had them in those days."

In fact, far from embracing the sandals-and-cheesecloth 'counter-culture' style, some of the players looked more like the city toffs or 'bread heads' the hippies actively despised. "Eddie McCreadie was the best-dressed man of the squad," claims Alan Birchenall, who joined Chelsea shortly after the hedonistic, psychedelia-soaked 'Summer of Love' in 1967. "He's the only guy I ever met who would come to training wearing a three-piece suit: jacket, waistcoat, trousers. He looked like a banker, more of a city investor than a footballer. He even had the rolled up umbrella."

It's unlikely that Eddie, by then Chelsea manager, would have chosen to buy his clothes from the shop on Elleston Green that his old team-mates Tommy Baldwin and Charlie Cooke opened in 1977 along with Baldwin's wife, Gabrielle, and former *Ready, Steady, Go* presenter Cathy McGowan. "We sold second hand stage gear we'd got from pop stars, people like Elton John," says Tommy. "It was quite successful. I used to serve in the shop sometimes with Charlie who was still at Chelsea at the time."

The Elton John connection went back a few years when Tommy was offered the chance to provide financial backing for the singer, who was then just beginning his showbiz career and was still in the process of casting off his old identity as plain Reg Dwight from Pinner. "I knew his PR guy, Ray, who was looking for a couple of investors to put in £1,500 to start Elton off," recalls Tommy. "Everyone was saying he was going to be the next big thing, but I didn't think much of the demo tape Ray sent me. In fact, I threw it out of the car window. Then I was invited to his first gig at a club called the Speakeasy. Everyone was raving about him but I was more interested in having a few drinks. Anyway, I was always more into country and western. I didn't take Ray up on his offer."

Unlike some of his players, manager Dave Sexton was an infrequent visitor to the King's Road, preferring to buy his clothes in Mayfair. A conservative man who had served with the army in Greece, Sexton preferred the clean cut style of an earlier period and was unimpressed by the increasingly scruffy appearance of his players. On one famous occasion, he even dropped David Webb for growing a beard.

"Dave was a very nice man and would come in every so often to buy a suit," says his tailor Doug Hayward. "One day he came in and gave me the tracksuit they wore at Wembley – blue trousers and a red top with the 1970 FA Cup Final motif on it. I had it upstairs for years until my daughter found it and she started wearing it to Chelsea games. Lots of people would come up to her and ask her where she got it. It caused quite a stir."

Doug, who still runs Hayward's outfitters in Mount Street W1, was a regular at the Bridge throughout the sixties, and organised tickets for a group of fans who included actors and film directors. "I used to buy 12 season tickets every year and everyone would pay for one," he says. "I would hold the tickets during the week and if a couple of people were away filming or whatever we had a list of substitutes to fill in. We used to meet before the game at a small restaurant on the King's Road. Then, when Alvaro's opened, he invited us along for the opening night. The paint was still wet and everyone was getting white marks on their jackets. Custom was a bit slow at first so he asked us all to come along and have lunch every Saturday before going to the football. He only charged £1 a head, which was a really good gesture as the meal was probably worth £5. But he just wanted a regular group of people to come every Saturday.

"That £1 a head continued for about eight or nine years and he never put the price up. It was lovely food too. Tommy Steele used to pop into my shop and say, 'Have you got a spare ticket this week?' He'd come along to lunch at Alvaro's and when it was time to put the £1 in he used to hold the note in his hand above the pot and then take it back without dropping the pound in. I bought an old taxi – I think it cost me £15 – and we used it to deliver stuff to the shop. But on Saturday afternoons we had this boy who came by and we used to give him two bob each to pick us up at Alvaro's and run us to Chelsea. Then he'd go away and come back at ten past five and we'd all pile in again. We got about ten or 12 people in that taxi, it was a real crush. Even then Tommy Steele wouldn't cough up the two bob. I couldn't believe it!"

One of those subsidising the long-pocketed entertainer was the photographer Terry O'Neill. In 1972 he created one of the iconic images of football in that decade when he snapped a group of London players, including Alan Hudson, David Webb and Terry Venables, smoking cigars and drinking brandies in a Fleet Street restaurant. "The idea was to make them look like the football mafia," he says. "I did that one in London and another in Manchester with Malcolm Allison, Rodney Marsh and Francis Lee. "I did film stars normally but I loved sports. *The Sun* had just launched and was the first paper to go for pictures of footballers off the pitch. So I thought up this 'clan' idea and sold them the pictures. It was difficult to get all the players together; if you think they're unreliable now they were mega-unreliable then. But I got them all together somehow, although it was all a last minute rush."

Chelsea have always had a showbiz following, but in the 1960s the Bridge could probably have supported a branch of Equity. Among the many actors following the Blues during the Docherty and Sexton eras were Dennis Waterman, Michael Crawford, *Man About the House* star Richard O'Sullivan,

Bill Gaunt and Rodney Bewes, better known at the time as Bob Ferris from *The Likely Lads*.

"Because of *The Likely Lads* and all the other filming I've done in the north east, people think I'm a Geordie," Bewes said a few years ago. "Actually, I was born in the middle of Yorkshire and then came down to London at 14. I used to stand in the Shed at every home match and travel away a lot, too. I was one of a group of North Country actors who followed Chelsea all over the place. The players were heroes of mine and I always made a conscious effort not to meet them. When you appear on TV you can normally get to meet most people, but I went out of my way to avoid the Chelsea players – I didn't want my illusions shattered.

"I was offered tickets for the Chelsea Ball and that type of thing, but always flatly refused. But then I bumped into Peter Bonetti in a King's Road restaurant. We'd never met, but it was as if we'd known each other for years. First name terms and an instant friendship. Then Peter turned to me and said: 'Who's that tasty looking blonde in the corner?' I told him that it was my wife Daphne and thought to myself that even the great Chelsea players have human instincts like the rest of us. I actually took Daphne to Stamford Bridge on my first date with her. I met her at a midweek party and asked her to Chelsea the following Saturday. She told me that she'd been frantically trying to get hold of me to say she didn't fancy going to watch a football match. But as I was ex-directory, she couldn't make contact. In the end, though, she enjoyed herself."

Bewes would often attend the Bridge with the actor Tom Courtenay, a Hull City fan who also adopted Chelsea as his London team. "I remember one occasion when Tom was having enormous success in the title role in the film Billy Liar. Tom was a little reluctant to go, because he thought people might start pulling his leg. But I managed to persuade him. Sure enough, after a few minutes of the match, some wag started shouting: 'Billy Liar, Billy Liar.' Tom told me that he should have stayed at home. 'No, I replied, it's okay. Just smile at the chap.' Tom did just that and promptly had an orange thrown in his face!"

Based in a studio next door to Stamford Bridge, fashion photographer Eric Swayne knew just about everyone who was anyone on the King's Road scene in the Sixties. Mary Quant and Vidal Sassoon were among his clients, he was on friendly terms with members of The Who and Rolling Stones and, even more impressively, Jane Birkin and Patti Boyd figured among his many girlfriends. Over the years he got to know a number of Chelsea players, although he might never have met any of them if the Blues had been able to keep the ball on the ground . . .

"In 1962 I went freelance and rented my first studio. It was in a block called West London Studios right next to the main entrance of Stamford Bridge. Our block was packed with really well known photographers, which I wasn't at the beginning. It was a bit of a celebrity photographer and model block, a lovely place. At that time the Chelsea team used to have a kickaround every morning in the car park. Their practice balls would occasionally come over the wall, so I often used to rush down to nick one. The players used to come round looking for the balls, but if I'd been around they very rarely found one. I had quite a collection, and I used to take them along to Parsons Green for a kickaround. Anyway, that's how I got to know the players – when they called round to ask for their ball back.

"Three of us in the block of studios had season tickets at Chelsea in the old East Stand and we had two spares as well. There was me, two art directors and in our little cluster of seats we were near Alan Price, Tom Courtenay, and the actor from *The Likely Lads*, Rodney Bewes. Pricey used to come along on one of my tickets sometimes. We had fantastic seats right next to the Directors' Box. I started supporting them the year they came up from the Second Division, 1963. I was immediately hooked on the Blues, like my son now who has a couple of season tickets. It was a very exciting team at the time. They had a devil-may-care attitude which made them great to watch. Alright, they didn't have the discipline of some of the players today and they probably didn't do the same amount of training but they had lovely talent. They were real stars, kind of like pop stars. They were marvellous. A super set of guys.

"Throughout this time I was very busy with my work as a photographer. Ian Quick, who was an art director with a design group called Yellowhammer wanted to do a poster of me for my own publicity. His father, Norman, was the sports photographer with *The Daily Express* and he arranged that some of the Chelsea team would appear in a photo shoot for me at Stamford Bridge.

"I paid a small fee, £50 or so, which was enough in those days. The idea was to have Peter Bonetti in goal with a defensive wall in front of him consisting of me, Johnny Boyle, Keith Weller and Tommy Baldwin. In the end we never did the poster because the guys weren't allowed to wear their Chelsea kit. We took the photos but it would have meant a lot of retouching and stripping the crowd in at the Shed end so we scrapped the idea. Anyway, I remember being very proud that I was wearing Ossie's shorts, which I'd found in the dressing room. Before the photo shoot started we were mucking around and having a kickabout with Keith Weller and the others. Keith put in a cross from the right and I hit it on the volley – pretty well, I felt. I thought 'Yes, goal!' but Peter Bonetti just nonchalantly flicked out a leg and kicked the ball clear. That was annoying enough, but what really got me was that at the time he had his back to me and was deep in conversation with the groundsman!"

In September 1973 Eric was asked by John Boyle to take the photos at his wedding in Walworth, south-east London. Peter Osgood was best man and most of the other Chelsea players were guests. "I knew the footballers who were there but I hadn't met his wife, Madelaine, before or any of his and her family," says Eric. "I just photographed anything that moved, sent off the contacts to John Boyle at Chelsea FC with a little note saying, 'Phone me, when you want to order prints' and he never phoned me. So, I thought, 'Funny bloke, doesn't like the pictures', which I found a bit strange because I did about ten or twelve cassettes of film. I really went for it."

What Eric didn't realise is that Boylers had gone out on loan to Brighton and the photos hadn't been forwarded to him. The pair lost contact and the wedding photos remained lost somewhere in the bowels of Stamford Bridge. Eventually, 28 years later, after Boyle had put out an appeal to readers of the official *Chelsea Magazine* to help him find the photographer, John, Eric and a copy of the snaps were reunited in a heart-warming encounter at the Shed Bar which would surely have brought a tear to the nation's eye had it been captured by daytime TV.

Interestingly, although he was on friendly terms with some of the team, Eric used to steer clear of the players' favourite King's Road pub, the Markham Arms. "I avoided it because the Kray twins used to drink there," he says. "I used to go to the Chelsea Potter instead."

Yet, it was the Potter which was the scene of a massive police raid in 1968 when the Met were on the tail of Great Train Robber Bruce Reynolds. The police had intercepted a telephone message from Reynolds in which he said he would meet his associate at the pub. What they failed to realise, though, was that 'Chelsea Potter' was code for 'Sloane Square tube' so the police ended up missing their prey by a mere couple of hundred yards.

Such excitement was unusual. Most of the time, the King's Road was simply a place to chill out and watch the beautiful people stroll by. "The King's Road was a just marvellous place to be back then," says Eric. "On Saturday mornings I'd drive down the road in my Mini Cooper S with the window down and the stereo on and the number of attractive women you'd see was amazing. In the King's Road I found, so to speak, Roy Boulting's daughter, Enid and Jane Birkin, who I went out with for a while – both stunning girls. The King's Road was a magnet for them."

Fellow photographer Terry O'Neill agrees. "It was always a happy place, everyone was eyeing up the girls. It's not the same now, although the excitement's come back a bit. The girls were all in mini skirts – it was a bit like the south of France, St Tropez or somewhere. It was definitely the best place to go to see beautiful girls in London. Some of them were models, others were ordinary girls but they were all good-looking. You didn't see any rubbish down there!"

London's top totty, some of the capital's best shops, restaurants and bars and all on the doorstep of Stamford Bridge. No wonder the players couldn't keep away from the King's Road.

THE END OF THE DOC

CHAPTER FIVE
THE END OF THE DOC

After playing a series of matches against local opposition and fellow tourists Dundee in North America on their 1967 summer tour, the Blues moved on to Bermuda where they were lined up to play three more games. Often described as 'an island paradise', Bermuda proved to be anything but as one of the matches threatened to spiral out of control.

"We were playing a Caribbean Select XI," remembers Docherty, "and we were six or seven goals up when the local referee sent off Tony Hateley and Peter Houseman for arguing – which was quite unlike either of them. Anyway, they wouldn't go off; so I went on the pitch to sort it out. The ref said, 'Get off my pitch, or I'll report you.' I told him to 'fuck off', and he reported me for swearing."

Tommy Baldwin, meanwhile, has a totally different recollection of the incident which, in time, would come back to haunt Docherty. "We played this game in Bermuda against a local island team and we were about five goals up just before half-time. We were attacking and someone crossed the ball when the lights went out. The lights came on again, went off again and it carried on like that all through the second half. Tommy got fed up with this and took us off the pitch at one stage, which made the referee go mad. We finished the game eventually – I think we won 8-0 or something. After the game we had to walk from the ground along a sandy lane back to the hotel. As I walked along with the other players I could hear Tommy still ranting and raving at the referee, and he was having a go back. Tommy must have said something – I don't know what exactly – and the referee reported it to the English FA."

Whether it centred on a debatable double sending off or faulty Caribbean floodlights, the incident didn't go down well with the Football Association, particularly as the Doc had appeared before their disciplinary panel only the previous year. On that occasion he had been fined £100 for 'ungentlemanly remarks' to a referee after a Youth Cup match at QPR.

As usual, the FA's convoluted disciplinary procedures took a while to whir into motion so Docherty's case was not heard until the start of October 1967. The new season was already well under way by then, with Chelsea having got off to a desperately poor start. Not only were the Blues hovering in lower mid-table, but they had also suffered a couple of consecutive four-goal defeats by Newcastle and Southampton and been pitched out of the League Cup by Second Division Middlesborough. One reporter described the Blues at this time as "a machine for the moment run down, a team out of confidence and lacking their former character."

Charlie Cooke, a complicated individual who was prone to self-doubt, was suffering a low period and was one of those out of form. Meanwhile Peter Osgood, back from injury and leading the attack again following the departure of Hateley to Liverpool, was understandably rusty. The fact that he had put on weight during his long lay-off hadn't helped, and increased the perception among some fans that, although gloriously gifted, Osgood was also a 'lazy' player.

As well as the bad results, Docherty's strained relationship with Chelsea chairman Charles Pratt, who had taken on the role in July 1966 after the death of Joe Mears, provided him with another headache. "Joe Mears died, which was real tragedy for Chelsea," says the Doc. "The new chairman, Charles Pratt, really lived up to his name. I fell out with him at our first meeting when I told him if I wanted his advice I'd ask for it. He didn't like that. Things came to a head when I took a team to the London five-a-side tournament. He asked me what my team was for the first game, and I said, 'I haven't got a team, I've got 12 players.' But he insisted on knowing my team. 'Well,' I thought, 'if that's how he is over a five-a-side, what'll it be like when we play a big match?' I knew I wouldn't be able to work with him, so the next day I told him it would be better if I left."

Docherty, who had signed a five-year contract with Chelsea in December 1966, resigned on the same day as the FA announced their verdict on the incident in Bermuda – a 28-day suspension from all aspects of the game. Under the terms of the suspension Docherty would not even be able to pay to see a game at the turnstiles, let alone coach or manage.

"There was no pressure brought to bear on Mr Docherty to resign, but I can say we were not very pleased at the FA suspension," Chairman Pratt told reporters. "This was something derogatory to a club of which we are very proud." Docherty himself issued a short statement, saying, "This was the time to part company".

The team's dismal form and the FA suspension didn't help but, ultimately, it was the mutual lack of trust and respect between manager and chairman which led to Docherty's departure. Like many Chelsea bosses after him, the Doc had discovered that when manager and chairman fall out there is usually only one winner.

The players were shocked by the news of their manager's departure and were clearly adversely affected the following day when they slumped to a 7-0 defeat at Leeds. Today, affection for the man is still apparent, even amongst those players who suffered the full whirlwind force of the Doc's frequently unpredictable nature. "Tommy was a good motivator," says Docherty lovebite victim Marvin Hinton. "He made you feel you were a much better player than the one you were up against. He was great at building you up."

Tommy Baldwin, who Docherty helped transform from a bit-part player at Arsenal to a Shed legend, is another big fan. "He was very different to my Arsenal manager, Bertie Mee. He was still quite young, about 38 to 40, and he wasn't the tough regimental man that people make out. He didn't mind us having a beer – not before a game, of course – and he would come and join us and have a beer himself. I got on well with him, I think we all did in the team I played in."

John Boyle, one of many young players to be given his Chelsea debut by the Doc, says simply, "He was a wonderful manager, he just encouraged all us youngsters to play."

In assessing Docherty's managerial reign at Stamford Bridge, it is clear that the positives hugely outweigh the negatives on the balance sheet. When he arrived at the club Chelsea were widely regarded as something of a joke and were wholly lacking in direction. A few months earlier the club had failed to hang onto their prize asset, Jimmy Greaves, and 'The Pensioners' tag, despite Ted Drake's best efforts, still attached itself to the team – appropriately, in many ways, considering the large numbers of veteran players in the squad. By clearing out the old stagers and promoting a generation of home-grown youth players to take their places Docherty not only produced a new, energetic young team, he also helped to create a fresh image for the club: dynamic, progressive and forward-thinking. The introduction of the new all-blue kit was symptomatic of this root-and-branch transformation. On the whole, his transfer policy was a success, too, with the likes of Eddie McCreadie, Marvin Hinton and George Graham proving to be genuine bargains. The fact, too, that attendances at the Bridge increased by 30% over the course of his period in charge, rising from an average 27,000 in 1961/62 to 35,000 in 1966/67, demonstrated that Docherty's efforts had the support of the fans.

On the debit side, critics will point to the lack of tangible success of the Docherty era. Yes, his side won the League Cup in 1965 but then, as now, this was not a competition regarded particularly highly by the leading clubs. This criticism, though, is harsh. Chelsea, after all, had only ever won one trophy in the 55 years of their existence prior to Docherty's arrival. To win silverware – of any sort – was a major achievement in that historical context. Nor should the numerous near misses of his reign be dismissed lightly: they showed the football world that Chelsea were a force to be reckoned with, raised the collective pulse of the fans and, crucially, provided the players with all-important big match experience.

A more pertinent criticism is that Docherty's volatile personality sometimes clouded his judgement and, ultimately, led to his downfall. His heavy-handed handling of the Blackpool Incident is a case in point. Was it really necessary to send the players home? And was it wise to sell four of the miscreants soon afterwards? On this second point, though, Docherty can point to his swift purchases of Charlie Cooke and Tommy Baldwin and his careful nurturing of the young Peter Osgood. Few would argue that these were inferior players to the trio they replaced – Terry Venables, George Graham and Barry Bridges.

On the other hand, there is no doubt that Docherty's sharp tongue and fluctuating temper sometimes created problems for himself. It is perhaps significant that of his many run ins with referees Docherty's most violent outbursts came in two essentially meaningless matches – he simply couldn't restrain himself. Nor could he resist some blunt straight talking with the new chairman when another manager might have opted for a more tactful approach. As it turned out, if Docherty had tried harder to muddle along with Pratt he would only have had to put up with his interfering ways for a few months longer. The Chelsea chairman died in March 1968 to be succeeded by Leonard Whithey, and then the following year by Joe Mears' son, Brian.

The past, though, cannot be altered; the ifs, buts and maybes count for nothing. So how will Chelsea history judge Tommy Docherty? Flawed though he was, there can surely only be one answer: despite the limited trophy return, the dressing room bust ups and his cavalier attitude towards the bigwigs in the boardroom, the Doc will be remembered as one of the club's finest and most influential managers.

In the immediate aftermath of Docherty's departure the players publicly lobbied the board to appoint ex-Blues coach Dave Sexton, formerly a player with West Ham, Brighton and Leyton Orient, as his successor.

"We are not trying to tell the directors their job," an unnamed spokesman was quoted as saying, "but we feel it is a good idea if they give us the chance to help choose the new manager. If Ron Stuart [acting manager] takes over, that will be fine by us. But if the board are going to look outside for a new man, we would like them to consider Dave Sexton for the job. He proved he was a great coach when he was here a couple of years ago. He would do a great job for club morale, and his coaching technique could take us right to the top."

For once, the board appeared to listen to the players and offered the job to Sexton, who by now was working as Bertie Mee's assistant at Arsenal. Sexton accepted the offer, and was warmly welcomed back to west London by Charles Pratt. "We regard him as the best man in the world to do the job for which he has come back to Stamford Bridge," said the delighted Chelsea chairman.

Certainly, considering Sexton's track record, it seemed a good choice. After resigning as manager of Leyton Orient in December 1965, Sexton had moved to Fulham as coach and played a big part in saving the Cottagers from relegation to the Second Division. In August 1966 he joined Arsenal, initially as coach, and helped guide the Gunners to their highest place for eight years. True, 7th place didn't exactly turn Islington into a sea of red-and-white bunting, but it represented an improvement in what had been a dire decade for the north Londoners. Above all, Sexton's abilities as a coach and his potential as a manager were well known to the board after his previous spell at the Bridge. Reserved and mild-mannered, Sexton was a very different personality to the maverick Docherty. Not that this counted against him – quite the opposite, in fact. After the turbulence of the Doc's reign, the directors were anxious to appoint a manager who would steer the club into calmer seas.

One of the few people at the Bridge to have reservations about Sexton's appointment was Tommy Baldwin, who confronted the new manager after his first game in charge, a 1–1 home draw with Everton.

"When he got the Chelsea job I thought, 'Oh no, he got rid of me when I was at Arsenal.' The night after the Everton game he had a party for the supporters. We were all at that and I bumped into him and said, 'Are you going to boot me out again, like you did at Arsenal?' He told me to go and see him in his office on Monday but I never went."

Sexton had inherited a talented squad from his predecessor, but one which was under-performing in a manner which would become all too familiar to Chelsea fans over the years. The team was struggling at the wrong end of the table and shipping goals at an alarming rate, so the new manager might have been tempted to concentrate his attention on defensive matters. Sexton, though, had different priorities.

"I got some good advice from Malcolm Allison when I started the Chelsea job," he said some years later. "He said attack should be your number one priority. It's okay boxing clever and all that – but if you want something, you've got to go and get it, haven't you? We never used to take the brakes off. In the long run, it paid off. That's the beauty of taking a positive approach."

Sexton signalled his commitment to attack by his first signing, Sheffield United striker Alan Birchenall. The blond forward, who possessed a sweet left foot he dubbed 'the Claw', arrived with a handy reputation, having struck an average of one goal every three games in a low scoring side. With Osgood, Baldwin and Tambling all still on the payroll, the Chelsea manager now had the luxury of selecting from four quality forwards, or rather he would once the £100,000 new boy had managed to find Stamford Bridge in the A-Z . . .

"I'll never forget my first day at Chelsea," says Birchenall. "I drove down in this red Triumph Spitfire soft top that I'd just bought, thinking I looked the dog's whatsits. So what happens? I only go and get myself lost in the backstreets of west London and end up having to stop and ask this cockney where the ground is. 'Jesus Christ,' this bloke splutters. 'We've lashed out a hundred grand on you and you can't even find your way to the poxy ground. Tell you what, piss off back to Sheffield, you big ponce.' So I'm thinking, 'Well, that's a great start.'"

Once he'd got his bearings, however, Birchenall quickly adjusted to his new surroundings, scoring on his Chelsea debut in a 3–2 win at Sunderland and hitting both goals later that month in a 2–1 Boxing Day defeat of

Arsenal at the Bridge. "I should have had a hat-trick, too," he recalls. "We got a penalty near the end, Johnny Hollins let me take it and I almost hit the corner flag!"

Thanks to improved form after Sexton's arrival the Blues eventually finished in sixth place and qualified again for the Fairs Cup, a creditable achievement given their early season troubles. Peter Osgood's 16 goals made him the club's leading scorer, and allayed fears that he wouldn't be so effective a player after his bad injury. The clean sheet count had picked up, too, especially towards the end of the season when Sexton bought uncompromising defender David Webb from Southampton, with Joe Kirkup moving in the opposite direction in part exchange.

Webb, who had played under Sexton at Orient, was so keen to join Chelsea he even agreed to take a pay cut to join the Blues – an unselfish attitude that epitomised his unflagging commitment to the club in the years that followed. Although he sometimes dived in unnecessarily, Webb tackled like a tank at full speed, passed the ball simply and effectively and, to the initial surprise of his team-mates and the Bridge crowd, proved to be a handy emergency striker when required to play that role.

Webb, though, was cup-tied for the crucial sixth round FA Cup tie at Second Division Birmingham, who included former Docherty Diamonds Barry Bridges and Bert Murray in their line up. The old boys had the last laugh, too, as City beat the Blues 1-0. The Cup would have to wait for at least another year.

At the end of the season Chelsea played QPR in a testimonial for Ken Shellito, who after numerous attempted comebacks had retired from the game through injury. There was a surprise for the 21,000 fans when Alan Birchenall trooped off to be replaced by Jimmy Tarbuck. "Dave Sexton decided to take off one comedian and put on another," quips the Birch. "Tarby was a Liverpool fan but like a lot of London-based showbiz people at the time he adopted Chelsea as his second team. But the main thing was we got a decent crowd along because Ken had been a good servant to Chelsea."

Sad though it was, Shellito's retirement represented another broken link with the Docherty era. Gradually, over the course of the 1968/69 season and beyond, Sexton began to forge a team which was increasingly in his own image. But it was most definitely a process of evolution rather revolution. Trimming his squad, Sexton moved on a number of fringe players, including occasional winger Joe Fascione, and back-up defenders Geoff Butler, Colin Waldron and Jim Thomson.

Among those to benefit from the Sexton regime, meanwhile, were Peter
Houseman and Ian Hutchinson. After five years in the squad, during
which he had made fewer than 100 first-team appearances, Houseman
finally made the left-wing slot his own in the 1968/69 season. Many fans
had doubts about a player who lacked two ingredients often thought
essential to the winger's craft: pace and trickery. However, Sexton gradually became convinced that Houseman's crossing ability, allied to his
stamina and the natural balance his left-footedness gave the side, merited
his inclusion in the team.

Ian Hutchinson, a rough-round-the-edges striker with then non-league
Cambridge United, was spotted by Sexton's assistant Ron Suart and snapped
up by the Blues for a bargain £5,000 in July 1968. Initially raw, awkward
and lacking in self-confidence, Hutch took a while to adapt to life at the
Bridge and seemed destined to be used mainly as cover for the likes of
Osgood, Baldwin, Tambling and Birchenhall. In only his second game for
the Blues, though, he unleashed his party piece, a massive long-throw
which flicked off Ipswich's Bill Baxter and into the net. Sexton was
impressed: this was a new tactic which clearly unsettled defences and,
along with Hutchinson's strength in the air and fearlessness in the box,
made the newcomer a more interesting proposition than he first appeared.
The only problem facing Sexton was how to best utilise the vast attacking
talent at his disposal. This dilemma led him to employing Peter Osgood
in midfield for much of the season, an experiment which was only
partially successful.

The battle for places in defence was equally fierce, particularly after
Sexton bought Fulham centre half John Dempsey in January 1969. An
uncomplicated stopper who was commanding in the air, a strong tackler
and tidy in his distribution from the back, Dempsey would go on to
form solid central defensive partnerships with both Ron Harris and, when
Chopper later moved across to full back, David Webb.

Inevitably, some players found themselves being less involved than they
had been under Docherty. Marvin Hinton was one player who found
himself watching from the bench or the stand more often than he would
have liked, while John Boyle was another who could no longer be sure
of a starting position.

"I don't think that Dave liked me as a player," he says candidly. "The
funny thing is, though, that he used to get the players to mark each
other out of 10 in different categories to find out if you'd had a good

game or not – and I always did well. We'd all put the marks down on a form, hand it to Dave and he'd work out the average. I usually figured near the top of the list because it was all about what Dave thought was important in the game – tracking back, chasing, tackling, lasting till the 90th minute and so on. I had all those qualities, you see. I remember it was always a problem what to put down for Ossie. I mean, chasing back . . . o out of 10?"

Sexton had good cause to study his prototype Opta-style stats during the 1968/69 season, which followed a now familiar Chelsea pattern. The Blues finished fifth in the league, without ever seriously challenging runaway champions Leeds. Again, the various cups promised much but delivered nothing but disappointment. In the League Cup Chelsea were once more the victims of a giant-killing, going out to Second Division Derby County in the third round. In the Fairs Cup, the Blues had an even more unpleasant shock, succumbing to little-known Dutch outfit DWS Amsterdam on the toss of a coin following two 0–0 draws.

Yet again, the FA Cup appeared to offer the best chance of glory. After goals from Peter Osgood and Bobby Tambling saw off Carlisle in the third round, the Blues drew 0–0 at Preston and were leading 2–0 in the replay when the Bridge floodlights failed in the second half and play had to be abandoned. To prevent a possible repeat of this fiasco, the rematch was held on the following Monday afternoon yet still attracted a crowd of more than 36,000. Many local schools, perhaps appreciating that double maths couldn't compete with the prospect of seeing the Blues in action, simply threw in the towel and took their pupils along to the game. As it turned out, Chelsea provided a useful lesson for the youngsters in the merits of perseverance as Webb and Cooke scored in the closing minutes to wipe out Preston's first half lead.

After Stoke had been accounted for in the fifth round, the Blues were rewarded with a home draw in the quarter-finals against the Cup holders, West Bromwich Albion – a tricky but eminently winnable tie. The result, a 2–1 defeat, had pessimistic fans in the 52,285 crowd wondering whether the Londoners' name would ever appear on the Cup. Frustratingly, the Blues travelled to the Hawthorns the following week for a run-of-the-mill league match and cruised to a 3–0 win. "That summed up how inconsistent we were at that time," admits John Dempsey.

You could, it seemed, change the manager, change the team and change the chairman. Changing the Blues' erratic nature was another story.

CHAPTER SIX

THE BOOZE

CHAPTER SIX
THE BOOZE

few years ago, an hour or so after Chelsea had famously thrashed Manchester United 5-0, Blues fans celebrating in a Fulham Road pub were a little surprised but nonetheless thrilled when Dennis Wise walked through the doors for a post-match pint. For the lager-swilling, blue-clad throng, life couldn't get much better than this: a hugely enjoyable massacre of the despised 'Manure' followed by the sight of their beloved skipper joining them in a few rousing choruses of 'Carefree', 'Blue Flag' and 'Who put the ball in the United net?'

Although it was only a fleeting, incident-free visit, Wise's swift half in an unfashionable Fulham boozer still made the tabloids. It wasn't exactly 'Scoop of the Year' material but, in an age when Premiership players have become increasingly remote from their public, enjoying mind-boggling salaries and glittering lifestyles almost beyond the comprehension of the average supporter, the Chelsea's captain's unexpected pub appearance was seen as worthy of a few column inches.

Rewind the clock 30 years, however, and any hack who suggested to his editor that 'Chelsea player spotted in King's Road pub' might make a good splash would be given short shrift and, quite possibly, his P45. News, after all, by its very definition, is something that is out-of-the-ordinary rather than an everyday occurrence and, much to manager Dave Sexton's dismay, the sight of one or more of his star players knocking back a pint or six in one of the local hostelries around the Bridge was far from uncommon.

Back in the sixties and seventies most teams had players who spent more time in the pub than on the training ground, but the Chelsea lads could make a good claim for being top of the unofficial drinking league.

By all accounts, their appetite for alcohol was truly gargantuan. Yes, there were some notable exceptions, with the clean-living trio of Peter Bonetti, John Hollins and Peter Houseman, in particular, preferring to disappear off to their families in the suburbs rather than going out on the town. Little matter, the rest of the team, led by Peter Osgood, Charlie Cooke, Tommy Baldwin and Alan Hudson, did their boozing for them as they bar-hopped their way down the King's Road on a regular basis. Indeed, Baldwin's capacity for beers and spirits was so immense it earned him the nickname 'the Sponge'.

"It was John Hollins who coined it," says Tommy. "When I first came to Chelsea I was introduced to all the players and John said to me, 'Hello, you're the Sponge, aren't you?' I just laughed, but later on I asked him, 'What's with the Sponge?' He said he'd been away with England Under 23s and Jon Sammels, who played with me at Arsenal, had told him all about me. 'You drink so much you must have a sponge in your stomach,' John said, and the nickname stuck." From time to time the name would even appear in the club programme, although the implication was always that the unusual moniker stemmed from the striker's shirt-drenching efforts on the field rather than his insatiable thirst off it.

When it came to finding a place to sup, Baldwin and co had no shortage of choices. Among the numerous pubs within walking distance of the Bridge, the players' favourites included the Lord Palmerston, at the top of the King's Road near the old Shed entrance; the Ifield Tavern, around the corner from the ground in Ifield Road; and the Markham Arms, a dark, cavernous pub halfway down the King's Road, next door to Alexander's restaurant. Sadly, none of these pubs are what they were in their seventies heyday: the Lord Palmerston, once a famous boxing-themed pub, is now the characterless Morrison's; the Ifield has been transformed into a yuppie gastro-pub; and, saddest of all, the Markham is now a branch of the Abbey National.

As Alan Birchenall recalls, the Markham was the most popular pub among the Chelsea boys for a lunchtime session. "We'd finished training at Mitcham and then, a bit later, we'd be on the King's Road sat in the Markham Arms with shepherd's pie and beans, looking out of the window at all the sights the street had to offer at the time. You didn't have all-day opening in those days but the pubs were never in a rush to throw us Chelsea players out at half two, and we managed to keep going through the afternoon. It was a similar story at the Ifield and the Lord Palmerston after evening games. We'd go round there, they'd pull the curtains and we'd stay in for a few after closing time."

In those days, 'lock-ins' were a part of London pub culture and, although illegal, the police tended to turn a blind eye as long as there were no complaints about rowdy, drunken behaviour. They might have adopted a more hardline approach, however, if they'd known what some of the late-night drinkers were planning.

"After the Fairs Cup tie against DWS Amsterdam in 1968 I went to the Lord Palmerston with Ossie," remembers the Birch. "The match was boring, a 0–0 draw. It was an early season game, a balmy evening, and everyone was in shirt sleeves. Ossie was by the fireplace, I went to get the drinks in at the bar where there was a guy with a thick black Crombie coat on. I looked at him and thought, 'God, he looks a bit dodgy.' He turned to me and said, 'You were fucking rubbish, you lot tonight.'

"He was a big bloke so I thought it best to agree with him. I wasn't going to argue. The bar was crowded and while we were waiting to get served, just as a matter of conversation, I said to him 'Blimey, aren't you hot in that?' pointing at his coat. He looked at me and said 'Yes I am, but there's a reason I'm wearing it.' Then he pulled open the coat and when I peered inside I saw the handle of a double-barrelled shotgun. I crapped myself, picked up the pints and went over to Ossie and whispered in his ear, 'Come on, let's get out of here!' He said 'Why? We've just got a pint in!' But I insisted we got out, because I thought the guy was about to do someone in the pub. You've got to remember those were the days of the Richardsons and the Krays, so there was no point taking chances.

"Anyway, the next day we forgot about it until we picked up an *Evening Standard* on our way back home from training. There was a huge great headline – 'Gangland Shooting on Fulham Palace Road.' Apparently a car pulled up outside a house, a guy got out, then another car came alongside and blew both the bloke's legs off. I said to Ossie, 'That's the geezer I was with last night in the pub.' A week later I was back in the Palmerston and asked the landlord about the bloke in the Crombie and he told me to zip it. I didn't need to be told twice, I can tell you."

If that was a case of a drinking bout coming to a premature end, the Birch more than made up for it on another occasion when he joined Charlie Cooke, Peter Osgood and John Boyle for possibly the longest and most inebriated lunch in Chelsea history. "We were all slightly injured," recalls Boylers, "and to stop us from swinging the lead, we had to report for treatment every few hours. Anyway, we went off to Barbarella's – the restaurant just outside Stamford Bridge – for lunch and the waiter said, 'Why not have a bottle of wine with your meal?' So we had a bottle which, inevitably, led to another one.

"Meanwhile, Dave Sexton had already been in, had his lunch and left. When a third bottle of wine arrived, the Birch actually went off for treatment leaving the three of us there; then a few minutes later he came running back and told us that Harry Medhurst, our physio, was doing his nut. But we had another bottle of wine opened, so we didn't want to leave. Fourteen bottles of wine later, there's Charlie waving a pen around, trying to sign a cheque. He needn't have bothered, the bank sent it back later as the signature was totally illegible. Unfortunately, one of the newspapers got hold of the story and Dave left us all out for the next match at Southampton."

One of the players to benefit from Sexton's crackdown was Alan Hudson, who replaced Cooke and made his Chelsea debut at The Dell in an eminently forgettable 5–0 defeat. It wasn't long, though, before Hudson himself had fallen foul of the manager in very similar circumstances, although the amount of alcohol involved on this occasion was a mere dribble in comparison. All the same, the incident is worth relating as it reveals the extent to which Sexton was angered and frustrated by what he perceived to be the dominant 'drinking culture' at the Bridge.

"The first team were having a bad time and me, Bill Garner and Stevie Kember were injured and having treatment," remembers 'Huddy'. "At lunchtime we went down the Markham to have lunch. They used to do a nice shepherd's pie so we had that and a couple of pints of lager. Then we went back for more treatment. We got back to the Bridge and Dave was waiting for us. He glared at us and said, 'Where have you three been?' We told him we'd been out for our lunch break but he still didn't look happy. 'You've been down the pub!' he said, and I replied 'Yeah, we've been down the Markham, but we're not fit to train this afternoon'. He went mad, absolutely crazy: 'Do you realise our team is struggling? And you're down the pub!' But I said, 'What can we do? We're not fit, we won't be playing on Saturday and we haven't gone down there to have 12 pints, we just had a couple.' But that just made him madder."

Incidents like that one, and the infamous 'Barberella's lunch' a few years earlier, led the Chelsea manager to take a number of unpopular measures in an effort to stop his players from drinking.

"Sexton used to get really upset when he saw the players in the old East Stand before the game drinking with the showbiz stars – people like Dennis Waterman, Michael Crawford, John Cleese, Sean Connery, Richard O'Sullivan and Rodney Bewes," says Hudson. "He really didn't like us hanging out with them. Of course, you only did that when you were injured or hadn't been picked. But he'd do really stupid things like put a note up saying anybody who wasn't playing should not be seen with alcohol. It didn't make any difference, mind you. We'd still go up to the East Stand, where we used to watch the games, and have a nice large brandy in a coffee cup. When he walked by us, we'd smile at him and although he knew what was going on he wouldn't stop us. There were supporters around and there would have been trouble if he'd had a go at us. Anyway, if you're not playing what's the harm? It was almost as if he was on a crusade – you mustn't do this, you mustn't do that."

Top of the list of 'no-noes', of course, was getting plastered the evening before a game. To be fair to the players, it seems that they were sufficiently professional to realise that this was a reasonable demand and, when questioned, they'll usually say that they never drank on the eve of a match. The big boozy sessions, they stress, happened after games not before them.

That may be true, but it's equally the case that the players didn't always switch to orange juice or Coca-Cola on Friday nights. Even Alan Birchenall – who insists "You couldn't play at that level and abuse your body drinking all the time" – admits that there were occasions when the players' pre-match preparation included a few beers. In particular, he remembers a night out in Manchester before the Blues were due to play at Old Trafford.

"We went out of the hotel for a look around and popped into the local Mecca. It was the usual suspects – Ossie, the Sponge and so on. It was one of my first away trips and it amazed me that we were out at all. I thought, 'We're going to get an arseholing tomorrow' because we were up against George Best, Bobby Charlton and Denis Law – basically the United side that won the European Cup. But we won it easily, 4–0, and I got one of the goals. I couldn't believe it. I was thinking, 'Is this the way Chelsea do things? Go out and have a couple of pints before a game and then go and put in a performance like that?' But it was just a couple of pints, not a session. Some of the boys were on a scouting mission for talent, but not the football type. One or two had a bit of success but I wasn't interested. I just stood in a dark corner because I couldn't believe what I was doing on a Friday night before such a big game. Friday night was sacrosanct at Sheffield United, you just never went out anywhere."

Stuffed like a plump Christmas turkey on their own patch, the United players would probably agree that the Blues showed no ill effects from their night on the town – quite the reverse, if anything. A year earlier, though, it had been a different story as a hungover Chelsea team crashed to one of their heaviest all-time defeats, 7–0 against arch rivals Leeds.

"It was the game after Tommy Docherty was sacked," says John Boyle. "We were leaving to go to Leeds on Friday lunchtime and we said goodbye to the Doc outside the gates at Stamford Bridge. It was a funny situation, the whole club seemed to be in turmoil. We got up there and after we went out to the cinema we brought a bottle of vodka back to the hotel. There were about five or six of us, including Eddie McCreadie who was the captain, sitting around getting drunk on the stuff. I wouldn't say we were especially affected by it the next day because we were so fit you could just work it out of your system. But it's not the sort of thing that you could do every week and, in fact, it was the only time in my ten years at the club that we went drinking the night before a game.

"The funny thing is we had a team meeting afterwards and McCreadie said something like 'Don't blame me, I played like three men out there', and somebody else said, 'Yeah, you played like Boyle, Baldwin and Cooke', because we'd all had shockers. 'You played like them three.'"

The Leeds debacle may have been the absolute low point of the period, but it was far from being unique. Some other surprising results from the Docherty and Sexton eras included a 5–1 defeat at Newcastle in August 1967, a 6–2 home thrashing by Southampton the following month and a 5–2 reverse at champions-to-be Everton in March 1970. Simple off days, the likes of which happen to all teams every now and then? Or could alcohol have played a part in the maulings, as surely it did at Elland Road? Certainly, Alan Hudson reckons that Chelsea's poor performance at Goodison Park could at least partially be explained by the fact that two players, David Webb and John Dempsey, stayed out well beyond the curfew imposed by Dave Sexton.

"The last person you want to be marking when you're hungover is Joe Royle," he laughs, referring to Everton's powerfully-built centre forward at the time. "Sexton used to have a fellow called Bill Edwards come along with the staff. He would look after the kit, but he was also a kind of spy. He'd stay up in the hotel on a Friday night and make sure all the players were back at the appointed time. It wasn't a surprise about Webby being out, but John Dempsey was another matter, because that wasn't him. But it came back through Bill that the two of them had been out."

Dempsey, though, strongly denies that he left the hotel at all and, in any case, Chelsea historians usually point to the absence of Peter Bonetti – Tommy Hughes, who had already conceded five against Leeds at Stamford Bridge earlier that season, replaced him in goal – as a crucial contributing factor to the massacre. Hudson himself, meanwhile, admits to being hungover during a couple of matches, including one at the Bridge against Crystal Palace when he needed a 'livener' in the Adelaide pub on the King's Road before he felt up to playing.

More generally, though, Alvaro Maccioni, the owner of the exclusive King's Road niterie The Aretusa, suggests that the players' protestations that they were always tucked up in bed with a warm cup of Horlicks at ten pm on Friday nights should be taken with the proverbial pinch of salt, if not a whole fistful.

"They used to stay in the club until late," he chuckles, "sometimes when they should not have been there at all. And they were out the night before matches – not regularly, but occasionally. I certainly remember one or two nights when they were in the club the night before games. Usually it was the ones who were local, Charlie Cooke, Tommy Baldwin and so on.

"One particular evening, at around 11pm, Dave Sexton called at the door when quite a few of the players were in the club. I didn't want them to get caught so I quickly sent someone down to tell the players 'The Boss is here!' while I chatted to Dave at the door. That gave them time to sneak out of the back entrance. I didn't want them to get into trouble because they were all great boys. Yes, they had a drink but they never got drunk or caused any problems. They just enjoyed themselves, whether they were having a quiet drink together or dancing in the disco downstairs."

With friends like Alvaro on the look-out for them, the players could often conceal their alcohol-fuelled antics from the manager. Sometimes, though, they so overstepped the mark that it wasn't Dave Sexton they needed to worry about, but those other boys in blue, the Metropolitan Police. One player to fall foul of the law was Tommy Baldwin who, early in his Chelsea career, unwittingly found himself caught up in a scene straight out of an episode of the popular seventies TV show *The Sweeney*.

"I was in the White Hart pub in Southgate with a few of the Arsenal players. It was a popular footballers' pub and Tottenham players used to go there as well. Anyway, this guy who I knew from my Arsenal days was there – he was always around the players – and he suddenly announced, 'I've got this party to go to.' So I said, 'Right, let's go.'

We got a bottle of vodka from the pub and headed off to the party – which was not far away in somewhere like Wood Green – with a couple of girls we'd been out with. I was sitting at the back of the car with one of the girls, while the guy I knew was driving. Suddenly he said, 'Oh no, there's a police car following me.' I said, 'What's the problem?' and he told me he was either banned from driving or he didn't have a licence, I can't remember which.

"I tried to calm him down but he was getting very jittery. 'I can't stop, I've got to get away from here,' he said and he put his foot down and we shot off towards Hackney. The police were right behind us still and I could see that we would be stopped eventually. I wasn't worried about that but I couldn't help thinking about the bottle of vodka I had with me. I really didn't want Dave Sexton getting to hear that I'd been out drinking. So, as we went round a corner, I threw the bottle into a gap between the cars and it smashed into pieces on the road. We carried on, going down a one-way system the wrong way and banging into a few cars along the way. By now there were about 40 police cars chasing us and a roadblock had been set up at Old Street. To avoid the roadblock the driver turned off and we found ourselves in a back alley or dead end with a police car right behind us. I couldn't even get out of the car at first because it was jammed in – eventually I managed to get out of the back with the girl I was with.

"They took me to Old Street police station and the driver to another station. They kept saying, 'Who's the guy who threw the bottle at the police car?' In the police station there was a bit of a fracas when they tried to put me in a cell. I didn't want to go in there, and I just stopped dead. The sergeant blew his whistle, three or four policeman came running into the room and they literally picked me up, gave me a couple of belts around the face and threw me in a cell. They charged me with assaulting a policeman and throwing a bottle of vodka at a police car.

"It was all over the news that I'd been arrested. I went to Old Street magistrates' court for the case the next morning. I looked a right mess – my shirt was all ripped, I had dried blood all down my face and my nose was sticking out at a funny angle. I pleaded not guilty and the case went to Crown Court. I was charged with assault. 'You're joking aren't you,' I told my solicitor, 'drunk and disorderly maybe, but they can't do me for that!' But I was found guilty and I was given four months in prison.

"Back in the cells at Old Street police station I was sitting there thinking it through and, oddly enough, the one thing that kept going through my head was that at least I'd be able to get properly fit because I wouldn't be drinking inside. Then the solicitor came down and said, 'Sorry Tommy, I can't believe they've done that to you! What do you want me to do?' I said, 'I don't know, just get me out of here!' So he said he'd appeal against the sentence and ten minutes later he came back and told me they were letting me go, I was being let out on appeal.

"Chelsea were great about it, and Dave Sexton came along with me to court. At the appeal the police got into a bit of a muddle with their evidence and the magistrate decided their case wasn't proven, so he suspended the sentence."

The whole episode should have been a salutary lesson for the Sponge, but it wasn't long before he was in back in trouble – and, once again, drink was the root cause. "A bit later on I got done on the breathalyser," he admits, a touch sheepishly. "I got banned for a year. I think I must have been the first footballer to fall foul of the breathalyser because it was only introduced in 1967."

Baldwin was not the only Chelsea player to have a brush with the law. Peter Osgood was arrested after over-exuberantly celebrating the Blues' League Cup semi-final win in January 1972 (see Chapter 13, *Blue is the Colour*), although the fact that Chelsea's vanquished opponents were hated north London rivals Tottenham was surely a mitigating factor any judge or jury would have to take into account.

With incident piling on incident, Chelsea supporters must have been wondering whether Dave Sexton didn't have the right idea with his zealous anti-drink drive. At one point, in a bid to keep a closer eye on his wayward charges, Sexton persuaded the club to put the players up en masse at the Kensington Palace Hotel the night before home league games. The policy might have worked if the players hadn't started taking their dirty washing along for the hotel laundry to clean every week. Eventually, with the bills getting larger by the week, the expense could no longer be justified and the players were once again left to their own devices on Friday nights.

Drinking on aeroplanes was another issue Sexton tried to tackle, and during the Blues' European Cup Winners Cup campaign in 1970/71 he introduced a complete ban. "That didn't go down too well with everybody but it was sensible enough," says John Boyle, "because of the effects of drinking on a plane."

Other players, though, while accepting the policy for the outward journey, were unwilling to celebrate a good result on foreign soil with a glass of tonic water or lemonade. "We just had orange juice in our champagne and he didn't know then, did he?" laughs Peter Osgood. "We'd be at the back of the plane with the stewardesses having a great time, while Dave was up the front. The ban didn't work at all."

At times it sounds as though Dave Sexton would have had an easier life as headmaster of St Trinian's. However, he has always denied the suggestion that the players turned Stamford Bridge into an anarchic, drink-soaked playground. "My players weren't difficult – quite the opposite," he once said. "The problem is what success does. It's liable to change your outlook on life. When you haven't got anything, you get on with things – you're hungrier. Once you start getting money and fame, it becomes difficult.

"They were decent blokes, but they were subject to the same temptations as anybody else who comes into a degree of success. For example, you get invited to a lot of dinners and social events – and before you know it, they're professional athletes living the life of rich playboys. They're eating good food and drinking fine wines. With success come the trappings, and sometimes you get carried away. But basically they were good lads."

Nonetheless, he has admitted that there were occasions, such as the 'Barbarella's Incident', which tried his patience. "Mostly you're better off turning a blind eye, but sometimes you have to act. That day they were supposed to be back for treatment of their injuries."

Sexton's attitude to alcohol was very different to that of his predecessor, Tommy Docherty, who would often join his players for a beer. Indeed, as John Boyle recalls, the Doc was often the instigator of the drinking sessions. "When we were staying in a hotel Tommy Doc would order bottles of champagne in the bar and get them signed off as rounds of sandwiches and teas on the club bill. Another thing we used to do when we were on tour was to order drinks, get one in for the chairman Brain Mears as well, get him in a good mood and sign them off to the room number of the club secretary, John Battersby. And he used to pay it."

Compared to Docherty, Sexton must have come across at times as a right old party pooper yet, strangely, he didn't seem to mind the players having a quick pre-match snifter in the inner sanctum of the dressing room.

"There was tradition at both Arsenal and Chelsea where they used to have a bottle of whisky on the changing room table," explains the Sponge. "Everyone could have a nip to calm their nerves before they went out. A lot of them would go for it. Some players would have a cigarette or two, as well, especially Eddie McCreadie. He smoked 60 a day, but he was still one of the fittest players at the club. Before games you never saw him, he was always disappearing into the toilets for a fag."

Many famous footballers, including Bobby Charlton, Gianluca Vialli and Gerson, the midfield playmaker in Brazil's legendary 1970 World Cup-winning side, have been heavy smokers, so McCreadie was not alone in his addiction to the evil weed. More interesting, perhaps, is the question of whether the smokers in the Chelsea squad ever puffed on anything stronger than a John Player Special. This, after all, was a period when fashionable London was taking a lead from the growing hippy movement and starting to experiment with cannabis, thanks in part to its endorsement by leading celebrities such as Mick Jagger and Paul McCartney.

No doubt to Dave Sexton's huge relief, however, mind-altering drugs barely appear to have registered on the Chelsea players' collective radar. "To my knowledge, nobody in football dabbled in drugs in the sixties and seventies," insists Alan Birchenall. "We didn't need to get our kicks that way." Indeed, the Birch readily admits to being totally unaware of the burgeoning underground drugs scene in the country until he arrived in the capital following his transfer from Sheffield United.

"I went to a party at my agent's flat where Eric Burndon and the Animals, two Beatles and a Rolling Stone were among the guests," he recalls. "I'd just come down from Sheffield as one of the first £100,000 signings and I couldn't believe it. There I was, sat in the middle of a room surrounded by all these people who I'd only seen before on TV and in magazines. I sat on a settee next to a model, and we were chatting away although she didn't have a clue who I was. My agent was introducing me – 'This is Alan Birchenall, Chelsea's new £100,000 signing' and all this bollocks. The only thing I had in common with that lot was that I had long blond hair.

"The girl next to me was rolling her own. She lit it up, took a puff and then said, 'Can I interest you in this?' I looked at her a bit bemused and said, 'Sorry, I only smoke menthols.' So she took a couple of puffs and handed it to the woman on the other side of her. They both looked at me like I was from a different planet. Obviously it was the old wacky baccy. That's how ignorant I was about the drugs scene. Otherwise, you never saw it as a player.

"Over in California, where I played in the mid-seventies, it was a different ball game. Even the Mayor used to have a smoke of the stuff outside the town hall. It was almost obligatory. We had half a team of Americans smoking that stuff. My wife nearly got hooked by accident. One of the guys gave her a cookie one day and she didn't realise what sort of cookie it was – of course, it was one of those funny cookies and she was flying for about three days after eating it."

It seems pretty clear then that, although they may have looked like a bunch of toked-up hippies with their shoulder-length hair, pork chop sideburns and garish clothes the team weren't indulging in the illicit substances which, presumably, many Chelsea fans were enjoying in the late sixties and early seventies. On the other hand, some of the players with longstanding injury problems were already popping enough legal pills to fell an elephant.

"I was like a junkie," Ian Hutchinson told an interviewer a year before his death in 2002. "There was no way I would have passed a drugs test if they'd had them then. I used to be on eight anti-inflammatory tablets a day. And then there were the cortisone injections. You couldn't walk for two days afterwards, but the important thing was that you'd be all right for Saturday."

Hutch's dedication to the cause was well beyond the call to duty, but was by no means unique. Other Blues players, too, regularly played through the pain barrier in an effort to help the club gain valuable league points or go through to the next round of a cup. Little wonder, then, that once the final whistle went their thoughts turned pretty quickly to that first post-match pint.

As we've already seen, most of the players liked a drink or two, but just how much of the stuff were they putting away? As anyone who's ever had a skinful knows it all becomes a bit of a blur after the third or fourth pint so, unsurprisingly, the recollections of the players are not wholly reliable. Fortunately, the well-known London photographer Terry O'Neill, who was friendly with some members of the team, can shed some light on this crucial question.

"I used to go out with the players occasionally," he says. "At least I'd go out with them until a certain time, because they had a capacity to drink which was phenomenal. I don't know how they did it. I mean they'd start at lunchtime and they'd be drinking up to midnight and beyond. It was incredible. Most of the time it was Ossie, Alan Hudson, Charlie Cooke, Eddie McCreadie and a couple of others, John Boyle and John Dempsey. I'd stay with them as long as I could last, because I wasn't a big drinker. They always used to go round a set of the pubs and clubs in Chelsea.

"I only drank a couple of glasses of wine when I was out with them, and the wine wasn't much to shout about at the time. But they drank heavily. I kept a gap from them, really, because it was fun to talk to them about football but apart from that we didn't share the same mentality. I'm not being a snob, but they were lads looking to enjoy themselves and we had jobs to do, so you couldn't just disappear with them all day. They were a confident bunch but you couldn't help wondering what they'd do after football."

Dave Sexton may not have approved, but the fact that the players were using the same pubs as local Chelsea fans helped create a very special bond between the team and the supporters.

"We used to mix with the fans all the time, especially in the Lord Palmerston," says Tommy Baldwin. "The pub was run by the Mancinis, who were a big boxing family. The 'guvnor' was the uncle of Terry Mancini, who played for QPR and Arsenal. The pub was near the ground and it became our regular haunt. All the fans knew we'd be in there after games, so we used to get mobbed when we went in. We always had a whip but lots of the time, especially if we'd won, fans would come up to us and offer to buy drinks. Most of the time we'd tell them we were okay, because we didn't mind getting our own drinks. The fans weren't slow to let you know what they thought – if you'd had a bad game you got slaughtered but if you'd had a good game you got the applause.

"After night matches we'd stay in the pub till closing time and then go on to a club. Quite often we'd go to the Aretusa – I used to be in there all the time as I lived locally – or we'd go the Sportsman on Tottenham Court Road because it had a casino. More often than not I was out with Charlie Cooke because he lived in the same area as me. A lot of the other guys were married and lived further out so we didn't see them socially so often."

All the players, though, are adamant that there were no splits in the camp between the hellraisers and the stay-at-homes, the big boozers and the apple juice drinkers.

"I think the one thing we had going for us was a fantastic, happy dressing room," says Ron Harris. "We had about 16 or 18 players and near enough everybody got on well. There was never a little clique in one corner and another in another corner. If we went up to Blackpool to stay before a match everybody used to go out together. Not just five or six of us. Peter Bonetti and Johnny Hollins were maybe the ones who didn't go out, but everyone else did. We didn't shun them, we always asked them, but they usually said they weren't bothered. Which was fine." Possibly, Hollins' reluctance to join the others stemmed from his involvement in the Blackpool Incident.

Alan Hudson makes a similar point to Harris, saying, "The lads never had a problem with Peter Bonetti, Johnny Hollins and Peter Houseman living their lives the way they did. It didn't matter that they didn't come out with us. We had a mix of characters which was good. What would have happened if those three had been as bad as the rest of us, I don't know!"

Dave Sexton, for once, would surely find it impossible to disagree with Huddy on that point.

CHAPTER SEVEN
THE CUP AT LAST

CHAPTER SEVEN
THE CUP AT LAST

A few minutes before the start of the 1970 FA Cup Final at Wembley the players of Chelsea and Leeds were presented to the Royal Guest of Honour, Princess Margaret. "While we were chatting she said she hoped Chelsea would win," skipper Ron Harris told Blues programme editor Albert Sewell afterwards.

Now it's possible, of course, that the Princess' remarks were merely a part of Cup Final royal protocol and that she went on to make similarly encouraging comments to Leeds' captain, Billy Bremner. On the other hand, Mags might well have had a genuine affinity for Chelsea. The Blues were, after all, the local team to Buckingham Palace and her bohemian tastes often took her to some of the same King's Road haunts frequented by Ossie, Huddy and the Sponge. By contrast, the Princess was not known to have any close links with Leeds or, indeed, with Yorkshire.

Given Chelsea's appalling luck in the Cup in previous years they needed all the extra support they could get. And, for a change, they got a fair dose of good fortune throughout their 1970 campaign, never once being drawn to play outside London. The third round draw set the tone, with the Blues landing a home tie against Second Division Birmingham City.

In the build-up to the game with City Dave Sexton, along with five other managers, was asked by *The Times* to name his tips for the Cup. "May I give Chelsea as the winners?" he replied boldly. "We have gone close so often, I believe it is our turn. We are going well at the right time; confidence is sky-high, and Hollins and Hudson are now reliable midfield dynamos. There is skill on the ground, height near goal to knock in the crosses and we can play in any conditions."

The reference to Alan Hudson showed just how central the 18-year-old midfielder had become to Sexton's side. Having broken into the Chelsea team in the autumn, Hudson had swiftly become the Blues' playmaker, spreading passes around the pitch in the manner of his boyhood hero, former England captain Johnny Haynes.

Like many top-class players, he was an expert at shrugging off the attentions of opponents, either with his trademark drag back or by surging forward with the ball from deep positions. Perhaps, though, it was his ability to knit together team play with his unerringly accurate distribution which was his most valuable asset. Pre-Hudson, the Blues had often appeared somewhat disjointed, a collection of talented individuals lacking unity and cohesion; now, with the youngster directing play, his socks round his ankles and long hair flapping in the breeze, the Blues at last looked like a real team.

Apart from the introduction of Hudson, another important change came in defence where Sexton had switched from the man-to-man marking system most teams employed to zonal marking. "There were a few teething problems but it worked 90 per cent of the time," says John Dempsey. "Dave had bought me because he wanted somebody commanding in the air and, in my first season at Chelsea, I would always pick up the opposition's taller striker. Then, when we switched to zonal marking, I would mark the striker who was in my space. That was fine, but it would be a bit worrying if Ron Harris, who was quite short for a central defender, found himself on the far post marking a 6ft 3in striker like Tony Hateley or Ron Davies. Having said that, I can't remember any vital goals we conceded that way. I think Dave made the switch because he'd been influenced by the continental teams who used zonal marking."

As the 1969/70 season progressed, with Chelsea climbing the league after a slow start, Sexton's work with his players on the training ground could also be clearly seen in the team's shape and style of play.

"At the back our top priority was to defend," says Dempsey. "Eddie McCreadie, who had pace, would get forward down the left but we didn't really have an overlapping right-back. Both Ron Harris and David Webb played in that position, but they were not natural right-backs and didn't push forward much. In midfield, John Hollins was a very gritty player who would get up and down, he was the engine room of the team. Alongside him, Alan Hudson was very skilful and creative and would make a lot of openings. Peter Houseman on the left, who was a very underrated player, and Charlie Cooke on the right would both get forward and, when the opposition attacked, come back to help out the defence. Peter would tend to stay on the wing but Charlie, who had played in central midfield, would come inside more. They were both good crossers of the ball, which suited Peter Osgood and Ian Hutchinson, who were both very good in the air. So, we had a 4-2-4 when we were attacking which switched to 4-4-2 if the move broke down. The flexibility in the formation came from how the midfield was set up."

With the new midfield blending well, Chelsea's forwards had not gone short of scoring opportunities during the first half of the 1969/70 season. One of those to benefit was the rugged Ian Hutchinson, who established himself as Osgood's first choice strike partner ahead of Bobby Tambling, Tommy Baldwin and the injury-hit Alan Birchenall. And it was Hutchinson who wrapped up Chelsea's victory over Birmingham in the Cup, with two second half goals after Osgood had headed in a Hudson centre just before the break.

"Birmingham had knocked us out in the quarter-final two years earlier so we knew it wouldn't be easy," says Ossie. "In the end, though, it was a comfortable win for us. It was good to get revenge in front of our fans and get us off on our Cup run."

One spectator who was particularly impressed by Chelsea's performance was football commentator Brian Moore. "I would not bet against them reaching Wembley," he wrote in his match report for *The Times*.

In the fourth round the Blues were again drawn at home, but against stiffer opposition, Burnley. The Lancastrians were not as powerful a force as they had been a decade earlier when they had won the championship, but they were still a decent First Division outfit. "Burnley were a pretty good team in those days," confirms John Dempsey. "They had people like Ralph Coates, Martin Dobson and Steve Kindon who were all useful players."

Two goals in two minutes from Hollins and Osgood midway through the second half, though, appeared to have put an end to the northerners' challenge. But, with time ticking away, Dobson scored twice to earn Burnley a replay. The Chelsea supporters in the 48,000 crowd must have left the Bridge wondering whether this was to be another season of missed opportunities in the Cup.

Three days later at a foggy Turf Moor Ralph Coates, the proud owner of a wispy Bobby Charlton-style comb over, turned Chelsea fans' anxiety levels up a further notch or two by putting Burnley ahead in the first half. With 18 minutes left the Blues were still trailing when Peter Houseman scored a magnificent solo equaliser. It was Houseman, too, who crossed for Baldwin, deputising for the injured Osgood, to head Chelsea in front in extra-time and Houseman, again, who shot home the killer third goal.

"I think we really believed we could win the Cup after that game," says John Dempsey. "To fight back from 1-0 down to win 3-1 in extra time was the sort of result which gives you great confidence and we started thinking it could be our year."

The positive vibes only intensified when Chelsea were paired with strug- gling Crystal Palace in the fifth round. True, the Blues were the away team this time but a trip to Selhurst Park held few fears. "We'd already won 5-1 there in the league so it wasn't a bad draw," says Dempsey. "You'd look at it and think, 'yes, Chelsea should win'." Peter Osgood, who had scored four goals on that earlier visit to south London, headed the Blues in front on 37 minutes before Palace's Roger Hoy equalised shortly after half-time. Little matter, Dempsey restored Chelsea's lead with a powerful header from Hollins' free-kick and further goals from Houseman and Hutchinson secured another emphatic away victory.

The quarter-final draw produced four pleasantly symmetrical ties, with Second Division sides Watford, Swindon, Middlesbrough and QPR all playing hosts to First Division opposition: Liverpool, Leeds, Manchester United and Chelsea respectively. Of the four pairings, the west London derby naturally generated most interest, not least among the Chelsea players.

"QPR was a fantastic draw because of the rivalry between the clubs," says Alan Hudson. "For one thing, they had Terry Venables and Barry Bridges who had both played for Chelsea. Then there was Rodney Marsh, who some people were saying was better than Osgood. There were going to be duels all over the pitch. There was me and Venables, Ron Harris and Rodney Marsh, Osgood and Frank Sibley or someone like that. It was just set up to be a great game."

Marsh may have been the main Rangers threat, but he was no secret weapon. For John Dempsey, especially, the striker was far from an unknown quantity. "I knew his game pretty well because I'd played with him at Fulham," he says. "In training he'd put the ball through your legs, and then say 'nutmeg' over his shoulder as he sped off. As you can imagine, that was a bit annoying. Rodney was a difficult player to mark because he'd drift all over the field, so one minute he'd be up front with Mike

Leach and the next he'd disappear off to the left wing or somewhere. But that was Rodney, he loved to entertain the crowd and the fans loved him back."

For once, the 90 minutes lived up to all the pre-match hype. On a mud-clogged Loftus Road pitch Chelsea got off to the perfect start with two goals in the first eight minutes from Webb and Osgood. Venables pulled one back for Rangers with a twice-taken penalty after McCreadie fouled Bridges and for a while the home side threatened an equaliser. Then, close on half-time, Osgood restored the Blues' two-goal advantage when QPR goalkeeper Mike Kelly failed to hold onto Hollins' long range shot. The Chelsea number nine took advantage of a defensive mix up to complete his hat-trick in the second half and, before celebrating with his team-mates, couldn't resist having a quiet word in the ear of the Rangers keeper.

"Kelly had failed Ossie on a coaching course not long before and after the third one went in Ossie said to him, 'Stick to fucking coaching!'" chuckles Alan Hudson. "Kelly didn't like that much."

Twenty-five years later relations between the QPR keeper and the Chelsea players hadn't improved much, the on-going feud resulting in a much-publicised tunnel bust up at the Bridge between Kelly, by then Middlesbrough's goalkeeping coach, and Hudson, who was working at Chelsea as a matchday corporate host. "I was about to do a presentation on the pitch at half-time," recalls Huddy. "It was 4–0 or something, we were playing great stuff, we'd murdered them. Kelly spotted me in the tunnel as I was waiting to go on. He looked at me and said, 'You, it's in the car park with you afterwards!'"

"So I went out and did the presentation on the pitch, went back to the box I was in and Ossie was there. I told him about Kelly, and Ossie said, 'Don't worry about that, I'll handle him'. Ossie went down after the game and they were chatting like best friends, but when he saw me Kelly went crazy. There was a bit of a scuffle but it was completely blown out of proportion by the press. I had to go off and do my question and answer thing in Drakes so I just walked away from it, but I made sure I had the last word. I told him that he should concentrate on coaching his goalie who'd just let in five rather than fighting. I got sacked after that."

Anyway, back to the QPR match and Peter Osgood grabbed all the headlines the day after the game, which finished 4–2 to the Blues, but an outstanding midfield display from Hudson had been equally crucial to Chelsea's success.

"Terry Venables said afterwards that with the heavy pitch he felt I wouldn't be strong enough and he could put me off my game," reveals Huddy. "He admitted he tried to give me a few knocks, but I just shoved him aside. He said he couldn't believe I was so strong at that age. But we won every battle all over the field, really. Ron kicked Rodney Marsh and he wasn't seen again, and Ossie proved that he was London's top striker."

Hudson's all-action performance didn't only impress Venables. After the game England manager Sir Alf Ramsey, who had been watching from the stands, said of the Chelsea midfielder, "There is no limit to what this young boy can achieve." This was praise indeed from the normally taciturn Sir Alf, a man who wasn't given to hyperbole and was so in control of his emotions that he had famously remained seated when the ref's final whistle signalled that England had won the 1966 World Cup. Although Ramsey hadn't said it directly there was a strong implication in his words that, aged just 18 and with less than a season's first team football behind him, Huddy was being considered for England's summer defence of the Jules Rimet trophy in Mexico.

That, though, was for the future. Of more immediate interest was who Chelsea might play in the semi-final. As expected, Leeds and Manchester United had overcome their lower division opponents but there had been a surprise at Vicarage Road where Watford had beaten Liverpool 1–0. Down at Chelsea's training ground in Mitcham the players gathered around a radio on the Monday lunchtime to listen to the draw. Unsurprisingly, there wasn't much debate about which team they wanted to be paired with.

"Of course, we wanted to play Watford," says John Dempsey, "and when we came out of the hat together there was a huge roar. We weren't frightened of playing Leeds or Manchester United but, obviously, you'd choose Watford out of those three. Mind you, we weren't going to underestimate them after they'd beaten Liverpool."

The Blues, though, had every right to be confident because they were playing some superb stuff at the time. A week after their trip to Loftus Road Chelsea strolled to a 3–0 win at high-flying Coventry, thanks to goals by Webb, Hudson and Baldwin. For Geoffrey Green in The Times the performance suggested that, finally, the team was becoming more than the sum of its parts.

"The secret of Chelsea nowadays is the harnessing and blending of their several skills," he wrote. "Where once the artistry of players like Osgood and Cooke tended to bring no end product and were showpieces on their own, set aside, as it were, from their colleagues, now there is real teamwork and co-ordination, built on craft, strength and spirit."

There was a growing feeling in the camp that not only could Chelsea win the Cup, they might also pull off the Double. "We just didn't think anyone could beat us, in the Cup or the league," says Alan Hudson. "In the league we were going pretty well, especially considering we were down the bottom at the start." The title, though, was a long shot, as Everton had a healthy lead at the top.

For the semi-final against Watford, played on another heavy pitch at White Hart Lane, Chelsea were the overwhelming favourites. Events appeared to be following the expected script when Webb put the Blues in front after just three minutes, but Terry Garbett quickly equalised and at the break the scores remained level. Watford had defended well but the Chelsea performance had lacked its usual zip. In the west Londoners' dressing room the players were in no doubt about the reason for their flat display.

"A day or two before the game Dave Sexton took us into town to have a sauna, somewhere around Kensington," recalls Ron Harris. "It's a bit like when you sit out in the sun for a long time: you feel a bit drained afterwards and a few of the lads were saying that at half-time. What didn't help, too, was that they were a Second Division team and you think to yourself it's just a matter of turning up and winning. But we had a helluva struggle for 60 odd minutes."

The goal which broke Watford's stubborn resistance arrived on the hour and, in many ways, epitomised Chelsea's bright, vibrant football that season. The move began with Hutchinson laying the ball back to Hudson who, surrounded by yellow shirts, cleverly turned away from his markers and slipped a pass out to Houseman in space on the left. With both Osgood and Hutchinson to aim for, Houseman picked out Ossie who powered his header past Watford keeper (and future Norwich manager) Mike Smith before hurling himself into the net in joyous celebration. Three more goals in six minutes from Houseman (2), his first following a superb run past three defenders, and Hutchinson confirmed Chelsea's place at Wembley. The 5-1 final score was the biggest FA Cup semi-final win since Wolves beat Grimsby 5-0 in 1949, although it was a little harsh on Watford. "The scoreline at the end looked like we pissed all over them but that wasn't the case," says Ron Harris.

On the other hand, the quick-fire salvo of goals which settled the tie was not untypical of Chelsea that season. When the team hit a purple patch – usually, this would involve the complementary talents of Osgood, Cooke and Hudson combining together in a dazzling array of flicks, feints and flourishes – the Blues were capable of putting a match beyond reach of the opposition in a matter of minutes. Dave Sexton knew this, but he also knew that outrageous skill and swaggering self-confidence alone were not enough for the team to be successful.

"Football isn't peaches and cream the whole time," he said a few years later. "Although you can win a game 3-0, you can always look back at moments in the match and say, 'By jingo, if we hadn't survived that particular spell, we wouldn't have been able to get in front.' So as well as playing attractive football, you have to be able to resist when these crises come along in a game and, believe me, they're cast-iron certainties." As if to underline this pragmatic philosophy, Sexton had a sign on his office wall reading, 'When the going gets tough, the tough get tougher'.

Chelsea would have to wait to learn who their Cup Final opponents would be. In the other semi-final at Hillsborough Leeds and Manchester United had drawn 0-0. The replay at Villa Park also finished scoreless so the teams would have to meet for a third time at Bolton's Burnden Park.

While this mini-epic was continuing, the Chelsea players had ample opportunity to reflect on which of the two teams they would prefer to meet at Wembley. Manchester United appeared to represent the distinctly easier option. Yes, they had three superstars in their team in George Best, Bobby Charlton and Denis Law, but the Reds were not the force they had been in 1968 when they won the European Cup. Moreover, Chelsea possessed a psychological advantage over United, having beaten them twice that season. Certainly, Ian Hutchinson must have been desperate for the Reds to triumph: remarkably, he had scored all four of Chelsea's goals against United that year.

Leeds, on the other hand, were arguably the best team in the country. The previous season the Yorkshiremen had won the league championship for the first time in their history with a then record number of points, losing just two matches in the process. In 1970, despite Chelsea's best efforts, they appeared to be the only team with a realistic hope of halting Everton's title charge, and they had also battled their way through to the semi-finals of the European Cup where they were due to meet Celtic. The demanding schedule of games didn't seem to worry Leeds' manager,

Don Revie. His side were invariably referred to as the most 'professional' in the land – although, often, there was an implication that this was a euphemism for 'dirty' or 'cynical' – and would simply, as the football saying goes, 'take every match as it comes'.

Unlike Manchester United, who relied heavily on their glamorous forward line and were lacking in quality elsewhere, Leeds were very much a team. Virtually all of their players were internationals and there were no obvious weaknesses in their line-up, apart perhaps from their erratic goalkeeper, Gary Sprake. The rest of the side, which included famous names such as Jack Charlton, Norman 'Bites Yer Legs' Hunter, Billy Bremner, Johnny Giles and Allan 'Sniffer' Clarke combined skill, tenacity and hard-edged ruthlessness in equal measure. In short, Leeds were a fearsome proposition.

Leeds also held the upper hand in their head-to-head league meetings with Chelsea that season, having beaten the Blues 2–0 at Elland Road and 5–2 at the Bridge. Chelsea, though, had eased the Yorkshiremen's fixture congestion by knocking them out of the League Cup before falling themselves to Carlisle United – the third season on the trot that the Blues had gone out of the competition to lower league opposition.

On balance, taking into account all the different factors, the Chelsea players might have been expected to prefer a Manchester United victory at Burnden Park. Not so, according to Alan Hudson. "The glamour final would have been Chelsea and Manchester United, and it would have been George Best's only FA Cup Final," he says. "But I wanted to play Leeds because the rivalry with them was so intense. If there was one team we loved beating more than anybody else it was Leeds. Okay, they'd beaten us 5–2 in the league but we hammered them, we slaughtered them. Tommy Hughes threw a couple in and they didn't earn their goals at all. We played terrific that day and came off the field shaking our heads. It was probably the most unjust result of my time at Chelsea."

John Dempsey was equally unfazed at the prospect of meeting Leeds. "I didn't really mind who we played in the final," he says. "Just to be there was the important thing. Peter Bonetti didn't play in the game when they thrashed us 5–2 at the Bridge, and no disrespect to Tommy Hughes or John Phillips but I always felt we missed Peter when he wasn't in goal. As a defender he was great because you'd hear a shout and he'd come and catch the crosses, which took the pressure off you. Although he wasn't the tallest of keepers he had a great leap and he just used to command his area. You felt a lot more secure when he was playing."

In the event, it was Leeds who got through to Wembley to face Chelsea, thanks to a solitary Billy Bremner goal in the second replay. To have kept three consecutive clean sheets against Manchester United's prolific strikers was some feat, but one which only served to underline the meanness of the Leeds defence. Indeed, on their route to the Twin Towers – which also included wins over Swansea, non-league Sutton United, Mansfield and Swindon – Leeds had only conceded one goal.

At the end of March, two weeks before the final, Chelsea's Double hopes were ended in spectacular style as they were walloped 5–2 at Everton. This time there could be no complaints about the score which, but for late goals by Dempsey and Osgood, would have been even more embarrassing. Two days later there was even worse news for Chelsea fans as Alan Hudson suffered an ankle ligament injury during a 3–1 defeat at West Bromich Albion. With his left ankle in plaster and hobbling on crutches, Huddy's chances of making Wembley other than as a spectator looked bleak.

"There was nobody near me when it happened," he says. "I just landed badly, my foot went down a hole and that was it. I knew as soon as it happened that it was serious because I was in unbelievable pain. It was a terrible idea to put the ankle in plaster because it glued the whole joint up. I tried everything to be fit for Wembley: I had acupuncture and even went to see a spiritualist, a lady in Victoria. It was like a palm reading, only she 'read' the bottom of my foot. I was just laughing while she did it and thinking, 'This ain't gonna work'. Anyway, she told me I wouldn't score in the final and she was right about that, but she didn't say I wouldn't play."

Two days before the final, Hudson failed a fitness test at Stamford Bridge. Although expected, this was a blow to Sexton as the 18-year-old was the creative hub of his team. "Alan Hudson is a tremendously gifted player, possessing all the skills," Sexton had written in the Chelsea programme. "He has superb close control when he's in possession, especially when he's forced to play his way out of a tight situation. When Alan is carrying the ball forward he is exceptionally smart at drawing defenders towards him and then slipping the ball past them to a team-mate. And that's not all – Alan has an explosive right-foot shot, a genuine net-stretcher."

These qualities would be sorely missed at Wembley, especially as Leeds' own central midfielders, Billy Bremner and Johnny Giles, were key figures in Revie's team. Meanwhile, skipper Ron Harris was also a doubt for

Wembley, having sustained a hamstring injury against Sheffield Wednesday a couple of weeks before. If the worst came to the worst, Sexton could call on the experienced Marvin Hinton to fill the gap in defence, but the Chelsea manager was desperate not to lose his captain for such an important match.

"Ron was what I would politely describe as steadfast," he said later. "He was very mature for his age, and loyal to the club. Some players don't like getting moved around and being asked to play in different positions. That wasn't the case with Harris. You could ask him to play centre-forward, and he would. Ronnie Harris was a rock – and they're the sort of fellows you build your team on."

As it turned out, Sexton's 'rock' passed his fitness test, telling waiting reporters that he was "as fit as I'll ever be." The truth was somewhat different, as Harris now admits. "Until the Thursday before the final I couldn't even jog," he says. "I wouldn't have played if it had been a league game and I needed three cortisone injections just to get me out there."

With his skipper pencilled in, Sexton's main selection dilemma was who to pick to replace the absent Hudson. The natural alternative was hard-running midfielder John Boyle, but he had fallen out of favour that season and had barely appeared on the team sheet. The same applied to Bobby Tambling, whose long Chelsea career was nearing an end. Alan Birchenall, who had played the previous week against Tottenham when Ian Hutchinson was nursing a bruised hip, was another possibility but his own season had been marred by a knee injury. The obvious choice, then, was Tommy Baldwin, who had played in half of the Cup games anyway, and had pushed his case for inclusion by scoring the winner against Spurs. The only trouble was that the Sponge and Dave Sexton weren't seeing eye to eye.

"When I saw I wasn't on the team-sheet for the semi-final against Watford I slapped in a transfer request," says Tommy. It was by no means the first time Baldwin had demanded a move; in fact, it was an unusual week when he wasn't banging on Sexton's door, expressing a desire to quit the Bridge. "I know we had a lot of good players, but I couldn't understand why I was always the one who got dropped," he explains. "I put in loads of transfer requests but Dave never let me go. He just used to say, 'Get out of my office, you're worse than James Dean.' Well, I suppose I was a bit of a rebel."

While Sexton mulled over his team selection, the build-up to the Wembley clash in the outside world became increasingly intense. For football fans throughout England, the FA Cup Final was a hugely important occasion. Amazingly, considering the surfeit of football now served up on the small screen, it was the *only* domestic match of the entire season that fans were able to watch live on television. Seeing their club win the FA Cup, if only from the comfort of their sitting room, was the height of most supporters' ambitions – eclipsing even success in the league championship.

In those days both BBC1 and ITV had live coverage of the Cup Final, leaving only BBC2 as a possible televisual haven for non-football fans. In the *TV Times* and the *Radio Times*, which featured a picture of Manchester City celebrating their 1969 Cup win on the cover, the two main channels' schedules for the big day announced hours of preview material before the game itself, interrupted only by racing from Ascot on the beeb and all-in wrestling on ITV. If that wasn't enough, there was also the opportunity earlier in the week to see Peter Bonetti and John Hollins take on Billy Bremner and Johnny Giles in a special Cup Final edition of *A Question of Sport*, presented by David Vine.

For the newspapers, too, the Chelsea-Leeds clash was a massive story, not only on the day itself but in the week leading up to the match. Two days before the game, for instance, the *Mirror's* front page was devoted to a Cup Final hardy perennial, the trade in black market tickets. "Big probe into Cup tickets racket" screamed the headline, above a story about tickets marked 'Leeds AFC' being sold outside Stamford Bridge. Leeds chairman Percy Woodward was reported as promising a full investigation, saying, "If we find out that a player is involved, he will be in very serious trouble indeed."

Elsewhere, £4 stand tickets for the final were reportedly selling for £60. One tout gleefully told the *Mirror*, "You can't lose. Leeds are the team of the moment and every football fan in London is willing to pay to see Chelsea win the Cup for the first time."

Mind you, it was hard to see why anyone would pay over the odds when *Mirror* readers already knew the result of the match. "The *Mirror* has played the game by computer and it's . . . Leeds for the Cup," the paper's centre-page spread revealed. There followed a truly daft story about how a panel of experts, including three unnamed First Division managers, two Mirror sports writers, a scientific advisor and "the one girl in the side, a management scientist who helped with the mathematics", had fed in all the available information about the two sides into a computer and come up with the final score: Leeds 2 Chelsea 1.

Leeds were the slight favourites with the bookies, too, with William

Hill quoting 8/11 for the Yorkshiremen and 11/10 for Chelsea. The odds suggested a tight match but Don Revie appeared confident that his team would win more handsomely than many were predicting. "It will be a hard game," he said, "but I don't think it will be as close as most people seem to think."

The mood in the Chelsea camp was equally optimistic. "We have none of the nervousness we felt before the final against Spurs in 1967," Eddie McCreadie told reporters, "and it's the right kind of confidence, the best kind, the quiet kind."

Another game from the 1967 Cup run was also a motivating tool for the Chelsea players. As we've already heard, the Leeds-Chelsea semi-final that year had been a physical and bloody affair. "Gary Sprake had put his studs in the face of John Boyle in the semi-final," recalls Alan Hudson, "so there was a lot of 'previous' going into the final. It wasn't like disliking a person, but when they put their kit on and we put ours on it was like 'Game on'. Leeds didn't have any rules and they would go to any lengths to win. They were like the Mafia in that respect. No one was dirtier than Leeds. Probably only Peter Lorimer and Eddie Gray out of all their team wouldn't go in over the top if they got the chance."

Tommy Baldwin agrees: "There were a lot of scores being settled from previous games whenever we played them. It always just seemed to go mad, with everyone kicking each other. But afterwards we'd have a drink with them in the bar and we got on okay."

And Ron Harris adds: "Chelsea-Leeds was never a game for faint-hearts. Everybody knows Jackie Charlton kept a black book containing the names of players he wanted to gain revenge against and you can bet there were a few Chelsea players in there. I wasn't amongst them myself because I didn't get up the other end of the pitch much. Personally, I didn't find I needed a black book as I've always had a good memory."

Chopper's defensive partner John Dempsey, though, reckons Leeds' infamous reputation was slightly exaggerated. "People say they were dirty but I found Mick Jones and Allan Clarke up front were okay," he says. "Jones was all arms and elbows and you had to battle him, while Clarke was a skilful player with a touch of the Jimmy Greaves about him. People sometimes criticised him for being lazy but when he had a chance he was deadly. I think Leeds' reputation for being a dirty team came more in midfield and at the back where people like Bremner, Giles, Hunter and Charlton were all very competitive. They could be niggly, too, pulling your shirt and other things like that to put you off."

On the day of the final, Saturday April 11th – the earliest Cup Final date, incidentally, since Aston Villa beat Everton on April 10th in 1897 – the Chelsea squad ate a pre-match meal at the same Gloucester Road hotel they had visited before every Cup tie that season. "Manager Dave Sexton has asked me to keep to the usual menu," the proprietor told *The Mirror*. "It is beef fillets and toast, rice pudding and tea. I call it the Chelsea Special."

By now Sexton had settled on his team. As expected, Tommy Baldwin would fill the gap created by Hudson's absence, playing on the right side of midfield. Moreover, the Sponge was a key element in Sexton's game plan.

"In the team talk, Dave must have spoken to me for about ten minutes," he says. "'Tommy,' he told me, 'whatever happens I want you to make sure Terry Cooper doesn't go on those overlaps. Get to him straightaway. Norman Hunter might come through, so just nip between the two of them to stop them both. If Billy Bremner or Johnny Giles come across to your side just get your foot in . . . and don't forget Eddie Gray, make sure you have a snap at him. So I'm thinking, 'Great, just the five players to pick up . . .' Then Dave turns back to me and says, 'Oh, Tommy, if you get the chance, try to get up there and get us a goal'."

At the time, teams were only allowed to nominate one substitute. As in all the previous rounds, Sexton named versatile defender Marvin Hinton in the role. "Before the final I hadn't got off the bench once," he says. "In those days if a player got a knock he tended to play on rather than come off. Dave was very superstitious so, along with all the stuff about the lucky suit, having me on the bench almost became another super-stition. I suppose that worked out well for me – as there were other players who could have been sub – although, obviously, I would rather have been in the starting eleven."

Many of the players were equally superstitious, with a number of them – including David Webb, Ian Hutchinson and Charlie Cooke – having decided that it would be unlucky to have a haircut during the Cup run. By the time of the final the Blues, no doubt to the disgust of the old codgers at the FA, were probably the hairiest team ever to play at Wembley.

When they arrived at the stadium the players went out to inspect the pitch, which they discovered to be in appalling state. This wasn't a surprise. In the previous days the newspapers had been full of stories about the Wembley groundstaff's attempts to prepare a reasonable playing surface for the showpiece occasion. Bad weather was partly to blame but so, too, were the stadium authorities who, in a moment of collective madness, had agreed to the *Horse of the Year Show* being staged at Wembley. The famous hallowed turf had failed to recover from the pounding it received, and in an attempt to even out the bumpy, rutted surface for the Cup Final the groundstaff had resorted to covering the pitch in a hundred tons of sand. The result was an ugly, lumpy, clotted mess quite unsuited to flowing football.

Once the pre-match preliminaries were over, Leeds, wearing unfamiliar red socks so as not to clash with Chelsea's white ones, quickly took control of the match. Much of their threat came down the Chelsea right, where left-winger Eddie Gray had established early dominance over David Webb. Their opening goal, though, came from a corner from the other side. Peter Bonetti failed to reach Gray's inswinger in a crowded six-yard area, Jack Charlton headed goalwards and, although either Eddie McCreadie or Ron Harris appeared well-placed to clear the ball off the line, both were deceived by the lack of bounce off the soft pitch. As the pair kicked thin air, the ball dribbled past the Blues' last defensive barrier and came to a stop a few inches over the line. Chelsea protests that Bonetti had been fouled were ignored by referee Eric Jennings and, after 21 minutes, Leeds had the lead.

The goal knocked Chelsea back and, for a while, only the sure handling of Bonetti and the swift interceptions of Dempsey and Harris prevented Leeds from adding a second. Then, four minutes before half-time the Blues equalised with a goal as soft as Leeds', Peter Houseman's speculative 25-yard shot squirming under Sprake's dive.

Tommy Baldwin hadn't touched the ball in the build up, yet he remains convinced that simply by hovering on the edge of the six-yard box he played a vital role in distracting the Leeds keeper. "I remember talking to Norman Hunter at some stage between the 1967 semi and the 1970 final and I told him, 'If I get the chance I'm going to get Sprakey, I'll just leave my foot in when I go for a bobbling ball,'" he says. "And, funnily enough, in his book Sprake says that when Peter Houseman shot he looked up because I was running in. He took his eye off the ball and it bobbled under his dive. He knew I was out to do him because of what he did to John Boyle in the 1967 semi and that put him off a fraction."

The second half saw good chances fall to both teams, but the two goal-keepers redeemed their earlier errors with some fine saves. Then, ten minutes from the end of normal time, Eddie Gray's fierce shot beat Bonetti but crashed against the crossbar. Three minutes later the Blues were not so fortunate as Allan Clarke's header bounced off a post into the path of Mick Jones, who smashed a left-footer into the opposite corner. Much as it hurt, few Chelsea fans would deny that Leeds deserved their lead.

One of the great qualities of Sexton's side, though, was that they never gave up. Despite being outplayed for much of the game they had hung on and, with four minutes left on the clock, the Blues were awarded a free-kick for a push by Jack Charlton on Peter Osgood. Harris slipped the ball to Hollins who curled the ball to the near post, where Ian Hutchinson flung himself in front of Charlton to send a powerful header past Sprake.

"If you look back over the season, I must have scored eight to ten similar goals," Hutch said later. "Peter Houseman or John Hollins knew it was their job to deliver the ball either to the near or far post. Ossie tended to go far, because he didn't like the studs up his arse, and I normally went near. We scored a hell of a lot of goals that way. It was just sort of programmed into us from the training ground, really."

Minutes later the final whistle blew, signalling half an hour of extra time. Trudging to the sidelines to listen to Dave Sexton's pep talk, Hutchinson was asked by TV reporter Peter Lorenzo for a quick comment on his goal. "I forgot that we were going out live and replied honestly, 'Fuck! Extra time on the sand dunes . . .'"

A few years earlier the flamboyant theatre critic Kenneth Tynan had caused a huge stir when he became the first person to say the word 'fuck' on TV. Fortunately for Hutch, his unwitting slip caused no such outcry – possibly because the entire TV-watching nation had popped into the kitchen to put the kettle on.

At the start of extra time Marvin Hinton came on for Ron Harris, the cloying surface having exacerbated his hamstring injury. Leeds, again, had the clearer opportunities once play resumed: Clarke hitting the crossbar and then Giles shooting beyond Bonetti, only for Webb to stretch out a leg and send the ball spinning over the bar.

"I was just running on instinct when Johnny Giles hit his shot," says Webby of this crucial intervention. "The ball was flying into the roof of the net with Peter Bonetti stranded and I just flung myself up to get my boot on it. If God wasn't smiling on me it would have ended in the back of the net. Instead it went over the bar."

Seconds later Jennings blew the final whistle on the first FA Cup Final at Wembley to end in a draw. The exhausted players, many of whom were feeling the effects of cramp, still managed to drag themselves round the pitch one more time for a joint lap of honour. "Both sides had played so well under the worst possible conditions that it was right to take a bow together," said Eddie McCreadie, who had come up with the idea.

Having been on the back foot for much of the match – the corner count of 12-4 in favour of the Yorshiremen told much of the story – Chelsea were happier with the draw than Leeds. "In the first game we just about survived," admits John Dempsey. "They were on top for most of the match and hit the post and bar a couple of times. I think we missed Alan Hudson because his passing and ability on the ball had been so important for us that season. A lot of the problems for us came in midfield especially down the left where Eddie Gray had a lot of possession and gave David Webb a tough time. They should have won it really, but we hung in there and showed character to hit back again when they scored near the end."

"I think we were the luckiest team ever to come off Wembley with a draw," adds Ron Harris candidly. "I wouldn't say we were totally outplayed but of the two sides they were far better than us."

Back in the Chelsea dressing room, Dave Sexton had already made his mind up to make one important change for the replay which, because of the poor state of the Wembley pitch, the FA had decided would be staged at Old Trafford. David Webb, cruelly exposed at right back by Man of the Match Eddie Gray throughout the afternoon, would move to the centre of defence with Ron Harris switching to the flank.

"Eddie gave me a right royal runaround," Webb admitted afterwards. "I enjoyed the whole occasion right up until the kick-off, and after that everything I did was about ten minutes too late."

Showing astute management, Sexton bolstered Webb's confidence by quashing any press speculation that the defender might be dropped for the replay. "David showed real grit and character," he told reporters. "He stuck to his job right through to the end and there'll be the replay for him to show who is top man."

"This was a great effort by everybody involved," he continued. "But I must give a merit mention to Peter Bonetti who proved he is the greatest goalkeeper in the world. Indeed, without Bonetti, their best performer on the day, the Blues would surely have been sunk. Peter Osgood was equally admiring of his keeper. "It was like he had glue on his gloves," he said. "Catty can do that at Old Trafford or any time you ask him."

The press reports in the following two days all agreed that Leeds had been unlucky not to win, but neither did they overlook Chelsea's contribution to a thrilling match. "This was the finest Cup Final seen at Wembley since the war, better even than Manchester United and Blackpool of 1948 and lacking only the emotional impact of the last 20 minutes of the Stanley Matthews fiesta of 1953," suggested Geoffrey Green in *The Times*.

In *The Mirror*, meanwhile, reporter Nigel Clarke relived his eventful afternoon in the Chelsea end: "I stood among the Chelsea ranks, high up on the terraces and shared with them an experience that left me emotionally exhausted. Someone spilled a bottle of beer down my neck, a woman with bright blue hair slapped a Chelsea hat on my head. And when Chelsea scored I was pushed crazily, 30 feet down the terraces in a jumble of laughing, leaping people. It was fun."

The post-match comments of the Football Association chairman, Dr Andrew Stephen, featured prominently in all the papers. "This was not a classic," he said. "It was an epic."

The FA, though, was a little concerned that the so-called 'Carry-on Cup Final' might interfere with England's World Cup preparations. Asked what would happen if the replay was also drawn Stephen ruled out the possibility of the Cup being shared. "You would even have to consider tossing a coin for it," he said. Eventually they announced that, if necessary, a third game would be played at Coventry's Highfield Road three days after the replay.

In the 18 days between Wembley and Old Trafford Chelsea played three league games, beating Stoke and Liverpool and losing away to Burnley. The four points won cemented the Blues in third place, their highest finish since 1955. Ron Harris wasn't risked in any of the games but was pronounced fully fit for the replay. Alan Hudson, though, had again failed a fitness test, ending his hopes of making a dramatic return to the team.

As for Leeds, their season was in danger of turning into a disaster of Titanic proportions. Defeats by Manchester City and Ipswich had finally ended their championship ambitions, while Revie's men had also waved goodbye to the European Cup after losing both legs of their semi-final with Celtic. There was further bad news, too: goalkeeper Gary Sprake had been carried off against the Scottish champions with knee ligament damage and was extremely doubtful for the Cup Final replay.

A few hours before kick-off at Old Trafford, Sprake was declared unfit to play and was replaced by 23-year-old Scot David Harvey. Otherwise, the sides were unchanged from Wembley. In another slight change from the original game, Chelsea took to the field wearing yellow socks while Leeds reverted to the pristine all-white strip that Don Revie, inspired by the great Real Madrid side of the time, had chosen for his team a decade earlier.

If the cast was familiar, so too was the script as Leeds began menacingly, putting immediate pressure on the Chelsea goal. Once again Lorimer, Bremner and Giles had gained an early ascendancy in midfield, from where they maintained a steady supply of passes to the dangerous Clarke and Jones. However, left-winger Eddie Gray had not brought his Wembley form with him and looked to be feeling the effects of a wince-inducing Harris tackle which had sent him hurtling off the pitch in the opening minutes.

"I suppose I didn't do a bad tackle on him," says Ron modestly, "and I think that helped us because he didn't do a lot in the game, certainly not compared to Wembley. There were a few vendettas flying around, but we all just got on with it. It's not like today when you get players looking for free-kicks, falling over and rolling around. Personally, I used to thrive in those sort of games."

Softening Gray up wasn't a pre-planned tactic as such, it was just simply what Chopper did in every game. "Ronnie used to sort people out in the first five minutes, just to let them know what was in store for them for the rest of the game," says Peter Osgood. "On the pitch he was a serious man, a very serious man. He led from the front, and he didn't expect anybody else to do what he didn't do. He had a good engine on him, he was a strong boy and people feared him. Quite rightly so. He was the captain. Nobody would try to take the piss out of him on the pitch. Off the field he was a different character. He was one of the jokers, he loved a laugh and a giggle, and he liked a little drink although he wasn't one of the big drinkers. But on the pitch he was just an animal, he really was."

With Gray hobbling rather than flying down the wing, the Blues appeared to have removed one of Leeds' main potential threats. Chelsea, though, soon had a major injury concern of their own as Jones crashed into

Bonetti in mid-air while the pair challenged for a cross. The Cat fell to the ground clutching his left knee and required nearly five minutes' treatment from Blues physio Harry Medhurst. These were anxious moments for Chelsea: there were, of course, no substitute keepers in those days, so if Bonetti couldn't continue his green jersey would pass to Dave Webb, the Blues' emergency goalie.

Happily for the Chelsea camp and Webb in particular, Bonetti, although limping heavily, resumed his position in goal with John Dempsey taking over the goal-kicking duties. "Because they attacked us a quite a bit there were a lot of kicks to take," recalls Demps, "and I remember thinking it was important to reach the halfway line at least. That gave me time to go charging out so as not to leave their forwards onside if they won the ball and played it forward. Fortunately, I didn't skank any and I got good distance on my kicks."

Five minutes after injuring Bonetti, Jones dealt Chelsea an even more painful blow, rifling a shot beyond the Blues keeper after Clarke had skilfully negotiated his way past three tackles and played the ball into his co-striker's path. For the third time in the two games Leeds had the lead, and on this occasion Chelsea would have no quick reply.

Revie's men retained the upper hand until well into the second half when, against a background of constant 'Chel-sea!' chants from the thousands of London-based fans who had made the journey up north to pack out the Stretford End, the Blues at last edged into the game. Baldwin's header prompted Harvey's first proper save of the evening on the hour and, with Cooke and Hollins now gaining more control in central midfield, the chances of a Chelsea equaliser no longer seemed remote.

The goal the Blues fans had been patiently waiting for arrived on 78 minutes. Inevitably, perhaps, it was scored by Osgood, maintaining his record of having notched in every round of the Cup – a feat which no player since has matched.

"I did the crossover with Hutch and then Charlie took it off Hutch," he recalled later. "Charlie went one way, I went the other, he bent it in, and . . . it was a bit like being in a dream or a film. I was just there waiting for it in loads of space. Luckily, Gary Sprake wasn't playing, and David Harvey was in goal. I think if Sprake had been playing he might have come and clattered me, but David stayed on his line and that just gave me time to have a quick look at him and glance it the right way.

"I honestly thought I was offside, but I looked across and the linesman didn't have his flag up. I ran to our fans and I had goose pimples on my skin and the hairs on the back of my neck were standing on end. It was an incredible feeling . . . "

As both sides searched desperately for the winner, the game became increasingly physical. Hutchinson was booked for shoving Bremner in the chest, Leeds hit back with some vicious tackles of their own and then, with just five minutes to go, McCreadie flattened Bremner in the Chelsea area.

"Maybe we were lucky not to give away a penalty," admits John Dempsey. "It wasn't even a normal tackle, it was a chest high lunge which almost cut Bremner in half." However, Eric Jennings, officiating in his last match, was in lenient mood and waved away Leeds' appeals for a spot-kick.

Throughout the season Sexton had drummed into his players the need to keep going for 90 minutes. Now, as at Wembley, tired legs would have to cope with the demands of an additional half-hour. The psychological strain was enormous too, as every player on the pitch knew that just one mistake could settle the match.

Leeds created the first clear opportunity in extra-time, forcing Bonetti, now more mobile but by no means fully recovered, to make a fine save from Lorimer's shot. Osgood's goal, though, had given Chelsea a huge lift which was reflected in the fans' confident chants of 'We're gonna win the Cup!' and, a minute before half-time in extra-time, a Chelsea attack down the left resulted in a throw level with their opponents' 18-yard line. Leeds knew what to expect. At the time, Ian Hutchinson had the longest throw in English football, with his best effort having been measured at 122 ft. "I'm double jointed at both shoulders," Hutchinson once revealed. "It was a flick and then a follow through."

Hutch's long throw wasn't the prettiest or most sophisticated of tactics but it was highly effective. On this occasion, he rubbed the ball on his jersey, stretched back his arms, arched his back and flung the ball through the night air towards the near post. The missile flicked off the back of Jack Charlton's balding pate across the six-yard box to the far post where, in a mad scramble of jostling players, the ball glanced off David Webb and into the net.

"The ball hit me on the cheek," said Webby later. "I went up to head it in, and as I was leaning forward, Leeds players got underneath me to try to put me off. I was determined to connect with the ball, and I knew that if I threw myself in the right spot, I'd score. As I landed in the net I saw the ball in front of me. And, even then, because it was Leeds, the first thing I did was look to see if the linesman was flagging. Then I looked at the referee, and he'd already run to the halfway line. Only after that was I comfortable that I'd scored. Leeds were such a professional side they'd intimidate anybody, you see."

As with Peter Houseman's shot at Wembley, Tommy Baldwin also claims some of the credit for Webb's unconventional goal. "I was at the far post and, when I jumped for Jack Charlton's unintentional flick on, I pushed Terry Cooper into the back of the net and stood on Eddie Gray's thigh," he says. "Webby got the goal, of course, but he might not have scored if I hadn't been in there as well."

Ahead for the first time in 224 minutes of play, Chelsea were determined to protect their lead. Apart from a Hutchinson 'goal' ruled out for offside, the final 16 minutes were largely a rearguard action for the Blues. Finally using his substitute, Sexton replaced Osgood with Marvin Hinton for the last ten minutes to add another body in defence. The plan worked as Leeds, despite a period of relentless pressure towards the end, could find no way through the thicket of blue shirts.

With Blues fans howling for the final whistle, referee Jennings finally took the hint and signalled that Chelsea, for the first time in their 65-history, had won the FA Cup.

Princess Margaret, perhaps not such a big Chelsea fan after all, was not around to present the trophy to Blues skipper Ron Harris. Nor, for that matter, were any other members of the Royal Family. Instead Dr Andrew Stephen did the honours while cockney-twanged chants of 'Ee-aye-addio, we've won the Cup!" echoed around Old Trafford. Going up to collect their winners' medals, the hairy, mud-splashed and dishevelled Blues, half of whom were now wearing the white shirts of their defeated opponents, were possibly not much of a sight to put before Royalty anyway.

Speaking after the match, Dave Sexton said: "We were very nervous first half, the same as at Wembley. We didn't get into it for a long, long while, but if we're not playing well, we hang on and hang on. That's the quality of our football, and it's paid off. That's why we're a good side.

"When Peter Bonetti went down, it was a really bad moment. If he had not been able to carry on, it would have been very serious. Then came another blow when Leeds scored the first goal again, but I never doubted that we would come back once more.

"David Webb's winner was just typical of him. At Wembley, Leeds had given him the sort of game most players would want to forget, but he could hardly wait for the chance of another go at them. He's bounced back like a rubber ball, hasn't he! I'm terribly pleased for him."

Webb himself spoke of his feelings when his Cup Final almost became a Sunday League player's worst nightmare, with the manager handing him the goalkeeper's gloves. "At half-time, when I looked at Peter Bonetti's left knee and saw it had ballooned right up, I was afraid they'd be sticking me in goal for the second half. I told Harry (Medhurst), 'Do a good job on him, mate – he looks better in the green jersey than I do.'

"Don Revie said earlier in the season something about players down south not being as dedicated as those in the North," he added. "I wonder if he still thinks we're soft. If Leeds are the 'most professional' team in the business, what does that make us? Just too brave for them, we were." Brave, certainly, but also a little lucky.

"Looking at the two games overall, it was daylight robbery that we won it," admits Marvin Hinton. Certainly, the Blues had had their backs to the wall for much of the four hours playing time, and had only shown glimpses of the captivating, smooth-passing football which had characterised their season. Their triumph owed as much, if not more, to single-minded perseverance as pure skill. Still, Chelsea had the Cup and Leeds, for all their efforts, had nothing.

"We dominated them for 70 minutes and still we didn't win," moaned Jack Charlton, who stormed off in a taxi after the match without even bothering to collect his loser's medal. "Peter Bonetti got hurt and we never challenged him again. He's a friend of mine but we ought to have whacked him. Not dirty like, but got stuck in."

While Leeds sulked, Chelsea got on with the serious job of celebrating. "We got absolutely wrecked," says Tommy Baldwin. "We had loads to drink at the formal post-match dinner, then most of us went out to a nightclub in Manchester until about four o'clock. Lots of people were coming up to congratulate us, because everyone hated Leeds at the time. I can remember coming out of the nightclub and there were some railings along the road. For some reason – maybe because it could have been a short cut back to the hotel – Charlie (Cooke) decided to climb over the railings and fell flat on his face. When we got back to the hotel room there were bodies all over the place, all sorts of friends and relatives were crashed out there. Then, coming back on the train to London in the morning loads of fans came into our compartment and the celebrations continued until the buffet ran out of beer."

One of the fans who wangled his way into the players' carriage was the fashion photographer Eric Swayne. "They knew me a bit and invited me and my two mates in," he says. "They had the two middle coaches and we were in with them. John Hollins' wife, Linda, sat on my lap coming back from Manchester. She was a pretty little thing. I can remember getting off at Euston and being kissed by girls who thought I was a member of the team. Everyone was telling me how marvellous I was – it was great!"

Arriving at Euston, Eric and the rest of the Chelsea party were greeted by around 1,000 fans, many of whom had travelled over from the King's Road where they had been celebrating all night. A report by Hugh de Wet in *The Times* that morning suggested the fans' festivities had been at least as wild and unrestrained as the players'. "As the realization gradually sunk in that Chelsea had defeated Leeds 2–1 in the FA Cup Final, the King's Road late last night built up into a state of almost hysterical and disbelieving frenzy as supporters screamed themselves hoarse with pleasure.

"At closing time outside the pubs, clubs and discotheques the long-haired and elegantly velvet clad were, for once, at one with the skinheads as all joined in the chanting and scarf waving. The loud jubilation was echoed from the cars, a solid mass of almost stationary traffic as Lamborghinis and Bentleys hooted repeatedly with stately bravura, to be backed up by the shrill and piercing toots of the minis. The crowds were particularly thick towards the Wandsworth Bridge end of the King's Road, with the gentlemen of the Chelsea Conservative Club standing on the pavement, beer mugs in hand, vociferously urging on the crowds of youths to greater things."

The boisterous celebrations continued as the players climbed aboard an open-top bus, which took them from Euston through Paddington, Kensington and Earl's Court to Stamford Bridge. "All along the route you could see blue and white scarves and flags hanging from office windows and houses," recalls John Dempsey. "It gave you a real tingle along the back of your neck. Then, around the King's Road and Fulham Road, it was just a sea of blue with thousands of people lining the route. It didn't seem to matter that it was a working day. The place was just heaving with people." Nor was the party confined to west London: in Ilford a pub landlord ran out of beer after honouring a 20-year-old promise to serve free drinks when Chelsea finally won the Cup.

In a similarly generous gesture, Eric Swayne invited all the Chelsea squad out to dinner a few days after the Cup Final. "I booked a table at the Meridiana, this lovely posh restaurant I used to go to on the Brompton Road, for the whole team, my wife, Shirley, and four other girls that I brought along. The only players not there were Peter Bonetti and Peter Osgood who had just left for England World Cup duty in Mexico. During the meal I was thinking, 'This is going to set me back a bit, but it's worth it.' It was a wonderful, wonderful meal with marvellous food, lots of champagne and wine plus beer for some of the players.

"After we'd polished off some brandy I was sweating a little, I had slightly moist palms about what the bill was going to be. But at the end of the evening one of the two owners, Walter Mariti, came up and whispered, 'There's no bill, Eric. Tonight's on me.' That was a fantastic gesture, but I think it reflected how proud everyone was about what the boys had done. So we had a marvellous time, and I didn't have to cough up a small fortune."

The Chelsea boys were surely entitled to relax with a glass or two of the finest Courvoisier. According to Dave Sexton, it had taken a "super-human effort" to beat Leeds. And even if the Blues had enjoyed some luck along the way, nobody could deny that for sheer grit, determination and a cussed refusal to accept defeat they had deserved to become the first Chelsea side ever to get their hands on the world's oldest football trophy.

CHAPTER EIGHT

SEX IN THE CITY

CHAPTER EIGHT
SEX IN THE CITY

In the early seventies Raquel Welch was, in every sense, one of the biggest female film stars in the world. An authentic Hollywood sex symbol, the well-endowed actress's movie roles – which, famously, included an extended bout of dinosaur-grappling while wearing a revealing leopard skin loincloth in *One Million Years BC* – were not exactly masterpieces of subtlety or understatement. Not that her many fans cared. "Raquel is raw, unconquerable, antediluvian woman," gushed *Time* magazine in a cover feature. "She is the nubile savage crying out to be bashed on the skull and dragged to some lair by her wild auburn hair."

By 1972, the year in which she made a brief but memorable appearance on the Chelsea scene, Raquel had done a fair bit of skull-bashing and lair-dragging of her own. Aged 32 and with two children by her first husband, she was recently divorced from husband number two, Patrick Curtis, when she turned up at the Blues' home match against Leicester City on November 11th. Although she had appeared in four films in 1972, her visit to the Bridge wasn't simply a promotional stunt.

"I used to work with Raquel Welch all the time and she knew I loved football," says photographer Terry O'Neill, "and one day she said, 'I'd love to see Chelsea and that Peter Osgood', so I took her down there. She was living in Knightsbridge at the time in a mews behind where the Lanesborough Hotel is now.

"Ossie had an agent called Ken Adam who fixed it up for us to go down there, so I walked her round the ground. It was incredible – you never used to see sex symbol movie stars at football and it was quite a thing. Walking with her round the pitch, the shouting and cat calls from the crowd just got louder and louder. I felt totally embarrassed, but Raquel seemed to enjoy it. Then we took her into the dressing room to meet the players, who were all over her, cracking jokes and so on. I don't think Dave Sexton was that pleased but he was very polite. I really didn't mean to create that sort of stir. I just hoped to take her to the game anonymously, but somehow it didn't work out like that."

Playing for Leicester that day was one Alan Birchenall, the former Chelsea striker who had left the Bridge two years earlier. While catching up with his old mates, the Birch was in the home changing room when la Welch made her dramatic entrance. "Dickie Attenborough brought her into the dressing room," he recalls. "When she was introduced to the team she made a beeline for Ossie, so we knew straightaway that she fancied him."

It was by no means the first time that Attenborough had taken a film star into the dressing room to meet the team. On other famous occasion the players had been surprised to see Steve McQueen popping his head round the door. Spotting a fellow smoker, McQueen had sat down for a chat and a fag with Eddie McCreadie. The star of *The Great Escape* was a hard act to top but, at the time, Welch was in the same glittering league – and, as the players couldn't help noticing, she was a damn sight better looking.

"After the game an American guy, her agent or minder, came up to me and said, 'Is Peter Aasgood here?'" continues Alan Birchenall. "I said, 'Get over here, Ossie' and that's when he said, 'Miss Welch would like to invite you and any of the Chelsea boys to a cocktail party at the Dorchester hotel tonight'. Ossie invited me and we went along. We thought we'd stay for an hour or so and we finally got back home on Sunday afternoon. There was a Who's Who of the Swinging Sixties and Seventies there – a couple of Stones, a couple of Beatles, the Animals were there, a smattering of TV personalities. It was a big mixture, a big cocktail party. I lost Ossie for a while and when we surfaced the next morning we thought we'd better get on our bikes. The hour had turned into 12 or more."

Ossie himself has a more distinct memory of the initial meeting than the party afterwards. "We met before the game," he says, "and she was a lovely, beautiful lady. She gave me a little peck on the cheek. Then, with ten, minutes to go, she walked along the side of the pitch, waving at me and saying, 'Bye, Ossie!' So I got a good bollocking from Dave Sexton for that." Certainly, Osgood gave every indication of being slightly distracted, having a quiet game in a disappointing 1-1 draw.

Curiosity in these matters being what it is, Blues fans have long speculated that more than a kiss passed between Ossie and Raquel that day. The Chelsea star, though, maintains that's all that happened. In one sense, it hardly matters what actually took place. The myth of a steamy Osgood-Welch liaison will live on regardless, fuelled in no small way by Alan Birchenall's final, somewhat ambiguous words on the subject:

"Raquel's a tasty woman now but 30 years ago she was absolutely stunning, so if I was Peter Osgood I would certainly claim what happened as being, shall we say, a little more than a peck on the cheek. But I'm sure that Ossie, being the man he is, refrained from taking advantage of the situation. I can say that without a smile on my face – lucky bugger!"

Ossie wasn't the only Chelsea player to get acquainted with 60s celebrity totty. Before George Best claimed a monopoly in the department, it was every footballer's dream to go out with Miss World, and it didn't much matter whether the young lady hailed from America or Zululand. Soon after breaking into the Chelsea team in 1965 John Boyle had a chance to do 'a Bestie' when he ran into the tiara-sporting champion at a charity function. "I didn't know her but we got chatting and swapped phone numbers," he says. "A couple of days later she phoned back and said, 'It's Anne here, you know Anne Sydney, Miss World.' She'd won it the previous year for the United Kingdom. I thought I'd pulled, but I hadn't. She just wanted a chat." Close, Boylers, but no cigar.

Having struck out with Miss World, Boyle had better luck a few years later with Fiona Richmond, one of the original porn stars of the late sixties. "We were on tour in Trinidad and she was over there doing a film shoot. I'd already met her in London at a party and she told me she was going to Trinidad so I laughed and said, 'Oh, we're going there as well! I'll give you a ring and take you out to dinner.' We were staying at the Trinidad Hilton and I managed to track her down and we had dinner at the hotel. She was actually a vicar's daughter and I found her charming company. We had great fun at the dinner and, of course, when I got back it was a typical football scene with all the lads wanting to know how I'd got on. Being a typical man, I probably exaggerated how well the evening had gone, but that's all I'm prepared to say on the subject!"

Although the dinner was a one-off, Miss Richmond retained a strong interest in football, or rather footballers, and a few years later, during Malcolm Allison's reign at Crystal Palace, she was photographed topless in the Selhurst Park team bath surrounded by wide-eyed Palace players.

No doubt, if she'd asked, the Chelsea lads would gladly have posed for a similar photo opportunity while she was out in the Caribbean.

In the early seventies the highlight of any edition of *Top of the Pops*, at least for red-blooded males, was the appearance of the dancing troupe Pan's People. Swishing their long hair as they gyrated around the stage, the leggy dancers captivated the studio audience with their energetic routines, only occasionally eliciting giggles for their overly literal interpretations of the hits of the day. As Britain boasted no girl bands at the time – and even solo artists such as Lulu, Sandy Shaw, Dusty Springfield and Mary Hopkin were very much a rarity – the glamorous Pan's People were hot stuff, almost the Spice Girls of their era. At the start of the 1973/74 season a small item in the Chelsea programme revealed that one of the dancers in Pan's People was having treatment at the Bridge for an ankle injury. What the fans probably didn't know was that the connection between the girls and the Blues went a lot further than that.

"I used to go out with the tall dark one, Dee Dee Wilde," says Tommy Baldwin. "I think I met her down the Aretusa club, and we used to go out in the afternoon drinking after I'd finished training. I met all the other Pan's People, too. She wasn't my girlfriend as such, we were just good pals. She was great, she was a good mate and because she lived locally, up on Putney Hill with her brother, I used to see her regularly. We used to drink together and then she started going to games. When she injured her ankle it was my idea to send her down to Stamford Bridge for treatment."

Tommy eventually married another woman in the public eye, Michael Crawford's ex-wife, Gabrielle. "She used to be an actress," says the Sponge. "She was in *Emergency Ward 10* and a few other things. But when she married Michael she gave up her acting. I knew him first. He used to go down to Chelsea with David Webb. In his book he said he was always trying to get Gabrielle to come along to the Bridge. Eventually she went to a game and liked it so much she ran off with the centre forward! I'd split up with my missus and she'd split up with Michael and we just seemed to get it together." The couple had two children before divorcing in 1984.

When not chasing after Miss Worlds, porn stars, actresses or dancers, the Chelsea lads often used to look to the skies for potential girlfriends. "Most of the boys were going out with air hostesses at the time, that was their thing," says Alan Hudson. Peter Osgood's second wife, Pippa, was a stewardess while his strike partner Ian Hutchinson also had a long relationship with a trolley dolly.

"I was married when I signed for Chelsea, but we were young and broke up," Hutch revealed in an interview in 2001. "Then, I was seeing an air hostess called Sally for a while. We actually lived together for three years. But she worked long-haul flights mostly so we were apart a lot. One day she came back earlier than expected and caught me in bed with a young lady. How inconsiderate. She could have phoned me from the airport to warn me at least. So that was the end of that relationship."

For the unmarried Chelsea players, opportunities for casual flings were plentiful, as young women everywhere rejected the strict, almost Victorian morality of their parents' generation. The fear of unwanted pregnancy banished by the new contraceptive pill, they embraced the hippy concept of 'free love'. In the Docherty era George Graham – tall, dark and handsome but with a caddish glint in his eye – in particular took advantage of this happy state of affairs and, amongst the other players, was the acknowledged top 'bird-puller'.

"Gorgeous George we called him," says Peter Osgood. "He used to be immaculate everywhere he went; even in his football kit he was immaculate. He was a good-looking lad. We went to Australia for six weeks in 1965. We flew out of four or five different airports on the tour and there was a bird crying in each and every one over George. I think some of the other lads, especially the ones who'd got married young, were a little bit envious because George was pulling birds left, right and centre and they couldn't do that."

Sometimes, though, the married players did stray from the straight and narrow. One player who succumbed to temptation soon probably wished he hadn't, even though he had managed to keep the affair hidden from his wife. "This player had a little fling and the brother of the girl sent him a note saying he was going to shoot him on the pitch," recalls Ossie. "Anyway, the player was worried, understandably, and took the note to Tommy Docherty. Tom looked at it and said, 'Well, you'd better keep running, then, because a moving target is always harder to hit.'"

The chat up lines used by the players to butter up of their potential conquests could be unconventional. John Boyle, for example, was dubbed 'Trampus' by his team-mates after being heard talking to a girl at some length about the character of that name from the TV series *The Virginian*. Not necessarily a winning routine, you would have thought, but possibly more likely to be successful than a regular chat up line employed by Ron Harris.

"We were down in Bournemouth before an FA Cup tie," remembers Alan Birchenall. "We went to a club in town, brought a couple of birds back to the hotel and I was trying to chat this girl up when Ron Harris came in with a watchstrap round his wendle, and said, 'Have you got the time on you, cock?' This bird just screamed and ran out of the room. I don't think she was that bothered about seeing his knob, she was actually looking at his face."

Another Chelsea player, who even after all these years must remain nameless, and Eric Swayne, a friend of some of the team, found that a slightly more sophisticated approach worked rather better. "We pulled a couple of good-looking girls in the King's Road," remembers Eric. "My favourite trick then was to sit in a restaurant with a mate and if there were two pretty girls at another table we'd just call the wine waiter over and say, 'See the two ladies over there? Please give them a bottle of Dom Perignon with Eric's compliments.' Then you'd join them or they'd join you and you'd take it from there.

"Well, everything went to plan on this occasion and we all went back to my studio in Thurloe Square round the back of South Kensington tube station. My bedroom wasn't a room as such, it was part of the studio, a beautifully made pine gallery. So I was up there with one girl and the Chelsea man, who was married, was downstairs with the other girl. It was a fantastic evening and I didn't start to fall asleep until about half past three. Even then, I remember I kept being woken up by the Chelsea player and his girl until about six o'clock!"

As now, for many young women the prospect of going out with, or even marrying, a famous footballer was an attractive one in the sixties. Aware of this common fantasy, it was not unknown for some cocky chancers to pretend to be a well-known star to increase their chances of pulling. Of course, it would be absurd to introduce yourself as George Best or Bobby Moore – not even the most gullible, dim-witted 'bird' would fall for that. But, if you looked vaguely sporty and unless the girl was an avid reader of *Shoot!* or a regular viewer of *Match of the Day*, you might well get away with claiming to be a lesser name – say, Chelsea's Alan Birchenall, for example.

"One day Ossie said to me, 'I see you're getting married again'," recalls Birchenall. "I said, 'What do you mean, I've only been married for three months?' Then he told me one of his mum's neighbours in Windsor had heard a woman boasting in the corner shop that her daughter had got engaged to Alan Birchenall, the Chelsea footballer. Ossie had also heard another story about me running up debts at a golf course. This was news to me, too, because I didn't play golf. After much scratching of heads, we came to the conclusion that the only possible explanation was that somebody must be impersonating me."

Determined to unveil the shadowy doppelganger, the two players turned detective and soon tracked down Birch's 'fiancee' to an address in Bracknell. "When we went round to the house the girl who I was 'engaged' to was out but her mother flatly denied that I was Alan Birchenall," says the Birch. "So we got the Chelsea team line up photo out and I told her, 'Look, that's me, Alan Birchenall!' But she just said, 'My daughter's engaged to Alan Birchenall. I think I know what he looks like, thanks'. I kept saying 'But I'm Alan!' and she kept replying 'No, you're not!' We went on for about ten minutes like that, until she started to believe I was the genuine article."

The police were informed and the story was covered extensively in the newspapers at the time. The girl's mother, Mrs Ethel Evans, told reporters: "My daughter, Eileen, met this man in a pub in Bracknell where he was known as Alan Birchenall the footballer. He used to come around here nearly every day and his knowledge of football was exceptional. My husband, who is a keen fan, could not trip him up. He was a smooth talker with lots of charm and nerve. He borrowed £25 off me. I took it out of the rent money I had saved. But he was always making excuses and when I asked about the money he said he had left his cheque book in his flat in Chelsea and was going to fetch it to repay me. He never did. My daughter was crazy about him and believed he was the Chelsea footballer. They were going to be married."

Generously overlooking the fact that the Evans family were unlikely ever to appear on *Brain of Britain*, an outraged Birchenall told *The Sunday Express*, "If I ever catch up with this character he will wish he never started this business. I don't mind a bloke pretending to be me if he just wants to impress a new girlfriend at a dance or something. But this is different and has done my name a lot of harm."

Eventually, police in Birmingham caught the man, who had committed a string of similar scams across the South East, and he was sent to prison.

"It was a bit worrying," admits Alan now. "There wasn't always room in the Chelsea team for one Birch, let alone two."

CHAPTER NINE

KINGS OF EUROPE

CHAPTER NINE
KINGS OF EUROPE

I f the Chelsea board of the 1950s had been a little more adventurous, it's just possible that the Blues, rather than Real Madrid, might have dominated the European Cup in its early years. An unlikely scenario, admittedly, but still conceivable in a 'Scotland might have won the World Cup if they'd qualified' kind of way.

What actually happened was this: Chelsea, as league champions in 1955, were invited to take part in the inaugural European Cup the following season. However, the Football Association, concerned about the possible impact on domestic attendances and generally suspicious about 'foreign' initiatives, advised Chelsea not to participate. To the disappointment of the players, Chelsea chairman Joe Mears, an FA councillor, decided to heed this advice. Instead, Manchester United became the first English club to enter the fledgling competition in 1956/57. As it turned out, Chelsea's championship-winning heroes would never have another chance to enter the European pantheon occupied by Real legends Puskas, Di Stefano and Gento.

The Blues finally got their passports out in 1958/59 for the Inter-Cities Fairs Cup, the precursor of the UEFA Cup. The competition was open to teams, other than the reigning league champions, from selected cities around Europe. Normally, the highest placed team from a particular city in the preceding season was invited to take part. On this basis, London's representatives in the Fairs Cup in 1958 should have been Tottenham, who had finished the 1957/58 season in third place, eight places above Chelsea. There was a feeling in UEFA, though, that Chelsea were 'owed' a European invitation from 1955 and so the Blues, rather than Spurs, carried the flag for London. After beating BK Frem of Denmark in the first round, Chelsea went out 4–2 on aggregate to Ville de Belgrade.

Seven years later, in 1965, Tommy Docherty's 'Diamonds' returned to the Fairs Cup on their own merits, as London's top club in the previous season. Despite lacking competitive experience in Europe, the Blues were confident of doing well, after having defeated numerous top continental sides and the West German national team, in a series of high-profile friendly matches.

In the first round Chelsea were handed a tough draw, being paired with former Fairs Cup winners Roma. The Italian side lived up to their nickname, *I Lupi* (the Wolves), in the first leg at the Bridge with some blood-curdling challenges. Roma right back Francesco Carpenetti picked on the wrong man, though, when he took a swipe at Eddie McCreadie.

"I went on an overlap, got my cross in, and this guy came across and kicked me in the shins," Eddie recalled later. "Then he put his hand right round my throat. And I was, well, have some of that, you know. And I decked him." The referee's response was a formality: while the Roma physio administered smelling salts to the befuddled victim, McCreadie was ordered off.

For Peter Osgood, just 18, and playing in only his second ever senior Chelsea match the experience of playing against such cynical opponents was something of an eye-opener. "It was a very hard, physical game," he says. "I didn't really understand it for the first half, to be honest. I just thought, 'What's going on here?' They were pinching and pushing, nudging you and scraping their studs down the back of your leg when the referee wasn't looking. They just tried to intimidate you the whole time, and get you to react – which Eddie did, unfortunately. He never used to lose his cool, he just used to sort people out but, on this occasion, he turned round and whacked this guy and got sent off."

Despite being down to ten men, the Blues still managed to win the game 4–1, Terry Venables scoring a hat-trick. A bad night for the Italians got worse when the multi-lingual Bridge crowd greeted the final whistle with a rousing chorus of 'Arrivederci, Roma!' Predictably, the newspaper reports the following morning concentrated on the fisticuffs rather than the football.

"At one time, as the first half developed, I felt there would be nothing but a police report or a despatch from the battlefront when the time was over – casualty figures for each headquarters," wrote the man from *The Times*. "The fact is that for almost three-quarters of an hour the match developed into nothing better than a Roman orgy, the roars for blood of the Stamford Bridge Coliseum in one's ears."

If the first leg was a cross between *Gladiator* and *Caligula*, the second leg resembled the famous scene at the end of *Frankenstein* where the pitchfork-wielding peasants storm the castle intent on destroying all those within it. And, while Chelsea might have contributed to the bad-tempered opening act at the Bridge, this time the fault lay entirely with the Italians.

"Roma got the hump," says Marvin Hinton bluntly. "When they got back to Italy they complained that they hadn't been treated properly by Chelsea, that the pitch had been watered by Tommy Docherty and so on. The Italian press blew it all out of proportion and when we went over for the return leg there was a really hostile atmosphere building against us. Roma pulled a bit of a trick by switching the game from their normal stadium to a smaller ground where the fans were right on top of the pitch. That was a surprise for us, but it was nothing compared to the reception we got when we walked out to have a look at the pitch. The crowd pelted us with everything they could lay their hands on: eggs, tomatoes, the lot."

Flying foodstuffs were a minor worry, though, compared to the fans' next choice of weapons. "They chucked everything on the pitch, metal seats and all," recalled Terry Venables. "And then a great big ice block went over the top of the fences. I don't know where they got that from. It must have taken about ten people to carry it."

Once the game started, the Blues had two main aims: first, to protect their first leg lead and second, to avoid any incidents that might incite the frenzied, near hysterical crowd still further.

"We just tried to be as calm as possible," says Hinton, whose famously unflappable temperament was ideally suited to the difficult circumstances. "One of their players punched me after I tackled him, but I just walked away. I think if I had hit him back the crowd would have climbed over the fences."

Apart from the occasional uppercut or left hook, Roma, for whom Carlo Cudicini's father, Fabio, was playing in goal, also tried to unsettle the Chelsea players with the type of sneaky, underhand and downright crooked tactics which were then virtually unknown in the English game.

"They would obstruct you, pinch you or pull the hair under your arms in an attempt to make you lose your cool," says John Boyle. "They also didn't like it when you went in for a full bloodied tackle; if you tackled them they would fall over and writhe on the ground. But we learned to cope with it all and, if you look at the stats, you'll see we rarely got booked in Europe."

With Hinton having a masterful game at sweeper, the match ended in 0–0 draw. "I was the first English sweeper, and it was a role I found very enjoyable," he says. "Tommy Docherty developed the idea when we played in Europe against teams who were technically better than us. He was worried that the quick passing and one-twos these teams played around our box would cut through our defence so he wanted someone in there to cover the central defenders. It suited my style of play to be the sweeper, because one of my strengths was reading the game and I liked to pass the ball out from the back. I wasn't the most physical of players so that free role was perfect for me."

Safely through to the next round, now the only worry for the Blues was how to give the irate Roma supporters the slip on the way back to the airport. "After the game we waited in the dressing room until we thought all the fans would have gone home," says Marvin. "But when we got on the team bus there were loads of Roma fans waiting for us. A lot of them had bricks and they smashed all the windows in. We all threw ourselves on the floor but the chairman's wife was cut by flying glass. It was awful, I'd never seen anything like it before. What made it worse was that there were policemen standing around, but they just stood back and watched us getting attacked."

Thankfully, the second round was an altogether quieter affair, Chelsea beating Wiener Sport-Club of Austria 2–1 on aggregate. The third round, however, saw the Blues involved in another pulsating, edge-of-the seat Italian drama. Drawn against an AC Milan side which included cultured midfielder Gianni Rivera and Paolo Maldini's father, Cesare, Chelsea went down 2–1 in the San Siro before winning the return leg by the same score at the Bridge to the delight of the near 60,000 crowd. In those days tied matches were settled by a play-off and, after Milan had won the toss for choice of venues, the players returned to the San Siro for the decider. That, too, finished level, Barry Bridges scoring Chelsea's goal in a 1–1 draw. The penalty shoot-out had not been invented then; instead, UEFA had devised an altogether simpler though spectator-unfriendly method of settling drawn ties – the toss of a coin.

"I went out on the pitch with Cesare Maldini, Tommy Doc and the referee," recalls Ron Harris, who had replaced Terry Venables as skipper in the aftermath of the 'Blackpool Incident'. "I called right and we went through. I can't remember if I called heads or tails but I know I was the first captain to win a toss of the coin in Europe."

The Blues' luck held in the quarter-finals, when they inched past Munich 1860 3–2 on aggregate, Peter Osgood scoring the all-important winner at the Bridge in the second leg. That victory set up a mouth-watering semi-final with Barcelona, who already had a couple of Fairs Cup trophies to their name. However, the tie arrived at a bad time for Chelsea: dressing-room morale was low after defeat in the FA Cup semi-final four days before the first leg and Blues boss Tommy Docherty had fallen out with several senior players who he had dropped from the team. "We are beset by internal strife," one unnamed player told the press.

Under the circumstances, a 2–0 defeat in front of 70,000 noisy fans in the Nou Camp was hardly surprising. "They were a very good side – it could have been 10–0," admits Ron Harris. Outclassed in Barcelona, Chelsea, with Charlie Cooke making his debut, were gifted two own goals by the Catalans in the return leg to level up the tie. "We were a bit unlucky because I scored a goal in the last few minutes which was disallowed," says Ron. "Then we lost on the draw of straws so we had to go back to Barcelona for the play-off."

In the mid-sixties European club tournaments were still very much in their infancy, and UEFA was uncertain whether the new competitions would appeal to the public. Chelsea fans, though, had responded positively to the Blues' Fairs Cup campaign. More than 200,000 supporters had poured through the Bridge turnstiles for the team's five European home games, but not many of them would be making the long journey to north-east Spain. In an effort to keep the fans involved, the club arranged to show the play-off match live on six large screens erected on the Stamford Bridge pitch – the first time a European game had been transmitted back to England by closed-circuit TV. Chelsea even produced a special souvenir programme to mark the occasion, which turned out to be a forgettable one for the 9,000 fans present as the Blues crashed to a 5–0 defeat.

"It was a disappointing way to go out," says John Boyle, "although just to be out there playing against Barcelona was a great experience. We played them at the end of a long season and it caught up with us a bit. I think by then we were shot."

Chelsea returned to the Fairs Cup three years later in the 1968/69 season, a year after Dave Sexton had replaced Tommy Docherty as manager. After Scottish side Morton had been summarily dismissed 9–3 on aggregate – curiously, Chelsea's goals over the two legs were shared out among eight different players – the Blues were drawn against DWS Amsterdam. The Dutch side had won their country's championship in 1964 but were now beginning the long, slow decline that would eventually see them sink into Sunday League obscurity. Another emphatic Chelsea victory looked likely.

The Blues, though, hadn't reckoned with DWS' goalkeeper Jan Jongbloed who would go on to appear in two World Cup Finals with Holland in the 1970s. Over the two legs he saved everything Chelsea threw at him and was instrumental in keeping the aggregate score at 0–0. Once more, Chelsea's fate depended on the coin-tossing skills of Ron Harris. This time, however, there was no happy ending: Chopper called incorrectly as a Dutch silver guilder spun to the turf, and Chelsea were out.

"We missed some simple chances," said Ron afterwards, "and the DWS goalkeeper played a blinder. Yet, if we had to face the Dutch side again we would have tackled the problem in exactly the same way. Our two 0–0 draws were, to my mind, just one of those things that happen in football."

Maybe, but the Blues had to pay a heavy price for their failure: against all odds, Newcastle, who had finished the previous season four places behind Chelsea in 10th position and had only qualified for the Fairs Cup through a series of unlikely coincidences, went on to win the competition in a two-legged final with Hungary's Ujpest Dozsa. Still, any jealousy Chelsea fans might have felt towards the Geordies would surely have been dissipated had they known that this would be the Magpies last acquaintance with meaningful silverware for 35 years.

The Blues just missed out on a European place at the end of the 1968/69 season after finishing one place behind Arsenal, who claimed London's Fairs Cup slot and went on to win the competition. In 1970, though, Chelsea resumed their continental adventures. By then, of course, the FA Cup was in the Stamford Bridge trophy cabinet and with it came a passport to the European Cup Winners Cup. In terms of prestige this tournament was rated slightly more highly than the Fairs Cup but it was probably easier to win, simply because the leading European football nations only provided one entrant each. In the Fairs Cup, on the other hand, countries with strong domestic leagues like Italy, Germany and Spain usually had three entrants, so the chances of meeting top-quality opposition in any given round were higher.

In the first decade of its existence, British clubs had fared extremely well in the Cup Winners Cup. Tottenham (1963), West Ham (1965) and Manchester City (1970) had all won the competition, while Rangers and Liverpool had been beaten finalists. Unsurprisingly, Chelsea were also expected to do well, being listed among the pre-tournament favourites along with Real Madrid, Benfica, Bologna and Bruges.

Certainly, the Blues' subtle mix of stylishness, resilience and old-fashioned English powerplay looked suited to European football. The likes of Osgood, Cooke and Hudson had the necessary technique, artistry and flair to unlock the tightest of continental defences; Hollins, Baldwin and Boyle would match all comers for effort, perseverance and commitment; and at the back Chopper Harris and co might have struggled to spell *catenaccio* but they still provided as intimidating a barrier as any in *Serie A*. Chelsea, too, had other weapons that could surprise unsuspecting overseas opponents: Ian Hutchinson's jaw-dropping long throws, the aerial threat of Webb and Dempsey at set pieces and, although it was sometimes unappreciated by the fans, Peter Houseman's deadly accurate crossing ability.

Moreover in Dave Sexton Chelsea possessed a manager who knew how to blend all these disparate elements into an effective unit. "Generally speaking, I tried to get a method of playing that suited the players I had," he said later. "That sounds obvious, but it's not. You have to enable them to produce their best, trying to improve them as you work with them. Some players are very clever, imaginative and creative, but they haven't got much fight or spirit to them, so you try to help them to toughen up. And the other way round. Your hard blokes – your David Webbs, your Ronnie Harrises – you strengthen their passing and their touch. The end result is that you have tough guys who can play football, and vice versa."

In the summer of 1970 Sexton had shuffled his squad, selling strikers Bobby Tambling and Alan Birchenall to Crystal Palace and bringing in Tony Curtis-lookalike Keith Weller from Millwall for £100,000. Weller had mostly played in central midfield at The Den and in his limited appearances for his previous club Tottenham, where his literary-minded team-mates had nicknamed him 'Sammy' after the character Samuel Weller in Dickens' *David Copperfield*. Sexton, though, planned to use Weller as an attacking right-winger, believing that his pace, directness and powerful right-footed shooting would be of more value further up the field.

Along with these personnel changes came a slightly altered playing style, influenced by Sexton's summer trip to watch the 1970 World Cup. "Over in Mexico, I watched Brazil three or four times," he said. "One particular move they did was that somebody on the left-hand side of midfield, instead of playing the ball into the striker's feet, would lift it over the top as the striker came towards him. The forward would then spin off his marker, leaving him completely clean through on goal. I promised I'd pay the bloke who played the pass and the one who scored the goal a fiver each." Sexton's bank manager had no need to worry, though, as Dave admitted, "I never once had to pay out."

The Blues were still struggling to get to grips with the so-called 'fiver ball' when they played their first European game of the season against Aris Salonika. Chelsea's opponents had a reputation as a dirty side and, on a dry, bumpy pitch, it soon became clear that the Greeks were more interested in kicking their English visitors than playing football. Indeed, it seemed only a matter of time before one of their number was given his marching orders by the Hungarian referee, a Mr G. Emsberger. Sure enough, the ref was soon waving a red card – however, the player he was waving it at was John Dempsey.

"It started when their guy tried to kick the ball out of Peter Bonetti's hands while he was clearly holding it," explains John. "I just got myself in between Peter and their striker, there was a bit of pushing and then the guy started rolling on the floor. It was ridiculous, I hadn't done anything. The linesman came rushing on the pitch waving his flag and I was sent off. Ken Jones, who was covering the game for *The Daily Mirror* said it was one of the most ridiculous sendings off he'd seen."

A clear case of a miscarriage of justice, you might think. Yet, according to Dave Sexton, Dempsey was far from being the innocent victim of a combination of Greek play-acting and incompetent refereeing. "Demps was well-known for having a short fuse and players knew they could wind him up," he said. "In the dressing room I took him to one side and said, 'Look, Aris Salonika are going to do everything to get you mad. They'll call your mother names, you names, everybody names. Don't bite at all – ignore it and get on with the game.' John was like, 'Yes, Dave,' and 'Okay, Dave'.

"Five minutes before half-time Aris won a corner and, just as their fella's gone to cross the ball, their centre forward's got hold of Dempsey's bollocks and given them a right old squeeze. John's responded by smashing him with his fist. Down to ten men we did well to hold out for a 1–1 draw." In fact, the result would have been even better if Peter Osgood hadn't missed a penalty after a foul on Paddy Mulligan, an attack-minded full back signed from Shamrock Rovers, primarily as defensive cover, in December 1969.

In the return at the Bridge Chelsea put on a bravura attacking display, crushing the Greeks 5–1. The pick of the goals came from John Hollins, who powered in a drive from fully 35 yards. For the Blues' anorak brigade the fact that all the home side's goals were scored by players with surnames beginning with 'H' – Hollins (2), Hutchinson (2) and Hinton – was an additional thrill. Despite being humiliated on the pitch, Aris had toned down their roughhouse antics from the first leg and relations between the clubs were further improved when their President told Brian Mears, "If you reach the final in Athens next May you can be assured of our support."

In the second round Chelsea were given a tricky-looking draw against CSKA Sofia, the Bulgarian army side. Regular champions in their country, it was something of a surprise that they were in the Cup Winners Cup at all, rather than the European Cup. Moreover, CSKA had a formidable home record in Europe, never having lost to foreign opposition in 17 European games at their People's Army stadium. A strong all-round team featured five players from Bulgaria's 1970 World Cup squad, including European Golden Boot winner Petar Jenkov. For Chelsea, the trip behind the Iron Curtain for the first leg promised to be a demanding one. And so it proved.

"They were the most impressive side we played in the whole competition," reckons Ron Harris. "We won 1–0 over there, Tommy Baldwin scored and I think that was the only time we got out of our half. They were one of the best club sides I've seen. A really good, technical, well-organised, well-prepared side."

And Peter Osgood adds: "It was quite intimidating. All 40,000 of the crowd seemed to be in military uniforms. When you saw that you thought, 'This is serious' but we kept our heads, we did a good job and we came away winners. But they were a bloody good side."

The football may have been of a high standard, but the Blues were less taken with other aspects of Communist life. "You couldn't get Coca Cola or any other mixers," complains Tommy Baldwin, whose winning goal came from a Keith Weller cross just before half-time. "If you went for a drink you got vodka and water. Luckily, we weren't there long. We simply went in and came back out and we didn't really see the city. Most of the time we just stayed in the hotel." Ron Harris, though, maintains that Sofia wasn't really that bad at all. "It was a hell of a lot better than some places I went to with Chelsea: Haiti, El Salvador and so on," he says.

Another disciplined 1–0 win over CSKA at the Bridge, thanks this time to a bizarre David Webb header from a sitting position, sealed Chelsea's passage to the quarter-finals. After the match, the Bulgarians' manager Manol Manolov paid a fulsome tribute to the Blues' star performer over the two legs, goalkeeper Peter Bonetti. "Although Chelsea tackled very hard but very fair, our biggest problem was not their tackling but how to get the ball past Bonetti," he said. "What a magnificent goalkeeper he is!"

By the time the quarter-finals came around, in March 1971, Chelsea's season had taken a turn for the worse. Having already been knocked out of the League Cup in the autumn by Manchester United, the Blues had lost their hold on the FA Cup in January, losing 3–0 at home to Manchester City in the fourth round. Immediately after that game Peter Osgood was suspended for two months by the Football Association, which had just launched a crackdown on player misconduct.

"It was just three bookings," says Ossie, still amazed after all these years by the severity of the punishment. "What happened was that Bestie had appeared before the FA, and they said the next player who came up was going to be made an example of. That was me. So I was given a six-week suspension. Brian Mears, the chairman, said: 'We're going to fight this, Ossie, we'll take it to appeal.' So I went back and got an extra two weeks plus a £150 fine!"

The suspended Osgood was not the only notable absentee for Chelsea as they headed off to Belgium to meet Bruges in the first leg of the quarter-final. Also missing were the injured Ron Harris and Ian Hutchinson and pneumonia-sufferer Peter Bonetti. Fortunately, Bonetti's deputy, John Phillips, was in fine form, having kept clean sheets in four of the six league games he had played in since taking over in goal. Up front, Sexton was forced to throw in South African centre forward Derek Smethurst for his European debut, alongside Tommy Baldwin.

Already lacking four of his key players, Dave Sexton was confronted with another unwanted problem at the team's hotel. "We were playing cards on the afternoon of the game and somebody lost quite a lot of money," recalls John Boyle. "There was a bit of an argument about that, so Dave banned us from gambling."

All in all, Chelsea's preparations were not ideal for a match which looked like testing the team to the limit. Runners-up in Belgium's Jupiler league the season before, Bruges were gradually emerging as their country's dominant force and would go on to play Liverpool in two European finals in the 1970s. A number of their players, including powerful striker Raoul Lambert, had appeared for Belgium at the World Cup in Mexico the previous year and, like CSKA, they also boasted a good home record in Europe.

In front of their own fans, Bruges gave an under-strength Chelsea a torrid time in the compact, English-style De Klokke stadium. Both goals in the Blues' 2–0 defeat stemmed from in-swinging corners, with Lambert grabbing the first after just four minutes.

"Bruges battered us in the away game," admits Alan Hudson. "How we came out of there still in the tie is incredible. They should have put us away. They had us under us the cosh, but John Phillips was fantastic for us in goal. On the plane coming home that night from Bruges I remember thinking, 'How the hell are we going to get this back?'"

Two weeks later Bonetti and Hutchinson were still out, but Harris was fit to return for the second leg. Osgood, too, had completed his suspension and, banned from the training ground as part of his punishment, had maintained his fitness during his two month-break with regular runs on his own across Epsom Downs. All the same, Sexton was reluctant to pitch his star striker into such an important game without any match practice behind him.

"When we got them back to Stamford Bridge Dave Sexton wasn't sure whether to play Ossie or not because he didn't think he'd be match fit," says Tommy Baldwin. "But, in the end, he did play. We were 2–0 down, but we just went out with the attitude 'let's go for it'. I can remember the team talk quite clearly. Dave kept saying, 'We can do this, but we've got to be patient. We know we can score goals.'" Keeping a clean sheet was just as vital, as a Bruges goal would leave Chelsea requiring four under the away goals rule introduced by UEFA six years earlier.

On a balmy spring evening, the 45,000-plus Bridge crowd was in optimistic mood, generating a raucous atmosphere from the first whistle. For once, even the East and West stands joined in as the Shed went through its full repertoire, while the rickety North Stand almost seemed to sway from side to side as excited fans jumped to their feet to add their voices to the thunderous chants of 'Chel-sea!'

"It was absolutely electric," says Baldwin. "The noise from the fans was constant, they were amazing. Maybe it got to Bruges a bit. Don't forget we were 2–0 down, so you might have thought the fans would be a bit flat, but right from the start they were singing and chanting."

An early goal from Peter Houseman, slotting the ball home from close range after Osgood had headed down Baldwin's cross, intensified the pressure on Bruges. But, with nine minutes left, they were still hanging on to their aggregate lead when Charlie Cooke crossed for Osgood, sporting a magnificent Jackson Five-style 'afro' which he had grown during his suspension, to shoot home the equaliser. It was a vital goal and, typically, Ossie celebrated in flamboyant style, rushing across the greyhound track behind the goal towards the fans in the North Stand terrace.

Quite where he found the energy from for this little display was a mystery. "Ossie definitely wasn't match fit for the second leg," says Alan Hudson. "But it didn't matter with him, because you just needed to get the ball into him in the box. The bigger the game, the better he was." As if to prove this point, Hudson set up Osgood for the crucial third goal, deep into extra-time.

"I got to the byline on the left at the Shed end and looked up, played it across to Ossie and he scored. Me and Ossie used to have this move where he'd run in with the defenders and then pull out to give himself a yard or two yards of space. That would give you the chance to get the ball into him and he'd pick his spot. It was something instinctive we always had between us. It wasn't something we particularly spoke about, even when we were room-mates. Sexton used to hate me for it, but I always used to try to give the ball to Ossie. Football's all about getting your best players in the game, but Sexton had a go at me about it once. He said I was passing too much to Ossie and not getting the ball out to Peter Houseman on the left."

Maybe Sexton had a point, though, because it was the under-employed Houseman who created the fourth, clinching goal for Tommy Baldwin two minutes from the end. "Peter passed it to me, I was about six or seven yards out and just knocked it past the keeper," says Tommy. "That was it, game over. I got mobbed by everyone, they all just jumped on me. That was the best game I've ever been involved in, even including all the cup finals."

On an exhilarating night which would quickly pass into Chelsea folklore, Sexton's gamble in playing Osgood had paid off. "Only an English footballer could have done what Osgood did, playing so brilliantly after eight weeks without a game – not just for 90 minutes but extra-time as well," said Bruges manager Frank de Munck afterwards. "His height gave us real problems."

As for Ossie himself, he admitted that his long lay-off had left him feeling shattered. "It was as well it didn't show, but I felt jiggered after 45 minutes," he told reporters. "I just kept putting one leg in front of the other, but I forgot the tiredness once the goals came."

In the semi-final draw, Chelsea were paired with the holders, Manchester City, with the winners facing either Real Madrid or PSV Eindhoven in the final. City had stuttered in their defence of the trophy, scraping past Linfield on the away goals rule in the first round and then beating Hungarian side Honved in the second. In the quarter-finals they needed a play-off to beat Gornik Zabrze, the Polish side they had also defeated in the previous year's final.

City, though, had gained a win (in the FA Cup) and a draw (in the league) in their two visits to the Bridge that season and in Francis Lee, Mike Summerbee and Colin Bell had three potent attacking threats. Unfortunately for them, only one of that trio, England striker and future toilet roll entrepreneur Lee, was fit for the first leg at the Bridge. Chelsea, too, had injury problems, and lined up without Bonetti, Osgood, McCreadie and Hutchinson. Strangely, Sexton opted for a strike force of Smethurst and Webb, relegating Baldwin and Weller to the bench. At the back, gargantuan 19-year-old defender Micky Droy – a sort of non-green version of The Incredible Hulk – came in for his European debut alongside John Dempsey.

Unsurprisingly, given the cast list of understudies and novices, the match was an uninspiring affair and was decided by a solitary goal shortly after half-time. Weller, on as a substitute for Cooke, started the move with a cross to Webb, he headed down and the alert Smethurst nipped ahead of City defender Tony Towers to slide a shot under goalkeeper Joe Corrigan.

A 1-0 lead was a slender advantage for the away leg, but the Blues were given some encouragement by a 1-1 league draw in a dress rehearsal at Maine Road 10 days before the main event. Again, both teams were, as 'Arry Redknapp might put it, 'down to the bare bones' for the second leg. For Chelsea, Baldwin and Hollins had been added to the casualty list, while City were now without skipper Tony Book and Joe Corrigan. Corrigan's absence proved to be costly for City as his replacement, Ron Healey, literally handed Chelsea their winning goal in the first half. After Hudson won an indirect free-kick for obstruction, Weller bent his shot round the City wall and Healey fumbled the ball into the net.

"I didn't realise the referee had indicated it was an indirect free-kick," admits Keith. "So I had a pot and Healey got a touch, but the ball ended up in the net. If he had let it go, the ref would have disallowed it."

"The semi finals weren't good matches, they were scrappy," says Alan Hudson. "It was a relief we got through. They had a lot of players out but so did we, and anyway I think we were a better team than they were. But they had beaten us in the FA Cup that season when Dave Sexton left me out and played Marvin Hinton in midfield. It didn't work. If I'd played I reckon we'd have beaten them. In fact, I'll go as far to say that the two biggest mistakes Dave Sexton made were playing Marvin Hinton in midfield in that game and playing Webby at full back in the 1970 final. He got away with that one, though."

Meanwhile, in the other semi-final, Real Madrid had squeezed past PSV 2–1 on aggregate to set up an enticing final between the kings of the King's Road and the undisputed aristocrats of Spanish football. The stark truth, though, was that this Real side could not be compared to the one which had won five consecutive European Cups between 1956 and 1960, thrilling crowds wherever they played with their extravagant ball skills and incisive passing. Amazingly, Real's team still featured one survivor from that golden era, the clever winger Francisco Gento, nicknamed *El Supersonico*. Nearly 38, Gento was now the elder statesman in a side which also included Spanish internationals Pirri, Zoco and Amancio, the latter a scorer in Real's most recent European Cup triumph in 1966 against Partizan Belgrade.

Real's path to the final had been less than convincing. In the first round the Spaniards had been held 0–0 by the Maltese minnows Hibernians in Valletta before delivering a crushing *coup de grace*, 5–0, in the Bernabeu. A 2–1 aggregate victory over Austria's Wacker Innsbruck put Real in the quarter-finals where they met reigning Welsh Cup holders Cardiff City. To the astonishment of the football world, the Second Division side beat Real 1–0 in the first leg at Ninian Park. A seismic shock was on the cards, but not for long: Real triumphed 2–0 in the return to book their semi-final with PSV.

Real may have been one of the most famous names in European football, but they were still largely an unknown quantity to the Blues. "We didn't know a lot about their players," says John Dempsey. "You didn't have the videos of other teams in those days, so it was more a case of concentrating on your own game rather than thinking about the opposition."

Chelsea arrived in Athens two days before the final, basing themselves in a hotel outside the city. This was a calculated decision by Dave Sexton, who didn't want his players being tempted into a retsina-guzzling, plate-breaking exploration of Athenian nightlife. "The directors were staying at the Athens Hilton," says Tommy Baldwin, "but we were in a hotel right out in the country. Dave Sexton always put us in hotels outside the city, away from all the bars and clubs. If we went out it was always a long, costly taxi ride to get back wherever we stayed."

While the squad prepared for the final with some light training, Sexton agonised over his team selection. The big question was who to play in goal: young John Phillips, who had performed so capably in Bonetti's absence or the ultra-experienced 'Cat', now recovered from his bout of pneumonia. To Phillips' dismay Bonetti, who had returned to the side for the final league game of the season at Ipswich and kept a clean sheet in a 0–0 draw, got the nod. "I thought I'd done enough to replace him," Phillips said later. "We'd conceded very few goals during my spell in the side and I believed I should have played in the final."

Another disappointed player was Tommy Baldwin, although he'd already had an inkling he wouldn't make the starting eleven. "For the game against Real Madrid I was substitute," he says. "I got a notion I wouldn't be in the team when Dave put me in the wall in training while the others were practising free kicks." There was better news for John Boyle, who was chosen ahead of Paddy Mulligan for the full back spot left vacant by the injury to Eddie McCreadie.

The venue for the final, Olympiakos' Karaiskakis Stadium, was situated in one of the less salubrious parts of town, the grubby port area of Piraeus. Four thousand Chelsea fans had made the journey out to Greece and they were joined in their support for the Blues by the majority of locals in the 45,000 crowd. In return, the Chelsea supporters had promised their hosts that English fans would back Panathinaikos, rather than Ajax, in the European Cup Final at Wembley the following month – although quite how they could guarantee this happening was unclear.

Chelsea lined up against Real in a 4–3–3 formation with Cooke, Hudson and Hollins in midfield, and Osgood a lone central striker supported by Houseman and Weller on the flanks. Cooke, mesmerising the Real defence with his intricate footwork, was in wonderful form although Chelsea created few chances until Boyle crossed for Osgood on 55 minutes. His first shot was blocked, but when the ball rebounded to him he buried it in the corner. As the game moved into injury time it was still 1–0. The Cup seemed destined for Stamford Bridge, but disaster was looming.

"There was just a minute to go," recalls John Dempsey. "The trophy, with blue and white ribbons attached, had already been brought to the side of the pitch. Then I miscued a clearance, and the ball skimmed off my boot straight to one of three Real players who would all have been offside if I hadn't touched it. I think it was Zoco who scored. I was really distraught, I was thinking it's my fault we haven't won the Cup. But you just have to try to put those thoughts out of your head and concentrate on the rest of the game, because we had to play extra-time."

In the additional 30 minutes Chelsea came under increasing pressure from Real but, thanks to a combination of stalwart defending and a couple of extraordinary saves from Bonetti, the Blues hung on for a draw.

"That was one of my best ever performances for Chelsea," said David Webb later. "I can't remember putting a foot wrong. Everything I did just seemed to go right. Extra time against Real Madrid was phenomenal. I was clearing the ball away off the line, repelling all their attacks."

Having come so close to winning the Cup, Chelsea might easily have lost it. "I thought we were very fortunate to stay in it the game," says Alan Hudson. "They had a guy called Pirri who was superb for them."

The man from *The Times* took a similar view. "At moments Real seemed to be taunting Chelsea like a matador teasing the bull," he wrote. The *Madristas'* strong finish also seemed to make them slight favourites for the replay, which was scheduled for two days later. "The Spaniards have established a technical and psychological advantage which they could well turn their way in 48 hours time," *The Times'* reporter concluded.

With a day to kill between the matches, Dave Sexton made an unexpected announcement. "After the first game, I got the players together and told them I wasn't going to put any restrictions on them whatsoever," he said. "They'd performed terrifically for me over a long, hard season. I left them to sort out their own arrangements."

Some of the players, including John Dempsey, spent their day off relaxing at the team hotel. Others, Alan Hudson and back-up striker Derek Smethurst amongst them, set off to explore the Athens flea market. A third group, made up of Peter Osgood, Charlie Cooke and Tommy Baldwin, headed to the Athens Hilton where they changed into their swimming gear, settled down by the pool and set about preparing for the big game in their inimitable fashion. For the Sponge, in particular, this was more like it. After all, he hadn't come all this way to stand around in a human wall. "We had some lunch, talked about the following day's game and got stuck into the rum punches," says Baldwin. "No, I'm only joking, but we had some beers and we were a bit pissed when we got backed to our hotel rooms."

Ask two people for their recollections of a mega booze-up and the accounts are likely to be significantly different. Such is the case here. Peter Osgood fundamentally disagrees with Baldwin: cocktails, rum punches or otherwise, were definitely on the pre-match menu . . .

"Tom might have been on beer but me and Charlie were definitely on cocktails," says Ossie. "I had quite a few, I admit. I remember Alan Hudson going past and saying, 'C'mon lads . . . ' and I said, 'Look, son, don't worry about us, we're on the top of our form, just worry about your own game.'"

"On the way back from the flea market we called in at the Athens Hilton and we saw Ossie and co by the pool," remembers Alan Hudson. "A very good friend of mine called Johnny Fennell was there, and I think he was the instigator of their drinking session. Ossie said to me, 'You go home and have an early night because you've got to do my running for me tomorrow'. They were already pretty pissed."

The mammoth drinking bout, which had begun around 11am, finally finished some nine hours later. "We were supposed to be back at the hotel at 7pm for dinner," says Baldwin, "but we didn't get back until about 8.30pm so I got fined again. Then Dave said, 'By the way, you're playing tomorrow.' It didn't really bother me, I probably would have gone out anyway."

Baldwin's unexpected promotion from sub had come about because of an injury to John Hollins, who was reduced to watching the replay as an expert summariser for the BBC. This was a big blow. Although rarely a headline-grabber, Hollins' drive and stamina made him a vital component of the team. He had a fearsome shot, too, and could be relied on to get his quota of goals. His nine goals in 1970/71 included one against Arsenal at the Bridge – a chip over Gunners goalkeeper Bob Wilson which had struck the bar, only for Hollins to hook the rebound over his shoulder and into the roof of the net from the edge of the penalty area – which had won ITV's 'Goal of the Season' competition. To cap a great year for the midfielder, Chelsea fans had voted him their 'Player of the Season' for the second season running.

Hollins, clearly, would be missed. What Sexton didn't know, though, was that another member of his midfield trio was also far from fit. "In the first game I was clean through on goal and I thought I was going to score, which would have been fantastic," recalls Alan Hudson. "But I got a whack and was brought down. The tackle gave me a dead leg and with the replay being on the Friday I thought, 'Here we go, I'm going to miss another final'. Sexton asked me how I was, and I said, 'Fine', but I wasn't really. If it had been a league game I definitely wouldn't have played."

There were also doubts about the fitness of Peter Osgood, who was suffering from a knee ligament injury and had only managed to play in the first game after having a cortisone injection. "I didn't think I was going to play because I could hardly walk," he says. "In the first game the injection wore off and I had to come off. On the Thursday I thought I had no chance of making Friday. I'd resigned myself to missing it, so that was the reason I had a good bender down by the pool. I didn't think I'd be playing. But on the Friday morning the doctor stuck the needle in again. He said we could do it again and, fortunately, it worked out for us."

With Baldwin joining Osgood up front, Chelsea reverted to a more orthodox 4–4–2 formation for the replay. Without the missing Hollins, always a dynamic presence, a lot would depend on whether Cooke and Hudson could establish supremacy in midfield. Fortunately, Madrid had injury concerns of their own in this area.

"As luck would have it Pirri, their top midfielder, sprained his arm and wasn't as mobile in the replay," says Huddy. "I actually think that turned the game our way. I was feeling the dead leg but as the game went on I was more or less able to run it off."

"If we stop Cooke, we will win," Real's Amancio was quoted as saying after the first match. That, though, was easier said than done. Again, Charlie was in sparkling form and, on the half hour, sent over the corner from which Chelsea took the lead.

"I headed the ball towards goal," says John Dempsey, "their goalie punched it in the air and I just hit it on the volley into the top of the net. It flew in. It was a wonderful feeling to score. I just felt I'd made up for my mistake in the first game. It was not only the most important goal I'd scored but also the best."

It was indeed a stunning goal, so good in fact that many Chelsea fans couldn't quite believe that Dempsey had scored it. What they didn't know was that the confidence with which Demps struck his shot probably stemmed from a successful run he'd enjoyed as a striker with his previous club, Fulham.

"A few years before the final I'd scored a hat-trick for Fulham as an emergency centre forward against Northampton in the League Cup," he smiles. "I'd played there as a schoolboy and the manager, Vic Buckingham, put me up front when we were short of forwards. I scored a couple more in the next few games, too, and there was an article in one of the papers saying, 'Fulham have found a new striker'. But the next week they signed Allan Clarke and I was back in defence."

Not to be outdone, Osgood soon scored an equally brilliant second. "Tommy Baldwin had the ball, he gave it to me and made a run forward," recalls Ossie. "As he went he was screaming for me to knock it through, but all of a sudden a big gap opened up because he'd taken two of their defenders with him. I just bent it, the ball hit the post and went right in the corner. So, really, Tommy had done a lot of the work for me. He would always do that for you. He probably saw me score more goals than him but he wasn't worried about that. His contribution was great for the team: he'd hold the ball up, lay the ball off, make chances for you and he took chances himself, obviously. He was one of the lads who worked really hard for the team."

For the second time in three days the Cup was within Chelsea's grasp. However, with 15 minutes to go Fleitas pulled one back for the Spaniards and the pressure grew on the Chelsea goal. Bonetti dived to save a Zoco header, Webb blocked Amancio almost on the goal line and then, suddenly, it was all over – the Blues had won their first ever European trophy. As Chelsea players embraced each other and were mobbed by the ecstatic Blues fans who stormed onto the pitch, John Boyle made a beeline for the Real substitute who had made a fleeting appearance towards the end.

"The great thing for me was that in both games I had marked Gento, who had played for Real in the best game that I ever saw, the 1960

European Cup Final between them and Eintracht Frankfurt. Thank goodness, he was slower by the time of our final – probably about my pace. I made sure I got his shirt at the end, too, and Keith Weller reckons that when I ran over to swap shirts at the final whistle that was the fastest I ran all night! Unfortunately, I lent the shirt to someone when I was out playing in America and never saw it again."

Later Peter Osgood paid tribute to Boyle's performances in the two games. "He was a Ray Parlour-type player, the sort who doesn't get the recognition he deserves," says Ossie. "Dave Sexton put him at right-back against Gento and he marked him out of the game. John wasn't the quickest and he was up against a very tricky player but he did a good job on him."

Dave Sexton's tactical switch, bringing in Tommy Baldwin to support Peter Osgood in attack, had also paid dividends. "We set out to take the initiative," the Chelsea boss said afterwards, "and here we are with the Cup. Yes, we had to fight for it, but in the end we fought harder than Real. They were much better in the second half because they were more attack-minded. But the way our boys never faltered made me feel proud of them."

Booked in at the Athens Hilton for the last night, the celebrating players were able to properly sample the delights of the Greek capital for the first time. "Me, Charlie Cooke and a reporter Charlie knew went to a restaurant where there were belly dancers," says Tommy Baldwin. "When we got there the reporter guy said, 'Have what you want, it's on me'. So, we ate our food and at the end the waiters were throwing plates as they do in Greece. As we were leaving the manager came over and said, 'Excuse me, you haven't paid your bill'. I said, 'He's paying', pointing to the reporter, but he said, 'Sorry, I haven't got any money on me, I've lost my wallet'. There was a massive doorman there who wouldn't have let us out, so we decided the best thing was to pay up."

"Everywhere you turned there were players celebrating with fans," adds Alan Hudson. All round the hotel, there were loads of people there. When you think that the fans stayed over there when they had no money, they'd missed their flights home after the first match, it was amazing. It was the first thing we'd ever won in Europe, so it was quite something."

Despite Sexton's alcohol ban, the champagne was out on the flight home the following morning. "I mean, how could he stop us? We'd just won the Cup," says Hudson. Hundreds of jubilant fans were waiting for the team at Heathrow and, from the airport, the players boarded an open-top bus which took them all the way to Stamford Bridge. A year earlier the team had paraded the FA Cup in their dull club suits. This time, reflecting the laid back 'anything goes' philosophy of the times, they were allowed to wear their civvies and took full advantage, donning a variety of flowery shirts that wouldn't have looked out of place on a King's Road dance floor.

"It was a Saturday morning so people were out shopping," says John Boyle, who had grabbed a prime spot with Keith Weller, Alan Hudson and the trophy at the front of the bus, "but they'd all put their bags down and wave to us. By the time we got to Hammersmith there were fans lining the streets and when we got to Fulham Broadway there was just a massive party going on. I was pretty tired but I had some friends to catch up with after the parade and they were all ready to celebrate as well. We had another party at home in South London on Saturday evening – in fact, there were parties going on all over the place – and I didn't get to bed until about two in the morning."

For Alan Hudson, who had missed out on the FA Cup celebrations the previous year, the joyous homecoming was particularly emotional. "I went to the Adelaide pub, next door to the Imperial on the King's Road, had a couple of drinks with my family there and then I almost collapsed. Partly, it was because I was knackered by then – I hadn't got any sleep – but it was also the euphoria. And we'd been drinking champagne all through the flight home!"

As Cup Winners Cup holders, Chelsea automatically received an entry to the competition the following season. Naturally, the Blues were among the favourites again, with Barcelona, Bayern Munich, Torino and Glasgow Rangers their most likely challengers. But they avoided the big guns in the first round, and the medium-sized ones too. In fact, their opponents, Jeunesse Hautcharage from Luxembourg, were more like krill than minnows, hailing from a village with a population of just 704. Their domestic Cup triumph the previous season, against Jeunesse Esch, had been a major surprise as Hautcharage were then in the Third Division.

The first leg, switched from the club's 1,500-capacity ground to the 13,000 national stadium was, as expected, a rout. Chelsea won 8–0, with Peter Osgood helping himself to a hat-trick. "It was easier than training," was Ron Harris' verdict afterwards. Worryingly, for Jeunesse at least, the Blues seemed intent on hitting their opponents' net even more frequently in the return.

"I've backed myself to score," Chopper told *The Sun* the day before the teams met at the Bridge. "All sorts of bets have been struck by the lads and we are definitely trying for the biggest score in Chelsea history – ten!"

Among the many wagers was one for £5 between Peter Osgood and Peter Bonetti that the striker would score a double hat-trick, a feat previously recorded only once in Chelsea history, by prolific striker George 'Gatling Gun' Hilsdon in 1908. Tommy Baldwin, too, had an incentive to get among the goals. "Mike D'Abo, who was in the pop group Manfred Mann, had a restaurant on the King's Road and after the game in Luxembourg he said he'd give me a free meal for two if I scored a hat-trick in the second leg."

On the night, the 5p Chelsea programme had some intriguing information about the Jeunesse players. Five of them were steel workers, four of them were from one family, one wore glasses on the pitch and the inside left, a student, only had one arm. The rest of the team included a station-master, a car mechanic, a butcher, a blacksmith and – no doubt, to the great amusement of the Chelsea dressing room – a hairdresser.

At half-time it was 6–0. Harris had got the goal he wanted, but Osgood had been stuck on two since the 6th minute and Baldwin hadn't scored at all. "I'd forgotten all about my bet with Mike and I'd just been trying to set up Ossie," says Tommy. "Suddenly, a steward came into the dressing room at half-time and said, 'There's a note here for Tommy Baldwin'. It was from Mike and it said, 'Don't forget you've got a free meal if you score a hat-trick.' So I went out for the second half thinking, 'Sod Ossie, I'm going for it!'"

Suitably fired up, Baldwin clinched his hat-trick with the last kick of the match. Osgood, though, had to settle for 'just' five of the Blues' 13 goals. Needless to say, Jeunesse didn't manage a goal of their own. "I don't think Peter Bonetti had a shot to save," says Tommy. "He could easily have popped out of his goal for a chat with the Shed end." The 21–0 aggregate set a new record for European football which, although equalled by Feyenoord the following season, remains intact today.

Summing up one of the strangest matches ever played at the Bridge, Peter Osgood says: "No disrespect to their lads – I mean, they were lovely people – but they were useless. The guy with one arm even went to take a quick throw and he had to put the ball down. And then there was the guy in glasses – it was like *Dad's Army*. It was unbelievable."

In their own way, the events of the second round were equally unlikely.

Drawn against Swedish part-timers Atvidaberg, the Blues' strikers envis-aged another scoring spree. But, in blustery conditions on a slippery pitch, Chelsea failed to find the net once in Sweden. "We should have beaten Atvidaberg by ten over at their place but we just couldn't score," says Alan Hudson.

Still, a 0–0 draw was no disaster and, back at the Bridge, Huddy settled the crowd's nerves with a sumptuous volley shortly after the break. Fifteen minutes later the tie seemed to be over as Ron Harris, in search of another rare goal, was hacked down in the penalty area. John Hollins, normally so reliable from the spot, stepped up to take the penalty and struck his shot against a post. Despite continuous Chelsea pressure the second goal wouldn't come and then, to the horror of the home fans, Atvidaberg equalised. In a frenzied finish, John Dempsey hit the bar and other chances went begging before the final whistle signalled the holders' exit from the competition on the away goals rule.

"If we'd have got through that round I'm convinced we would have won it again," says Hudson.

Maybe, but the history books show that they didn't get through. What's more, they also show that, incredibly, it would be another 23 years before Chelsea would appear again on the European stage.

THE SHED

CHAPTER TEN
THE SHED

O n Wednesday 7th September 1966, Chelsea maintained their unbeaten start to the 1966/67 season with a 2–2 draw at home to Leicester City. Of more long-term importance than the result, though, was a letter which appeared in the match programme. Signed C. Webb of South Ockoden, Essex, it read: "From now on we wish the Fulham Road End to be called 'the Shed'. That is the section where the fanatics stand – and, while we are on fanatics, why don't more people come in the Shed and join in the singing and chanting, instead of just at big matches like last season's Fairs Cup? If we could have had that support all through the league and Cup, we would have won them both. This year we must have this attitude at every game, so please help us make the Shed as fanatical as the Kop."

The reference to Liverpool's Kop was significant. The Merseysiders had been the first fans in England to generate a fiercely partisan atmosphere at their team's home games, creating a wall of sound from the terraces. The Kop's repertoire wasn't huge – apart from chants for the team, it largely consisted of sing-a-longs to Beatles and Gerry and the Pacemakers hits, with the lyrics unchanged – but the constant noise helped turn Anfield into an intimidating fortress.

The 1965 FA Cup semi-final between Chelsea and Liverpool at Villa Park was a turning point for Blues fans, who realised how poor their support for the team was compared to that of the vocal Reds. "They outsung us, outchanted us, and they were just more passionate than we were," remembers Tony Easter, a Chelsea fan from west London, who had just started following the team. "We simply weren't organised like we became later to sing the songs."

The Kop had been a singing end since 1963, an *annus mirabalis* on Merseyside which saw both the start of Beatlemania and Liverpool's re-emergence as a football power after nearly a decade in the Second Division. At the same time, Chelsea were returning to the First Division in an altogether more genteel environment. Polite applause, the occasional witty remark shouted from the terraces and a spot of banter with the away fans were the order of the day.

The Bridge, as Tommy Docherty had already mentioned in a newspaper interview, was far from being a daunting venue for opposition teams. The bowl-like design of the stadium, with the greyhound track circling the pitch and the terraces pushed back some way behind the goal, meant that fans were distanced from the action – in contrast to other London grounds, such as Upton Park or White Hart Lane, where it felt like the crowd was almost spilling out from the stands and terraces onto the field.

"We had a good home record but it didn't help us that the fans were pushed back from the pitch," says Alan Hudson. "It cost us a few times, and I couldn't help thinking when I first saw the completed new stadium that we'd have won the league if we could have played there. The Bridge would have been our fortress. The only time the atmosphere became really electric was for the big night games – against Roma, Bruges and Spurs in the League Cup, for instance. Because it was dark you couldn't see how far away the fans were and the noise seemed to carry more at night. But even then you couldn't compare it to the atmosphere the fans created at Old Trafford in the Cup Final replay when they were right on top of the pitch at the Stretford End. They really pulled us through that night."

The longstanding Bridge tradition of swapping ends, which continued into the late sixties, also contributed to the lack of atmosphere. "At half-time we always used to change ends," recalls Fred Roll, who attended his first game at the Bridge as a 14-year-old in 1966. "You could walk under the tunnel of the old East Stand – where the traps for the greyhounds were – and you'd meet the opposing supporters halfway down the tunnel. Obviously, Chelsea still kept the area under the Shed but you wanted to stand behind the goal where your team was going to score. You didn't want to see defenders, you wanted to see goalscorers. So there would be home and away supporters at both ends as some of them would stay where they were."

Occasionally, Chelsea fans couldn't even get into the Shed at all, especially when Manchester United were the opponents. In the early 1960s
the United fans had the habit of turning up a few hours before the
game to stand en masse at the Fulham Road End. The fact, of course,
that virtually all of them were glory-hunting 'Cockney Reds' rather
than residents of Salford made arriving at the Bridge at 11am somewhat
easier.

"They would completely take over the Shed three hours before the
start," says Jim Luck, a Chelsea fan from East London, who began going
to games with a schoolmate at the age of 10. "You'd turn up to go in
your usual place and the turnstiles would be shut and you'd have to get
in somewhere else in the ground. There wasn't the segregation of fans
you got later."

Fortunately the Bridge's enormous capacity – around 70,000, dropping
to 62,000 after the West Stand sprung up on the West terrace in 1966 –
meant that most fans could usually squeeze in somewhere or other even
for the biggest matches. But outsung by Liverpool and outmanoeuvred by
Manchester United, Chelsea's support was lacking in direction. One fan,
in particular, realised this and set about giving Blues fans some leadership. Mick Greenaway, a 20-year-old Chelsea nut from Grove Park,
south-east London, had been impressed by the backing Liverpool's followers
gave their team and, with a group of equally passionate Blues fans, began
thinking up some songs and chants for the hardcore supporters in the
Shed to sing.

Early efforts included The Beatles-inspired 'Blue Submarine', and a homage
to Docherty's 'Chelsea Aces' sung to the tune of *The Blaydon Races*. The
famous 'Zigger Zagger' chant, which Greenaway adopted as his own
personal rallying cry, also became a matchday regular, with the whole of
the Shed joining in the finger-jabbing 'Oi, oi, oi!' response. There were
songs, too, for the most popular members of the team, including this one
for Peter Osgood, set to the tune of *The First Noel*:

The Shed looked up
And they saw a great star
Shooting goals past Pat Jennings
From near and far
And Chelsea won
And the star of that team

Was Peter Osgood.
Osgood, Osgood, Osgood, Osgood,
Born is the King of Stamford Bridge

Not surprisingly, Ossie loved that one and even subtitled his recent autobiography, *King of Stamford Bridge*. After making an instant impact for the
Blues following his arrival at the Bridge in September 1966, Osgood's strike
partner Tommy Baldwin was also soon being serenaded by the Shed, this
time to the tune of *McNamara's Band*:

His name is Tommy Baldwin
He's the leader of the team – *what team?*
The finest football team
That the world has ever seen
We-e-e-e
Ar-r-r-r-e
The Fulham Road supporters
And we're louder than the Kop
If anyone wants to argue
We'll kill the fucking lot

"I remember the fans singing my song just a few weeks after I joined,"
recalls Tommy. "I think they liked me because I would always battle
for everything and I never used to give up. I could play a bit, too,
but they loved my tenacity and aggression." Even today, the Baldwin
song can still be heard on matchdays, sometimes in the stands but,
more often, in the bars around the Bridge. "It's brilliant, I love it," he
says. "I get embarrassed when fans recognise me in a pub and start
singing it, but I'm still proud of it. I always had a good rapport with
the fans."
The same couldn't be said for Peter Houseman who, over the years,
became something of a scapegoat for Chelsea fans when the team wasn't
performing well. He even got stick when the Blues were winning, most
famously when Chelsea thrashed Luxembourg minnows Jeunesse
Hautcharage 13–0 at the Bridge in 1971. Usually fans don't bother creating
a song for an unpopular player; in Houseman's case, however, the Shed
made an exception, although the player probably wished they hadn't. To
the tune of The Scaffold mega-hit *Lily the Pink*, it went:

Peter Houseman, played terrible football
And the Shed all called him names
So they gave him
A kick in the bollocks
And now he plays in all our games

This cruel ditty then segued into a tribute to Shed idol Charlie Cooke:

We'll drink a drink a drink
To Charlie the king the king the king
The saviour of our football team
For he invented professional football
And now we're gonna win the league

Poor Houseman must have been devastated – not only was his song merely the warm up act for Cooke's, it was downright hurtful to boot. Some supporters, though, felt that by openly criticising the fans in the Shed in a letter to the programme, Houseman had encouraged the mickey takers. The letter, which appeared in October 1966, was signed 'Peter House, Battersea', but Houseman, a Battersea resident, was widely believed to be the author:

"In reply to C. Webb, who wishes the Fulham Road End to be named 'the Shed', I would like to rename it 'the Foulmouthed End'. I find myself – and probably many more supporters are, too – sick and tired of hearing these so-called 'fanatics' finding any excuse to call players and officials of opposing clubs any filth which comes into their heads. These 'supporters' are a bad advert for the club and, in time, will only make the good name of Chelsea FC a bad one."

The letter, whoever had written it, had absolutely no effect. If anything, the four letter word count only increased as chants like 'Who the fucking hell are you?' (directed at the visiting team as they ran out of the tunnel), 'You're going home in a fucking ambulance' (directed at visiting supporters after their team had scored), and 'What the fucking hell was that?' (directed at opposition players who had shot miles over the bar) made their Bridge debuts in the late sixties.

The away fans or players weren't the only targets, either, as Robert Holliday, a fan from Uxbridge, recalls. "The first time I went in the Shed

Left: Peter Bonetti in action at Villa Park. Spectacular saves like this one earned him the nickname 'The Cat'.

Above: Manager Tommy Docherty and coach Dave Sexton run through team tactics with the help of a Subbuteo board during pre-season training in July 1963.

Right: Tommy Docherty speaks to the Stamford Bridge crowd after Chelsea had clinched promotion to the First Division with a 7–0 thrashing of Portsmouth in May 1963.

Right: Bobby Tambling scores for Chelsea during the League Cup Final first-leg against Leicester City at Stamford Bridge in February 1965. Chelsea won the match 3–2 and played out a dull scoreless draw at Filbert Street to take the trophy.

Below: Tommy Docherty makes up with the eight Chelsea players he had sent home after the 'Blackpool Incident' of April 1965 when they broke a club curfew.

Top right: The Chelsea squad train on Worthing beach in preparation for their FA Cup semi-final against Liverpool in March 1965.

Bottom right: Teenage prodigy Peter Osgood shoots against Nottingham Forest at Stamford Bridge in August 1966. A month later Osgood broke his leg and missed the rest of the season.

Top: The old
Stamford Bridge,
pictured from
the Shed end.
The greyhound
track running
round the pitch
was used for
race meetings
until 1966.

Above: Dave
Sexton with
Chelsea chairman
Charles Pratt
shortly after
Sexton had
replaced Tommy
Docherty as
manager in
October 1967.

Top right:
Chelsea captain
Ron Harris
shakes hands
with Tottenham
skipper Dave
Mackay before
the start of the
'Cockney Cup
Final' in 1967.

Right:
Marvin Hinton
closes down
Tottenham's
Jimmy Greaves
during the 1967
FA Cup Final.
Chelsea lost the
match 2–1.

Chelsea line up at the start of the 1969/70 season. Back row (left to right): Marvin Hinton, Ian Hutchinson, David Webb, Tommy Hughes, Peter Bonetti, John Dempsey, Eddie McCreadie, John Hollins. Front row: Alan Birchenall, Charlie Cooke, Alan Hudson, John Boyle, Ron Harris, Peter Houseman, Peter Osgood, Tommy Baldwin, Bobby Tambling PHOTO: COLORSPORT

ACTION IMAGES/MIRRORP

Above: Chelsea defend in numbers during the 1970 FA Cup Final against Leeds United at Wembley.

Below: Peter Osgood heads Chelsea's equaliser in the FA Cup Final replay at Old Trafford.

Right: Chelsea and Leeds players go on a joint lap of honour after the teams drew 2–2.

Below right: Osgood (9) and John Dempsey (5) celebrate David Webb's winner in the same match.

EMPICS

Left: Ron Harris lifts the FA Cup trophy following Chelsea's victory over Leeds. After a number of near misses in previous seasons, victory tasted all the sweeter for the players.

Below left: 'Chopper' poses with the FA Cup in a photo booth at Manchester Piccadilly train station shortly before the team returned to London.

Below: Jubilant Chelsea fans greet the Blues players as they show off the FA Cup along Fulham Broadway the morning after the replay.

EMPICS

ACTION IMAGES / MIRRORPIX

ACTION IMAGES/MIRRORPIX

EMPICS

Previous page: Tommy Baldwin, John Hollins, Peter Bonetti, David Webb and Peter Osgood (left to right) celebrate Chelsea's FA Cup triumph in the team bath at Old Trafford.

Top left: Eddie McCreadie, Ron Harris and Peter Osgood prepare to fly out to Greece for the European Cup Winners' Cup Final.

Top right: Tommy Baldwin, Ron Harris, and Charlie Cooke parade the European Cup Winners' Cup after the Blues had beaten Real Madrid in the final in Athens.

Above: Alan Hudson, Peter Bonetti and John Boyle pose with the Cup. The victory established Chelsea as one of the most successful English teams of the era.

Right: Jimmy Hill explains the offside rule to an excited Raquel Welch during the film star's visit to the Bridge in February 1972.

Blue is the Colour: the Chelsea squad record their 1972 League Cup Final anthem. The song reached number five in the charts and is still a much-loved part of pre-match entertainment at Stamford Bridge.   PHOTO: ACTION IMAGES/MIRRORPIX

Above: Alan Hudson and David Webb emerge from the tunnel at White Hart Lane

Right: Ian Britton, before suing his barber.

Far right top: Dave Sexton and Alan Hudson at Mitcham – before the rows began.

Far right bottom: Building work continues on the East Stand during a match at the Bridge.

Bottom right: Bill Garner in Chelsea's Hungary-style red, white and green away kit.

the TV cameras were there. The game was obviously going to be on *The Big Match* because we all spotted Brian Moore walking in front of the Shed before the match. The fans started waving at him and singing his name – 'Brian, Brian, Brian Moore, Brian Moore, Brian Moore, Brian, Brian, Brian Moore, Brian, Brian Moore' – to a sort of can-can tune, and he waved back. He really looked delighted to be recognised. Then came the 'second verse' to the same tune: "Oh, wank, wank, wank, wank, wank, wank, wank, wank, wank, wank . . ." complete with 'wanker' hand signs. It was a lot cleverer than 'Brian Moore is a wanker' but I think he got a dose of that as well as he scuttled off. Poor bloke, he looked completely crestfallen. But it was very funny."

Along with the 'foul-mouthed' lyrics came an increase in 'aggro' on the terraces. Football hooliganism was not a new phenomenon in the 1960s – Millwall's home ground, The Den, had been closed four times between 1920 and 1950 after outbreaks of crowd trouble, for example – but it did became more widespread, thanks in part to cheap 'football special' train services which encouraged greater numbers of over-excitable young fans to travel to away matches. From the mid-sixties onwards Stamford Bridge probably witnessed as many incidents of fan violence as any other ground, while Chelsea's massive away following became so notorious the Government tried – and failed – to ban Blues fans from travelling in 1977.

"The first hooligans came from Liverpool," says Andy Jackson, who started going to the Bridge in the early sixties when he was still at primary school. "The first time I saw fighting was at Easter 1965 when the Liverpool fans caused a lot of trouble at the Shed end. Loads of fans climbed over onto the dog track from the Shed and then it spilled all round the ground."

Liverpool fans may have started the trend, but soon it became a matter of honour for all large away followings to attempt to 'take' the home end. Even increasing segregation of rival fans at matches didn't stop the violence, as Fred Roll remembers.

"I was in the Shed once, around 1967/68, when all these fans came in wearing blue and white scarves. I thought it was a bit strange because there were so many of them in a big group. Then, all of a sudden, I got a whack on the side of my head. They were Arsenal fans in disguise and, of course, once everyone realised what was happening there was a huge fight.

"We used to establish ourselves more at away games," he adds, "because you'd get the high terracing and the tactic was to start at the top and force yourselves down. There was violence, but it wasn't violence as we know it today. It was more scuffling, a bit of pushing and shoving. It was territorial, more than violent. You might get the occasional slap round the back of the head, but that was it.

"I remember going to Burnley one year and it was all Chelsea – no Burnley supporters would come near us. This one copper came over with a big black stick with a brass bit on the end and he said, 'Any trouble from you lot and I'll have yer', so one wag at the back shouted out 'Quick, hide the shotgun!' One copper for the whole ground, it was unbelievable."

Around the same time, Andy Jackson attended his first Chelsea away game outside London, taking a football special up to Coventry. "In those days we used to only take 300-400 away fans," he says. "By the mid seventies it was more like 7,000-9,000, depending on who we were playing. All the same, there was a lot of trouble, with kids running around like idiots. There was a lot of damage to the town centre. Coventry was still being rebuilt after the war and I remember in the next day's papers the local chief of police said, 'Chelsea did more damage in 90 minutes than the Luftwaffe did in five years.' It was vandalism more than anything. Some fans went into a carpet shop on a street on a hill, stole some carpets and then started rolling them down the hill. That was a strange sight.

"When we got back to Coventry station the Chelsea chairman, Charles Pratt, was there. He had just cut the half-price concession for kids because some of them had been running on the pitch to celebrate goals or to mob the players at the end of games. So eventually, after a number of warnings, the concession was cut and all the youngsters had to pay full price. Obviously that wasn't popular, so while he was waiting for the train everyone was chanting, 'Our chairman is a prat!' I was quite naïve at the time and I didn't even know what 'a prat' was."

Throughout the 1960s the various youth cults of the decade – mods, rockers and hippies – had been well represented on the terraces at Chelsea. The newspapers had got themselves into a right old tizz about all three groups, but never specifically about their connection with football violence. It was a different matter, though, when the skinhead look swept through the Shed in 1969.

The skinheads had borrowed heavily from 'hard' mods and West Indian 'rude boys' to create their own unique style: typically, Ben Sherman shirts, Sta-press Levi's, Doc Martens boots, often worn a size or two too big for added effect, and a half-soldier, half-convict shaved head. To many the new look was both alarming and threatening, and the tabloid press was not slow to exploit these fears by making little or no distinction between 'football hooligans' and 'skinheads'.

Eventually, too, in the popular imagination, 'skinheads' would be synonymous with 'racist thugs', which rather overlooked the fact that the original skinheads were into black music in a big way, particularly ska and reggae. Ska stars like Laurel Aitken and Prince Buster returned the favour by writing affectionate songs about skinheads. It was, though, an instrumental reggae track which was to be adopted by the skins in the Shed as their own anthem.

Reaching number nine in the charts in November 1969, *The Liquidator* was a one-hit wonder for Harry J Allstars, the house band of Jamaican producer Harry Johnson. Featuring the swirling organ of Winston Wright, the record had an instantly catchy hook and, crucially, a series of pauses into which a staccato chant of 'Chel-sea!' could be inserted before the hypnotic riff re-started. Around the country fans of other clubs whose names contained two syllables – West Brom, West Ham and 'The Wolves', for instance – also latched onto *The Liquidator* but none could match the passion, intensity and sheer volume of the Shed's rendition. In the days before *Blue is the Colour*, which didn't come out until 1972, *The Liquidator* was *the* Chelsea song, and its airing ten minutes or so before kick-off would crank up the atmosphere in an already packed and expectant Shed to near fever pitch.

By the mid-seventies the skinhead cult had largely died out on the terraces. Hairstyles, influenced by bands like Sweet, Slade and T Rex, grew long and feathery; silk scarves, worn around the wrist à la Bay City Rollers became a necessary fashion accessory; wide flared trousers which could have doubled as curtains flapped around the lower leg; and huge platform soles, inspired by the stilt-like monstrosities worn on stage by Gary Glitter, David Bowie and Elton John, replaced the infamous skinhead 'bovver boot'.

Unfortunately, the new gear, especially the footwear, was totally unsuitable for football 'aggro': balancing was difficult during hand-to-hand combat and running away was virtually impossible when the police snatch squads moved in. As one vogue supplanted another, even the preferred style of terrace fighting changed: thanks to the popularity of the TV show *Kung Fu*, martial arts-style drop kicks and hand chops were favoured over

old-fashioned punches to the face or knees to the groin. By the time Chelsea
and Tottenham fans clashed on the pitch before a vital relegation decider
in April 1975 fans watching from the stands could easily have imagined
they were watching a surreal glam rock version of a Bruce Lee movie.

"The hooligan element got worse as the seventies went on," says John
Dempsey, who was on Chelsea's books for most of the decade. "But in
the early seventies it wasn't a big issue among the players. Yes, kids ran
on the pitch when a goal went in and the re-start would be delayed a
minute or two. Other than those occasions, I can't remember being
involved in a game which was held up for any length of time because
of pitch invasions or crowd trouble.

"At away games we would be escorted to the ground by the police and
when we got off the coach there would often by lots of home fans
hanging around the players' entrance. You'd get a lot of insults, but most
of them seemed to be directed at Ossie – 'Osgood, you're rubbish!', that
sort of thing. Then, when we got out on the pitch you'd see our fans
packed together in an end or a corner. If we were playing in London –
at Tottenham, Arsenal or West Ham – they would completely fill an end,
and even up at places like Old Trafford or Anfield the fans would be
there in large numbers. Coming from Fulham as I had, I wasn't used to
seeing so many fans at away games. The Chelsea away following really
was fantastic."

Cheap train travel and inexpensive, pay-at-the-turnstile entry on the day
encouraged increasing numbers of Chelsea fans to go to away games. The
prospect of 'aggro' was an added attraction for some. "There was always
an element who would try to 'take' the home supporters' end," says
Robert Holliday. "If you were in the away end you would suddenly see
them waving Chelsea scarves about, usually a few minutes after kick-off.
Then, the home fans would either back away, creating a gap around our
mob, or they'd steam in and a fight would break out. After a few minutes
the police would pile in and escort our fans to the away end, where
they'd get a heroes' reception.

"The first time I joined up with a Chelsea crew was for a game at
Arsenal in the mid-seventies and, bizarrely, we weren't even playing. We
were supposed to be playing at home in the FA Cup, but as the tube
train I was on pulled into Earl's Court there was an announcement that
the match had been called off because of a waterlogged pitch. Everyone
groaned and then somebody said, 'Let's go to Highbury, Arsenal are

playing Wolves!' A few people got off at this point but most of them stayed put. Everyone was very excited, banging the windows and singing 'We hate Arsenal!' and 'We're gonna take the North Bank!'

"As we got nearer the Arsenal tube stop, word went around that we should stop singing and hide our Chelsea scarves – we didn't want the Arsenal fans knowing who we were. When we left the station there were so many people milling around outside Highbury that it was impossible to say how many Chelsea fans were in our mob, but it must have been a few hundred. We all went in together at the North Bank end, which was absolutely heaving. Suddenly our gang seemed pitifully small and the idea of 'taking' the North Bank, where there were about 20,000 home fans, simply ludicrous.

"I was only 14 and rather small for my age. I didn't really fancy getting beaten up by irate Arsenal fans, so I decided the best thing to do would be just to melt into the crowd. As I was doing that, a huge 'Chel-sea!' chant went up and I could see dozens of blue and white scarves coming out. The Arsenal fans around me were genuinely surprised, they hadn't seen us coming. There was a lot of movement around me, people were either trying to get away from the Chelsea fans or were barging their way through to try to get nearer. The game was just about to start, but everyone's attention in the North Bank seemed to be on this one corner of the ground. Scuffles were breaking out and there was a lot of shouting – 'Fuck off, Chelsea!' 'You're gonna get your fuckin' heads kicked in!' and so on.

"By now, the police had realised something was happening and started to move in. Eventually they managed to herd the Chelsea fans into a corner and gradually shove them down the terracing towards the pitch. The Arsenal fans around them were absolutely livid. One guy spat at our fans but missed, and gobbed on a policeman's chest instead. He was quickly hauled off and I thought the police would chuck all our fans out, too, but instead they escorted about 200 of them down to the Clock End where all the Wolves fans were. The whole of Highbury seemed to explode with anti-Chelsea venom – even in the posh seats people were standing up and shaking their fists – but our mob just waltzed down to the other end waving their scarves triumphantly.

"The game was on *Match of the Day* that evening. At one point the camera showed a group of Chelsea fans twirling their scarves among the Wolves supporters. John Motson was commentating and he said something like: 'Oh I say, Chelsea fans there giving their support to Wolves after their match was postponed. They could have gone shopping or gone to the cinema but they chose to come to Highbury. In a way, that sums up the universal appeal of the FA Cup.' No mention of the big fight earlier – he must have been having a pre-match cup of tea!

"Of course, the next week back in the Shed, the chants were 'Arsenal run from Chelsea!' and 'We took the North Bank, the North Bank, the North Bank, Highbury!' Word had got around what happened and everyone joined in, even those who weren't there or, like me, had played a rather limited role on the day. It really felt like we'd got one over them, turning up like that when they weren't expecting us."

Despite the undercurrent of latent violence which existed at virtually every Chelsea match in the late sixties and throughout the seventies, for many young fans being part of the boisterous crowd massed in the Shed or on an away terrace was an incredibly exciting experience. No trip to the Bridge, though, could possibly match the thrill of seeing the Blues play in a cup final. Between 1967 and 1972 Chelsea reached four finals, providing the fans who attended the games with some of their most vivid football memories.

Like all Chelsea fans at the time, Tony Easter was desperate to go to the 1967 FA Cup Final against Tottenham, the first all-London final at Wembley. True, the fact that he hadn't got a ticket was a slight problem, but not by any means an insurmountable one.

"I was apprenticed at a garage in west London and, luckily, the senior mechanic's father worked at Wembley as a senior turnstile attendant. He wasn't going to be on the turnstiles on the day of the final, but he told me he could get me in to the game if I turned up at Wembley at around 12.30. I arrived on time with my father and we joined a queue of about 30 or 40 outside a door. We were on the list as St John's Ambulance workers and when the door was opened we both went in. We just had to pay the guy the going rate for a terrace ticket, although he didn't actually have any tickets on him. I knew the score because we'd got into Wembley for the England-Argentina match at the 1966 World Cup in exactly the same way.

"After about half an hour in the outer ring of Wembley we were shepherded to the next entrance where another guy was checking the tickets – and, of course, we didn't have any. But our contact just said, 'OK, Fred, these are the St John's Ambulance people', and we were in the ground at about 1pm. The only trouble was as the fans with tickets arrived we realised we were in the Tottenham end. We didn't fancy spending the match with the Spurs fans but we knew you could walk round Wembley and get to the other end. So we went down the Chelsea end, waited until one of the attendants was busy checking fans in with their tickets and ducked in to watch the game. It was a total scam, but I've always promised I'll learn how to take a pulse one day!"

In 1970 he didn't need to pull the same trick, having obtained a ticket through legitimate means for the FA Cup Final with Leeds. "I went to Wembley and the replay at Old Trafford," says Tony, one of 20,000 Blues fans who made the midweek trip up north. "Up in Manchester my mate and I were with two Manchester City supporters. They took us to a club in the city after the game, and we didn't leave until about 4am. Then I drove back to London, we arrived about 7am and came straight down the King's Road. We had breakfast in a café in the area, and waited for the boys to come along on the open-top bus. It was just fantastic, everyone was going crazy. We even got our pictures in the *Evening News*, which was a bit of a worry because I was supposed to be working and I'd phoned in sick."

Eric Swayne, who travelled back down to London with the team on the train from Manchester, had also enjoyed his night at Old Trafford – unlike the Leeds fans. "There was a huge Leeds supporter behind us and he kept going, 'That's it, stroke it around, that's beautiful, you're makin' 'em look silly.' This went on for ages until Ossie scored the equaliser and this guy was literally sick – he puked! At the end of the match he was crying his eyes out."

The following year, around 4,000 Chelsea fans travelled out to Athens for the European Cup Winners' Cup Final against Real Madrid. Unfortunately, most of them were booked on a short two-day package which didn't take into account the possibility of the final going to a replay which, of course, it did. Reluctantly, some fans took their scheduled flights back to England. Others, meanwhile, were determined to see the climax of Chelsea's European adventure and altered their travel arrangements. Short of funds, they relied on the generosity of other fans, donations from the players and the hospitality of the locals to provide them with bed, breakfast, beer and kebabs for the extra couple of days.

Concerned that there might be a replay, Jim Luck had erred on the side of safety and arranged a week's holiday in Greece. "Lots of fans who were supposed to go back after the first match stayed on in the rooms which the others had booked up," he says. "We ended up with about six fans in our room. The hotel staff must have realised what was going on. They can't have been too thrilled but there were so many people coming and going they probably couldn't tell who was a paying guest and who wasn't. We were staying outside Athens in a separate resort. After our victory in the replay we went over to a higher standard hotel where the better-off fans were staying. They'd put money behind the bar and we stayed up most of the night drinking and singing. In the morning there were loads of bodies crashed out all over the place surrounded by empty bottles. It was a great night. Then in the morning we got on the coach to the airport."

For stay-at-home fans, meanwhile, there was intense disappointment when they discovered the first match with Real Madrid would not be shown on television. From the perspective of today – when Sky will quite happily screen a mid-table Conference clash as part of its saturation coverage of the game – it seems extraordinary that no TV channel in 1971 was prepared to broadcast a major European final involving a British club. However, the fact is that very few games were shown live in the early seventies. In football circles there was a widespread belief that live coverage would adversely affect attendances, so fans had to make do with highlights of two matches on *Match of the Day* on Saturday night and three games the following afternoon on *The Big Match*. Unbelievably, Chelsea fans couldn't even look forward to highlights of the game with Real on *Sportsnight* as the Beeb had chosen instead to show snippets of England's Home International fixture with Wales at Wembley.

The only way for Blues fans to keep in touch with events in Athens was through the commentary on the radio. "I ended up on the King's Road in the Stanley Arms opposite the World's End," recalls Andy Jackson. "I went round there with a couple of friends to listen to the game on the radio. It wasn't that busy, I suppose most fans just stayed at home. I felt very deflated when Real Madrid equalised with last kick of the game, but at least they carried on with the commentary in extra-time rather than switching to some other programme that had been originally scheduled."

As it turned out, Real's last-ditch equaliser, while disrupting the travel plans of thousands of fans in Greece, proved to be a bit of a boon for the supporters back home as the BBC announced it would be showing the replay live on Friday evening. Hooray! Some bright spark had even recruited the injured John Hollins to act as expert summariser. This was more like it. The only question for Chelsea fans was where to watch the game – home or pub?

Andy Jackson chose the pub. "We went back to the Stanley for the replay and this time the place was absolutely heaving," he remembers. "I think the World's End and all the other local pubs were the same. It was so packed, we were literally swaying in the pub shoulder to shoulder. I used to wear glasses and when John Dempsey scored the first goal I jumped up to celebrate. I went one way and my glasses went the other way. I never saw them again. We were 2-0 up when Fleitas scored for Madrid, and I needed a leak so I battled my way to the toilet. It was just as packed in the bog because there were fans who were so tense they daren't come out. They were almost praying in there. At the final whistle the whole place erupted, tables and beer glasses went flying everywhere. It was sheer jubilation. Everybody spilled out on the King's Road and the party carried on in the street. The next day the estimates in the newspapers were that 5,000 people were still out on the street celebrating at two in the morning.

"In the early hours a group of us decided to go down to Trafalgar Square. The replay was the day before the England-Scotland match at Wembley and, of course, all the Scots were in the square. I don't think they were quite sure what to make of us. Some of our fans went in the fountains and splashed around for a while. Then we went straight back to Chelsea – we didn't bother going home – to see the victory parade. I was standing in the doorway of a dry cleaner's next to the old Supporters' Club on Fulham Broadway. There was an enormous crush and one of the shop windows went in just through the pressure of bodies. By this stage I'd had no sleep, little to eat, too much to drink but it was great – it wasn't like the recent victory parades at Chelsea which have all been very organised. There was no organisation, no crush barriers, nobody selling flags or T-shirts. It was just spontaneous mayhem. People were going right up to the open-top coach to scream and wave at the players and the police couldn't stop them."

The following year Chelsea reached a third consecutive final, this time in the League Cup. The competition couldn't really match the FA Cup or Cup Winners' Cup in the glamour stakes but, nonetheless, a ticket for the Wembley final against Stoke was still highly prized.

"I'd been to all the games and sent away for my tickets through the voucher system," remembers Ray Taylor, a fan from Fulham who had been supporting Chelsea since 1965. "The final was in March and in February I got married at Fulham Town Hall. I had a reception afterwards, a local family thing, and I was opening the telegrams and cards of congratulations when I came across a letter with writing I recognised. Of course, it was my writing and the letter contained the two tickets I'd applied for. I was over the moon – more so for having the tickets than for getting married. My euphoria completely overtook me; but what a disappointment in the end – the final and, as it turned out, the marriage as well."

While Ray Taylor, Andy Jackson and thousands of other Chelsea fans were slumming it on the terraces a handful of lucky supporters had VIP passes for the best seats in the house in the new East Stand. "I used to go in the directors' box on a 'comp' ticket provided by Brian Mears," says Mark Colby, who is now a season-ticket holder at the Bridge but admits to not being much of a fan at the time. "I had a mate at my school, a minor public school in Leatherhead, and his dad knew Brian Mears and some of the Chelsea players.

"We'd go up to games and, obviously, we got a very good view from the directors' box. Then, after the game, the players would come up in the lift and you could help yourself to sandwiches and drinks. It was all very safe and contained and you felt a huge discrepancy between the experience of being in the directors' box and, say, going in the Shed. Later I started going in the Shed and I preferred it there, really, being with the real supporters.

"I remember Henry Kissinger, who was American Secretary of State at the time, came to one game when I was there and he was surrounded by his secret service people. Every time Chelsea went close to scoring the secret service people would jump up and when we did score they were totally surrounding him. I think they got nervous because the fans kept shouting 'Shoot!'"

Thanks to his connections, the young Colby wasn't only rubbing shoulders with the players and other well-known faces on matchdays – he was bumping into them in the school holidays as well. "I'd go over to my mate's house in Cobham, Surrey and there would be all these young Chelsea players – people like Ian Britton and Steve Finnieston – hanging around the swimming pool," he remembers. "Michael Crawford's ex-wife, who was married to Tommy Baldwin by then, would quite often be there, too."

Another fan who became friendly with some of the players was Ron Hockings, the chairman of the original Chelsea Supporters Club which was founded in 1948. Ron is also author of *90 Years of the Blues*, a massive reference work which has helped settle many an argument between statistically-inclined Chelsea supporters.

Although slightly older than most members of Tommy Docherty's young team, Ron got to know the players fairly well during the sixties. "It started by accident, really," he recalls. "I used to drive a motorbike and in 1959 I had a smash and broke my leg. I was in plaster for five months and from January to the end of the season I used to go to the training ground at Welsh Harp, Hendon nearly every day. Peter Bonetti, Bobby Tambling and all those were there, so I knew them right from when they were kids. The youth system then was superb, it really was. We had so many good young players compared to other clubs. Jimmy Greaves, Ron Harris, a whole team came through from Chelsea youth. I used to go up there on crutches and the players used to bring me cups of tea after training. I was in a really privileged position and all because of my broken leg. I was married with kids but I used to get out of the house to see them train, it was a sort of therapy. That's what I told my wife anyway. So I got to know the players, although a lot of them never made it at Chelsea and had careers elsewhere.

"It was around that time I went up on the train to Newcastle for an FA Cup tie. I was still on crutches, we got all the way to Newcastle only to find the game was postponed because of the bad weather. So we went to another match, between Bishop Auckland and Whitley Bay. I was walking along in the snow with one leg in plaster covered by a blue sock. But I didn't need the blue sock because my toes were blue beneath it!"

Ron's relationship with the players grew as the youngsters were swiftly promoted by Docherty from the youth ranks. "Having known them as kids, the players became used to seeing me and a few other regular fans once they got in the first team. We'd see them at away games and they'd come out of the dressing room to chat to the supporters. Often we'd be coming back from away games and be on the same train as the team. They'd be on the platform waiting with us and then invite us in to their compartment to chat to them. It was great – you got to know the players as friends. We'd play cards with them sometimes. Eventually they got a bit selective about who they'd let in there because some fans would take liberties with players, smothering them basically. Tommy Docherty didn't like that very much. I was alright, luckily, because I was always there – that's the way to get known. By the late sixties, though, they started going by coach. I think they found the train too public. Another factor was that they were tied to the train timetables which weren't always necessarily the most convenient for them."

However, before the Blues swapped British Rail for National Express Ron had managed to have a few frank heart-to-hearts with the Doc, mostly while returning to London after away games up north. "I liked Tommy Docherty. He was very open. He told the fans things he perhaps shouldn't have been telling you. He'd say things about players after a game – 'what a lazy little sod' so and so was, for instance. He was brash, but friendly. You could talk to him, have your own say. I liked Dave Sexton too, but I thought he was a crap manager. He was a bloody good coach, mind you. But he couldn't manage a flea circus."

When he wasn't acting as an informal advisor to the Chelsea manager of the day Ron had an altogether less glamorous role at the Bridge – as a matchday steward. "In the sixties I was a steward in the enclosure in front of the old East stand. We just had to pack them in – 'Could you move along a little bit?' was our catchphrase. We didn't have uniforms or bibs, we just wore an armband and badge with 'steward' on it. We picked up ten bob (50p) a game, which was more than they got later. When the match started we just disappeared up to the back of the stands and watched the game from there. It wasn't like now where the stewards can't even watch the game. It was a cushy number, basically. Eventually they brought in another guy to organise the stewarding and he stuck me behind the gate in the old North Stand, the small stand on stilts above the terracing. The first game of the season, I think it was in 1970 or 1971, I was standing behind a door looking through a bloody window at the game. I said to him 'No way, mate' so I chucked it in and got Mick Mears in the ticket office to get me a season ticket up in the North Stand."

Ron and the other supporters interviewed in this chapter all agree that the late sixties and early seventies were a great time to follow the Blues. Apart from the team's successes on the pitch, the fans began to develop a strong collective identity through chants and songs – many of which, incidentally, remain essential components of the Chelsea canon. Meanwhile, cheap admission prices and bargain 'Soccer Special' train fares kept costs down for the dedicated travelling fan. On the down side, hooliganism was rampant, ground facilities were poor and club merchandise was virtually non-existent. For most supporters, though, these were minor inconveniences compared to the thrill of being part of the Blue army which roared on Ossie, Huddy and the rest.

Even today, a surprisingly large percentage of Chelsea's regular fans can date their support for the club back three decades to the double cup-winning side. The 1970 FA Cup Final was particularly important in this respect, acting as a highly effective recruiting sergeant of youngsters all around the country who were just beginning to become interested in the game. They didn't know it then, but for many of those kids glued to the TV that April night the Blues would become a central part of their lives in the years to come.

CHAPTER ELEVEN
TRAINING BLUES

CHAPTER ELEVEN
TRAINING BLUES

Exciting trips abroad, invitations to parties attended by the rich and famous, assignations with beautiful women, the adulation of thousands packed on the terraces: from a fan's point of view it must have seemed that the Chelsea players of the time were living the lives of gods rather than mere mortals.

Probably few supporters, though, fully appreciated the hard work which underlaid these trappings of success. If anything, the players' everyday experience, away from the snapping cameras of the sports photographers and society *paparazzi*, was just about as unglamorous as it can get. After all, most people would agree that the prospect of running around a field in south London, in weather conditions ranging from blisteringly hot to bone chillingly cold, is not in itself particularly alluring. Yet come rain, wind or raging blizzard, the Chelsea players would be out jogging on the club's training ground in Mitcham, no doubt uttering a few oaths under their breath when out of earshot of Dave Sexton.

Now the site of Tooting and Mitcham's Imperial Fields stadium, the complex contained three pitches – one, by the river Wandle, used to get very heavy in winter – and a pavilion where the players changed. It was here that Tommy Docherty and Dave Sexton would hone the players' fitness, develop tactics and create some of the defensive and attacking ploys which would be used in future games. Sexton is widely regarded as one of the best coaches this country has produced and in his two spells at Chelsea, first as Docherty's assistant then as manager, he did much to build his reputation as one of the game's great thinkers.

"Tommy, or 'Boss' as we called him, would do his bits but when I got into the first team squad Dave Sexton was already there as the coach," says Peter Osgood. "He was a brilliant, fantastic coach. He made everything interesting, different and new. One day we went in and he took us to Twickenham to watch a rugby match and then for three or four days we trained with a rugby ball – we didn't see a football. The reason for that was you couldn't pass the ball forward, you had to pass it back. What he was trying to get you to do was to get to the by-line and get crosses over for people coming in. It worked out brilliantly. Peter Houseman and Charlie Cooke would whip in the crosses and me and Hutch went flying in to get them. We got loads of goals that way.

And Alan Birchenall adds: "I was his first signing and whenever I bump into him I always say, 'After me, Dave, it all went downhill', but it didn't really. His coaching was superb. With all due respect to the other managers I played under, Dave Sexton was far and away the most innovative coach. He was years in front of his time, and some of the stuff we did on the training pitch was great.

"One of my first training sessions was at Winchester College on the Embankment. He wouldn't let me go until I'd bent two balls out of ten into the goal from the corner flag. I'd never done anything like that before and, at first, I couldn't see the point of it. I said, 'What am I doing this for? I'm the centre forward, not a winger.' Dave said, 'It doesn't matter, there are other aspects of your game I want to develop.' And, credit to Dave, I felt my all-round game really came on at Chelsea."

Skipper Ron Harris, too, has nothing but praise for Sexton's coaching skills. "He'd been there as the coach under Tommy Docherty a few years before so lots of the lads related to him straight away," he says. "One thing he did was to bring in zonal marking, which nobody did before. In the past, if I was playing right-back and Eddie McCreadie was playing left-back and my winger went over to Eddie's side we used to swap over. Dave changed all that. He brought these bollards in to training to mark out different zones on the pitch, then if a player moved into your zone you had to pick him up. So in training he'd say, for example, 'Hey, Webby, he's in your zone now' and that's how we switched to zonal marking. The training changed how we played, but he also made it enjoyable."

As well as working on the defence as a unit, Sexton was also determined to improve his defenders' individual skills. In the passing game that was Chelsea's hallmark at the time there was no use for the aimless long punt from the back which, dispiritingly, became all too common a feature of British football in the 1980s.

"Dave taught me a lot of stuff," says Micky Droy, who played his first games for Chelsea under Sexton as a teenager before eventually going on to become the Blues' skipper. "He was way ahead of his time, too. For example, he was the first manager to go abroad in the summer and study continental sides' methods – that was unheard of then. He used to have me and Gary Locke back for training in the afternoon at Mitcham and we'd spend hours whacking balls at each other and bringing them down – from 20, 30, then 40 yards. That made me comfortable on the ball. A lot of defenders just used to whack it, they didn't care where it went, but I did. That all came from Dave."

After the serious technical and tactical work the players would often be rewarded with a five-a-side game at the end of the session. On Fridays, the day before matches, the team trained at Stamford Bridge and these mini-matches were played in full view of the passing public in the ground's forecourt. "We used to play games between 'The Goodies' and The Baddies'," says Ron Harris. "The Baddies were me, Ossie, Hutch, Huddy and a couple of others. That was good fun, and fans would stop to watch as they walked past."

And Micky Droy adds: "It could get a bit tasty because the games always had an edge to them: North v South or England v Scotland. It was really competitive because we usually had the same teams each week and nobody liked to lose. There were a few tackles flying in – Ronnie Harris used to do slide tackles on the gravel – but I used to play up front out of the way. Looking back, it was unbelievable; but it was good for the spirit of the team and the players used to look forward all week to those games."

Droy wasn't the only defender to switch to an attacking role in these games. Indeed, David Webb claims that his scoring feats in training were instrumental in persuading Dave Sexton to try him out as an auxiliary or emergency striker in first team matches. "I was always the most prolific goalscorer in five-a-side games," he boasts, "so in league and cup games they'd throw me up front if we were behind. That old buccaneering spirit would turn matches. I threw so much effort and enthusiasm into it that it just sparked off everybody else off."

For new signings arriving at the club, the five-a-side game would generally be their initial taste of competitive action as a Chelsea player. Naturally, they would be eager to do well but, as Alan Birchenall recalls, a test of character rather than skill would often be the first challenge.

"I was introduced to the boys and we started off with a five-a-side game on the concrete forecourt outside. I got the ball for the first time and then, wallop, Ron Harris whacked me right up in the air and knocked me out. When I came round he was standing right over me, snarling, 'Welcome to Chelsea. You may have cost a hundred grand but you're still not earning more than me.' Ossie picked me up and said, 'Chopper runs things round here. That was your initiation and you reacted well; you didn't jump up and retaliate.' Well, the only reason I didn't jump up was because I was bloody concussed!"

Harris, though, denies that this incident was in any sense a formal 'initiation'. "Alan Birchenall says he got larruped and I said, 'Welcome to Chelsea Football Club'," he muses. "Well, put it this way, I used to play the same way in training as I did in a match. I could only play one way."

All the same, the idea that Chopper liked to test the mettle of new players – and the strength of their shinpads – certainly gained currency around the Bridge. "When I joined Chelsea, one of the players warned me to watch out for Harris in training," says Keith Weller who signed for the Blues three years after Birchenall in 1970. "I was told he topped all the new players to put them in their place. I'd never heard anything like it. I thought that was ridiculous. But nothing happened, until one day down at Mitcham when we had a very long training session.

"Ron didn't drive at the time and his wife used to come and pick him up. One day we were still playing when I saw her parking her car and casually remarked that we must be training late if old Chopper's missus had turned up. For some reason he took offence, I don't know why as I didn't mean anything by it, and soon after in our five-a-side game there was a 50–50 ball between the two of us. He went over the top and left me in a crumpled heap on the ground. He'd done my knee in and I missed the next game because of it. Dave Sexton was worried that I'd seek retribution. I told him he had nothing to worry about. I wasn't like that. If it had happened during a proper game, I might have but I was prepared to let the matter drop."

It went largely unnoticed by his terrified opponents, but Ron Harris did possess a sense of humour. Again, the new signings would often be the victims. "We were down the training ground at Mitcham and John Dempsey, who had just joined us from Fulham, was kicking lumps out of me," remembers Peter Osgood. "I said, 'Demps, listen, you're not playing for Fulham now, I'm your team-mate, what's going on?' But he kept kicking me so I said, 'Demps, if you do it again, I'm going to deck yer! What's the problem?' And he told me, 'Chopper Harris says you told him I put hair lacquer on my hair!' That was typical of Ronnie, winding somebody up, which is why we called him 'Buller' – because he was full of bullshit."

Ron Harris wasn't the only player with an eye on the new boys in training. Charlie Cooke, too, liked to set them a challenge which invariably resulted in the recent addition to the squad handing over the contents of his wallet to the canny Scotsman. "On the first day of training Cookie said, 'Bet you a tenner I can walk down the middle of Stamford Bridge with the ball on my head, turn round and come back'," recalls Alan Birchenall. "I'd never seen anybody do anything like that, so I said, 'Go on then, you won't be able to do it'. I was set up. I gave him the tenner, which was the equivalent of about £50 nowadays, and he just walked down to the bottom of the pitch and back again with the ball perfectly balanced on his head the whole way. I learnt a lesson that day!"

Such moments provided light relief for the players from the serious side of training. Since the abolition of the maximum wage in 1961 football clubs had required greater professionalism from their players, and this new ethic was reflected in training programmes which were much more gruelling and taxing than ever before. Certainly, by the mid-sixties the training regime at Chelsea was nothing like the relaxed and relatively undemanding one it had been under Ted Drake just a few years previously.

"A lot of what we did was tough – 100 yard sprints, 220s, 440s, 880s and cross countries," says Peter Osgood. Famously, Ossie wasn't so keen on the last of these exercises. "No, I fucking wasn't," he confirms. "I thought that football is to be played with a ball and if I didn't see a ball for two days I thought it was ridiculous. I think I should have been a Brazilian, to be honest. They play with the ball all the time and that would have suited me.

"Peter Bonetti was the best trainer at the club," he continues. "Chopper wasn't far behind. Johnny Hollins and John Boyle were good runners, too. Only me and Marvin Hinton were useless. When we went running on Epsom Downs Dave used to take his car to collect us because the minibus would have been gone about 20 minutes before me and Marvin finished."

Osgood particularly disliked pre-season training, which included regular cross-country runs around Epsom Downs in an attempt to build up stamina levels for the campaign ahead. "Ossie was a lazy so and so," says Alan Birchenall. "Every day, Ena (John Hollins) would come in first, I'd finish somewhere in the middle and Ossie would always come in last after we'd been sat in the van for 20 minutes. Dave Sexton had enough of this so he says to Ossie, 'Right, if you come in last tomorrow, everyone will have to go round again in the afternoon.'

"So, on the way home, I'm nagging Ossie to pull his finger out and he just says, 'Don't worry about me, there's no way I'll be last tomorrow.' Next day, exactly the same thing happens. Ena goes off in front, I'm in the middle of the pack, and Ossie's right at the back. We're coming into the final straight and there's no sign of Ossie. He's not even with the stragglers at the back. Just as we're cursing him and preparing to go round again, we hear the sound of galloping hooves. I turn round and there's Ossie riding this racehorse flat out and he comes charging past us giving it all the 'hi ho silvers!' and shouting, 'Come on, you lazy bastards, who's going to be last, then?' He'd only got his mate to bring a race-horse up, hidden the horsebox in the woods then nipped in the saddle when we were all sweating it out."

The club's pre-season tours abroad provided more opportunity for fun and games. Unlike the summer tours, which were essentially exotic holidays with a few exhibition games thrown in, these trips tended to be short haul rather than long haul, with Germany, Spain and Scandinavia among the favoured destinations. For Dave Sexton, the pre-season tour was a chance to whip his men into shape after the long summer break. Punishing training schedules would be drawn up; tough local opposition would be arranged; and, knowing his fun-loving players as he did, Sexton would be careful to find a training base which was miles away from the nearest bar or nightclub.

Both Sexton and his predecessor Tommy Docherty liked taking the team to Germany in the summer as the local training facilities were good and the longstanding rivalry between English and German teams added a competitive edge to otherwise inconsequential friendly fixtures. For the players, too, Germany provided the added attraction of first-rate lager served in *uber*-sized glasses by buxom, lederhosen-clad *frauleins*. Certainly, more than a few *steins* of the local brew were downed on the Blues' trip to the Rhineland in July 1968, as Alan Birchenall recalls.

"We were on a team night out in Kaiserslautern. Dave Sexton had told us the bus was leaving the town square at eleven but, of course, me,

Ossie, Marvin Hinton and Joe Fascione missed it and we got a lift back along the motorway from a German guy we'd met in a bar. I told him it was about 30 miles back to hotel, but he said it wasn't a problem so off we went. Marvin was in the back and was rapidly turning a pale green colour. Suddenly, he shouted out, 'I've got to be sick!' so the guy stopped his Merc and Marvin puked up in the middle of the *autobahn*.

"He got back in the car, we carried on driving for another four or five miles and then Marvin cried out, 'Turn back, I've lost my tooth'. He told us he had a single false tooth on a dental plate and it had fallen out while he was throwing up. 'You're never going to see that pile of puke, it'll be squashed!' we told him, but he insisted we turn back. Luckily for Marvin it was about three o'clock in the morning and there was no traffic, so we managed to spot the place where he'd been sick.

"Marv poked around in the sick in the headlights of the Merc and after a few minutes he triumphantly waved something in his hand. 'I've got it!' he yelled. Anyway, we got back to the hotel – a baronial German mansion in the middle of nowhere, which we dubbed Stalag 14 – and we couldn't get back in because it was all locked up. We didn't fancy waking Dave Sexton up by ringing the bell so, after looking around for a while, we found a skylight above the back entrance and we decided to shove the smallest one of us, Joe Fascione, through it. Small he may have been but he had a big arse, and although he got his upper body through his arse and legs got trapped. Well, we pushed him and he went like a blooming Exocet through the skylight, straight into the kitchen, knocking over a pile of saucepans in the process.

"Of course, the hotel security was alerted by the noise, as was Dave Sexton who came rushing down in his dressing gown. He was furious when he saw us and we all got hit with a big fine. I was upset about losing two weeks' wages but Ossie didn't seem that bothered and I soon saw why. When we got back to Heathrow he phoned up the *Daily Express* from a telephone kiosk. 'Do you want a hot one? Yes? Chelsea boys get fined after night out . . .' I couldn't believe it, I thought it would get us into more trouble. But Ossie just said, 'Don't worry, the money we get for the story will pay off the fine'. Fortunately for Marvin, Ossie left out the bit about his teeth." Needless to say, although Sexton took the Blues back to Germany in later years, he always gave Kaiserslautern a wide berth.

Three years later, in 1971, Sexton's meticulous pre-season arrangements came unstuck again when he booked the team into a remote Swedish hotel that turned out to be altogether livelier than he anticipated. "I got married on the Saturday and we went to Sweden on the Monday, so I had my honeymoon with the lads," remembers Alan Hudson. "We came from the airport and on the coach we were travelling down these country lanes and we didn't see any life anywhere. Finally, we pulled up outside this big hotel – a gigantic gaff – and all the boys were saying, 'What's he brought us to?' It looked like a concentration camp in the middle of nowhere. There was no sign of a bar, or any life whatsoever.

"We took up our gear to our rooms and then we walked up the back stairs to the restaurant for dinner. We opened the door and the place was packed with Swedish birds dancing, there was a band on the stage, and in the corner Dave Sexton was sitting at a table with his head in his hands. It was so funny. We all got there and went 'Great!' and, what's more, they had a nightclub downstairs. The hotel was the local entertainment centre and everybody would go there for a night out. I've never seen so many beautiful girls in one place at one time. What our boys got up to was unbelievable – we'd be out on the beach with the girls we'd met until five in the morning."

Which sounds fun, except the Chelsea boys were expected to be back out on the beach an hour later for the start of an arduous day's training. "We'd train at six o'clock in the morning, when half of us hadn't been to bed," says Huddy. "We'd just have time to go back to the hotel to get our kit on. After training, we'd come back to the hotel to have breakfast, train again at eleven o'clock, two o'clock and four o'clock.

"The first session was running along the beach, back and forth. Dave Sexton and Ron Suart had done their homework. They'd walked along the beach, and marked it all out. There were about five or six canoes or little boats, 50 yards apart as you went up the beach. So on the first morning they said, 'This morning you run to the first boat and back, second morning you run to the second boat and back and so on.'

"We went off in fours, the four quickest followed by the next four, down to the fourth group of four. I was in the front group with Peter Bonetti, Eddie McCeadie and Johnny Hollins. The worst runners were the last ones to go – Peter Osgood, David Webb, Tommy Baldwin and John Dempsey. We'd reached the last boat and turned back to see the others still coming. They were trotting along and chatting to each other and they said to us, 'Oi, slow down a bit'. But on the fourth day we didn't see them at all. We thought, 'What's happened to them?' Then we got back to the first boat and they were all lying in it with their feet up. It was a bit misty that morning so Dave and Ron couldn't see them and as the third group went by they all jumped out of the boat and ran in just behind them. When they got back Sexton and Ron Suart were really impressed. 'Well done boys,' they were saying, 'you boys at the back have done absolutely terrific'."

The management team were less impressed later that afternoon when the unusual seaside setting diverted Charlie Cooke's attention from the serious business of a five-a-side game. "We were playing at the waters' edge," Huddy remembers. "Someone got the ball and passed it out to Charlie, who was looking out to sea in a bit of a daze. Sexton went mad, he picked the ball up, and said, 'Charlie, if you don't want to play, we won't play. We'll run instead.' Charlie said, 'I'm only looking out to sea!' and everyone cracked up. We got back from pre-season in pretty poor shape and I don't think we won until about eight games into the season."

Significantly, Sexton switched the squad's training base to Holland the following season – staying well clear of the fleshpots of Amsterdam, of course – and the Blues never returned to Sweden while he was in charge.

CHAPTER TWELVE

OVER LAND AND SEA

CHAPTER TWELVE
OVER LAND AND SEA

Haiti, Iran, El Salvador, Mozambique: four countries where war, violent revolution, natural disasters and abject poverty have been pretty much the norm over recent decades. Despite the best efforts of their respective tourism ministries, none of the quartet is what you would call holiday brochure material yet, bizarrely, Chelsea went on summer tours to all four places during the 1960s and 1970s.

The decidedly oddball destinations, however, seem a little less unusual when viewed in a historical context. Over the years, the Blues have specialised in travelling to the sort of exotic locations normally favoured by the likes of Alan Whicker and Michael Palin. Africa, Asia, Australasia, Europe and America – Chelsea really have 'been, there, done that and got the T-shirt'. Way back in 1929, for example, the Londoners were one of the first teams from Britain to tour South America, playing games in Argentina, Brazil and Uruguay. Newspaper accounts from the period suggest the expedition wasn't an unqualified success.

"A Chelsea player was assaulted with a brutality that was the more regrettable because one of the principal assailants wore the uniform of a public service," reported *All Sports Weekly* of a match in Argentina, while the *Estado de Sao Paulo* correspondent appeared shocked by the spectacle he witnessed in Brazil. "The shouting and booing of the spectators and the violence of the game made it look like a bullfight," he wrote.

More recently, in 1986, the Blues accepted an invitation to play a match against the Iraqi national team in Baghdad – despite the fact that the Iran-Iraq war was still raging. Saddam Hussein was expected to attend the match and kick-off was delayed for over an hour as the two teams waited for him to appear. In the event, he didn't show up but, presumably, the Iraqi dictator would have been reasonably satisfied with his side's 1–1 draw.

As one of the most successful and well-known English clubs of the 1960s and early 1970s, the Blues wouldn't have had any shortage of tour offers from overseas clubs and national associations. In many cases, the tours would be sponsored by major international companies, allowing Chelsea to collect a handsome cheque for their participation as well as having all their costs covered.

The size of the financial inducement which enticed Chelsea to play two games in Mozambique in May 1969, both against the national team, is anyone's guess. What is certain is that the Blues pitched up in southern Africa at a time when the country, then still a Portuguese colony, was wracked by civil war between government forces and the anti-colonial resistance movement, Frelimo. Most of the fighting, though, was in the countryside and Chelsea were assured that the visiting party would be safe in the capital Maputo, then known as Lourenco Marques. Having toured the millionaire's playground of Bermuda on their previous summer club outing, the news that they'd be heading this year to a war-torn, fly-blown African outpost didn't have the Chelsea players exactly whistling with joy as they packed their suitcases – 'football boots, check . . . mosquito repellent, check . . . flak jacket, check.'

"With all due respect, Mozambique's not Trinidad and Tobago and 30 years ago it certainly wasn't," says Alan Birchenall, who had just missed out on the Bermuda trip, having signed for Chelsea from Sheffield United a couple of months later. "If you had a straw poll and had to choose between Bermuda and Mozambique I don't think there'd be a contest. I think we landed in a field, and the local airport was a hut. It was unbelievable. I thought, 'Of all the places in the world, what the hell are we doing here?' I'd like to know if Sir Dickie Attenborough was planning to do a film out there and our visit was supposed to spread a bit of goodwill."

Ian Hutchinson, another player on his first Chelsea summer tour, was at least prepared to give the place a chance. "I'd never been to another continent before and, naturally, I was excited about going," he recalled. "But when we arrived, it was the pits, starting with the hotel. Huddy was my room-mate at the time, and when we got upstairs there were lizards in the bedroom. We chased them round the room and swatted them. We woke the next morning covered in bites, and went down to reception to be told the lizards were there to catch the mosquitoes. You could just see their logic – but we really didn't fancy lizards crawling all over us."

First impressions may have been disappointing, but the Chelsea lads were still determined to search out the best in nightlife the Mozambique capital had to offer. "We did manage to find the only nightclub in Lourenco Marques," says Alan Birchenall. "Wherever you put the Chelsea boys we'd find a place with a bit of music and serving late beers. I've frequented most nightclubs throughout the world as a player and a businessman. I've seen the best and the worst, and this one was certainly one of the worst. The roof was just a corrugated iron sheet. But, on the other hand, music's music and a beer's a beer.

"Mozambique was a very sinister place back then, there was a civil war going on, you saw soldiers and tanks on the streets and it was quite scary. We'd been warned to stick together and not to go wandering off. Some of the single lads wanted to go off with the local ladies we met in the club but we'd been advised not to travel back to the hotel on our own, so in the end they didn't. It was that frightening you could have had Naomi Campbell on your arm and still not taken a chance by going off with her."

All very sensible. However, John Boyle has a different version of events altogether, in which a trio of players ignored the advice they'd been given – and almost paid a heavy price for their recklessness. "We were in this club and the young lady we'd been talking to invited us back to a party at her place," he recalls. "I went along with a couple of the other lads. It turned out to be back in a township, a very basic place – just a shack really. We arrived there at about two o'clock in the morning. It was just the four of us; there was no party as such. After a while, two of us went outside, leaving the other guy inside with the girl. While we waited, we could hear the bed springs squeaking. Then, the other one went in, and the same thing happened. When it came to my turn I said I wasn't bothered, but this young woman suddenly started shouting, 'Escudos! Money!' We shook our heads, but then she pulled out a knife. Well, of course, that changed the situation – we flung down some money and just ran. We didn't have a clue where we were going but eventually we managed to make it back to the hotel."

As for the two games, Chelsea won them both – the first by a ridiculous Sunday League-style scoreline, 9-3, and the second by two goals to one. "In the first match one of their guys played in bare feet," remembers

Tommy Baldwin, who admits to feeling somewhat the worse for wear after the previous night's drinking session.

"It was a baking hot day. In the first few minutes I made a couple of runs and threw up on the pitch on the edge of their penalty area. Ah, it was terrible and I felt awful. At half-time I came into the dressing room, ran some water in the sink and just sprawled out under the tap. All I could think of was getting loads of water on me. Dave Sexton came in and said, 'Where's that Tommy Baldwin? I want him off.' I just wailed, 'I'm over here'. He subbed me off and fined me."

Oh dear. The Blues had successfully avoided the worst Mozambique could throw at them – repugnant reptiles, bloodthirsty rebels and knife-wielding locals – only for one of their number to be felled by a raging hangover.

If Costa Rica is the Switzerland of Central America, then El Salvador is more like the Balkans. Government-backed 'death squads', moustachioed dictators and gun-toting guerrillas are all familiar features of the political scene in El Salvador, a country which on more than one occasion, rightly or wrongly, has been described as a 'banana republic'. Colourful and exciting it may be, but it's hardly somewhere you'd choose to go on holiday. Unless, of course, you're the players and staff of Chelsea FC.

Quite why the club decided to head off on a summer tour to El Salvador in May 1971 is a bit of a mystery. There are suggestions that a multi-national tobacco company wrote out a big cheque in front of the directors and this suddenly persuaded them, despite all the available evidence to the contrary, that San Salvador, the capital, would be a pleasant spot to spend a few days. Certainly tobacco – like bananas, coffee and state-sanctioned torture – is big business in El Salvador so this explanation sounds plausible.

Football, too, is hugely popular in this small, earthquake-afflicted country although passions can easily get out of control. Two years earlier, in 1969, El Salvador's World Cup qualifier play-off with neighbouring Honduras had ignited the so-called 'Soccer War' between the countries – a four-day conflict which left 2,000 dead. True, the nations had been squabbling for some time over various non-sporting issues, including those arising from the presence of hundreds of thousands of Salvadoran 'squatters' in Honduras, but the fact that a football match could spark such bloodshed and misery must have been a little worrying for the visiting Chelsea players. That unease could only have been increased on the first night the squad stayed in San Salvador.

OVER LAND AND SEA

"I could hear shots being fired outside the hotel," recalls Alan Hudson. "We really were in the middle of it." Quite what 'it' was – soldiers firing on demonstrators, possibly, although it could just as easily have been the other way round – remains unclear and, understandably, Huddy wasn't particularly keen to find out. "We just kept our heads down indoors, wondering what the hell we were doing there," he adds.

Fortunately, perhaps, the Blues' itinerary was a short one. First up was a game against Southampton, who were also in town, followed by a match two days later against the El Salvador national team. That promised to be a tough encounter as the El Salvadoreans, having won their local spat with Honduras, had made a first ever appearance at the World Cup finals in Mexico in 1970.

English pride would be at stake in the second game so the last thing the Blues needed was to be involved in a bruising fixture with the Saints, who were known as one of the most physical, if not downright dirty, teams in England at the time. Not that the boys from the Dell were looking for a fight – for them, like Chelsea, the game was primarily a bit of fun between boozing sessions.

Chatting away in a local bar together the night before the game, the two sets of players got stuck into a drinking contest. While lager followed lager, talk turned to the two matches the teams would be playing against each other, first in San Salvador the following day, then in the altogether more agreeable Caribbean island surroundings of Trinidad a week later. As the beers took hold, Tommy Baldwin and Southampton's Jimmy Gabriel struck a £100 bet on which player would score the most goals in the double-header. It was a bold wager by Gabriel, as he played in midfield, while the Sponge, of course, was a striker. The bet was discussed for a few minutes – then, as the night wore on, somebody came up with what seemed like a bright idea.

"We were in the bar all evening and along the way we sorted out what was going to happen when we played them the following day," remembers Alan Hudson. "We decided to have a high-scoring, friendly game, but to keep it a draw. So it would go 'you score, we score' and so on." Needless to say, neither Dave Sexton nor the Southampton manager, Ted Bates, were to be informed of the pact.

"The next day everything was going to plan on the field and it was something like 2–2 or 3–3 at half-time," continues Huddy. "The fans seemed happy, we were happy, but Dave Sexton wasn't. He came in the dressing room at half-time and we could tell he was angry. 'I fucking know what's going on,' he screamed, 'don't think I fucking don't know. I know where you all were last night, drinking with the Southampton mob. People have paid good money to see this game, the club have been paid good money to come out here and you're playing like this, thinking it's a joke. Now get out there and you show people how you can play.'

"We went out for the second half and tried to tell the Southampton players that the agreement was cancelled, but they thought we were joking. Pretty soon we scored, then straight away we scored again. The Southampton players were furious and it turned into a kicking match, a right war. They thought we'd turned them over on purpose." By the final whistle, a Sexton-energised Chelsea had banged in eight goals to Southampton's three, with Baldwin taking a seemingly unassailable four-one lead in the first leg of his personal duel with Gabriel.

The following day Baldwin, Gabriel, Charlie Cooke and Eddie McCreadie took a tour of the city. "The army was out on the streets and everywhere you looked there were people carrying guns," remembers the Sponge. "At one point Eddie asked a policeman if he could have a look at his gun. The guy gave it to him, but he quickly took it back when Eddie started waving it around like a cowboy in a western."

In a San Salvador nightclub the Scot managed to go one better – or should that be one worse. "There was a bloke at the end of the bar in an army sergeant's uniform," says David Webb. "Eddie proceeded to remove this guy's gun from his holster and started firing it as a joke. But the gun had real bullets in it and people started diving for cover."

Little wonder, then, that by now the locals were viewing the Chelsea players with some suspicion. "We took a taxi back to the hotel one night and I could tell we were going in the wrong direction," says Tommy Baldwin. "I tapped the driver on the shoulder and said, 'Hey, where are we going?' Immediately, he reached for the glove compartment and I could see there was in a gun in there. I just put my hands up and said, 'Carry on, señor!'"

Unaffected by that scare, Baldwin scored the winner as Chelsea beat El Salvador 1–0 in front of 18,000 fans and hundreds of gum-chewing, tooled-up soldiers. He continued his hot streak in Trinidad, grabbing another two goals as Chelsea thrashed Southampton again, 6–2 this time. With Gabriel only managing one for the Saints in reply, the Baldwin bet was in the bag. Three straight wins, a wager won and nobody hit by a stray

McCreadie bullet – the tour had been a rousing success. Which is more than you can say for the Blues' trip to Haiti although, given the country's reputation, perhaps that was no surprise.

The western half of the Caribbean island of Hispaniola, Haiti is the home of voodoo, a strange blend of Roman Catholicism and west African religion which apparently makes perfect sense to the locals but, thanks to numerous B-movies featuring pin-sticking witch doctors and sleep-walking zombies, has dark and sinister connotations elsewhere. Politically, the country is what is sometimes known in diplomatic circles as 'a basket case'. Democracy has the most tenuous of footholds here, and few eyebrows were raised when the Haitian leader President Aristide was overthrown in an armed rebellion in March 2004. His abrupt flight into exile led to scenes of mass looting and general chaos on the streets of the capital, Port-au-Prince, with order eventually being restored thanks to the intervention of a UN security force.

Happily, when Chelsea called in on the last stage of a three-week long Caribbean tour sponsored by the British/American Tobacco Company in June 1964, Haiti was more stable – if only because the notorious dictator 'Papa Doc' Duvalier had made himself President for life and crushed any dissenting voices by creating a terrifying civilian militia, the Tonton Macoute. Overall, it seems, the Blues players would have preferred to have been somewhere else.

"Haiti was a horrible, dirty, stinking place," is Ron Harris' terse summary. "When we got off the plane it was absolutely chucking it down and you could see cars floating down the street. I wouldn't fancy going out there at night – and we didn't. We were pleased to get out of there."

Chelsea were lined up to play two matches in Haiti, the first against fellow tourists Wolves – who they had already played four times in Barbados, Trinidad and Jamaica – and the second against the country's national team. The game against the Midlanders went off without incident, the Blues winning 2–0 to claim a 3–2 match aggregate victory. It was a different story, though, the following day when Chelsea met their hosts in Port-au-Prince.

"We were losing 2–1 against the Haiti national team at the time," recalls Chopper, "and it got a little bit physical. It's possible that Tommy Docherty come on and played. I know he came on in Malta in 1963 and we had a big ruck because he topped one of their players. I'm not sure whether he got involved in something in Haiti but the game definitely got abandoned.

It wasn't because of the rain, either, it was because so much was going on, either in the dug outs or on the pitch. I can't remember whether the referee was a bit biased and that kicked it off or whether there was a bit of a schemozzle between the players. But the ref took the teams off and that was the end of the game."

Tommy Docherty, however, is certain that it *was* the weather and nothing he or any of his players did which caused the abandonment. "There was absolutely no trouble between the players," he says. "What happened was that we were hit by a tropical storm – well, it was more like a hurricane – and the ref called the game off. The rain was lashing down, the wind was howling and it was quite frightening. When they get a storm like that there it's quite something. There were spectators on bicycles trying to get home by cycling across the pitch, but they weren't getting very far. It was a shame because the stadium was packed and Haiti, who had some good players, were giving us a decent game."

Whether the match was prematurely ended by torrential rain or violent scenes on the pitch, the upshot was the same: the abandonment allowed the Chelsea players to get out of Haiti a full half hour earlier than scheduled, so it's unlikely there were too many glum faces in the away dressing room.

Roman Abramovich may have more money than a double rollover lottery winner, but he is far from being the first multi-billionaire to take an interest Chelsea FC. That honour goes to the Shah of Iran who, before his overthrow in the 1979 revolution, was an occasional visitor to the Bridge. The Shah was also a big fan of Real Madrid and, in November 1966, sponsored a charity game between his two favourite teams at the Bridge.

"He was at the game and presented us all with a gift on the pitch," says Tommy Baldwin. "Real also gave us all a gold watch with the club crest on it. It was a really beautiful watch, but unfortunately I don't know what's happened to mine. The most interesting thing about the game was that Puskas, the great Hungarian player, was still playing for Real. He must have been in his late thirties by then and he was carrying a bit of weight. He couldn't get around the pitch very well, but he still had some lovely touches."

Chelsea won that game 2–0 but, more importantly for our story, the evening helped cement ties between the Shah and the club. And although the Iranian leader didn't invest any of his untold wealth in the Blues – "a shame," says Baldwin, "because he wasn't short of a few quid at the time" – he did invite the Londoners to tour Iran whenever they fancied. Seven years later, in 1973, Chelsea accepted the offer and headed off to Tehran.

Iran in the early 1970s was a very different place to the hardline Islamic society it is today. The Shah, Mohammed Reza Pahlavi, had ascended to the Peacock Throne in 1941 determined to exploit the country's huge oil reserves and transform Iran into a modern, westernised, economically successful Middle East power. With support from the West his dream soon became a reality but, by the 1970s, the Shah's authoritarian regime was facing increasing opposition. Before the decade was out he and his family would have to flee for their lives as popular discontent turned into full-scale revolution.

"It was a weird place," remembers Tommy Baldwin. "It was more decadent than it is today. You saw girls wearing make up and short skirts, and they didn't cover their faces with a veil. You could get Coca Cola and other western products. It wasn't the culture shock it would be today, but it was still very different. Again, we couldn't go out alone at night. Instead, we went to some big dinners every evening where English-speaking women would come along and sit between us – one player, one girl, one player and so on. Afterwards we went to a couple of shows, one with belly dancers and the other was a more western thing, with can-can dancers."

During the ten days they were in Iran the Blues played three matches against local opposition, including a game against a Tehran Combined XI – effectively, the national team. Then, as now, Iran had a useful side and were reigning Asian champions. Many of the players in the side that faced Chelsea would also go on to play in the 1978 World Cup in Argentina, where they famously held Scotland to a 1–1 draw. The Blues knew they would be in for a difficult match, especially as the conditions were so unlike the ones they were used to back in England.

"The biggest problem was the altitude," recalls Tommy. "Tehran is 5,000 ft above sea level and it was really hot as well. It was a very tight, hard, bumpy pitch, too. There was a big, noisy crowd in the stadium. We were told not go near the terraces, not to incite the crowd and not even to celebrate if we scored a goal – because the fans would throw anything they had at us. Anyway, there were a couple of controversial incidents in the game and when we came off there was stuff raining down from the stands and bouncing off the cover over the tunnel. And that was just a friendly!" Fortunately, perhaps, the Blues didn't score, losing the match 1–0.

To mark their visit the Shah presented the Chelsea players with a magnificent gift, a big tub each of beluga caviar – the world's best. Most people would have been thrilled to receive such a present but, it seems, the Chelsea boys were distinctly unimpressed. "Coming back on the flight home everyone was going 'Yuk, what's this?' and flicking it around the plane," says Tommy. "I opened my tub, which contained about a pint and a half of caviar, took a taste and flicked it around like the others. The stuff was all over the place. When we got back to London we found out that top-quality caviar costs something like 10 guineas an ounce, so the amount we each had was worth about five hundred quid. Shame we'd left it all over the plane, really. But I'm sure Peter Bonetti kept his because he was astute like that."

Wars, revolutions and hostile crowds may get the adrenaline running but, given the choice, most players' ideal summer tour would involve a spot of footy and a lot of chilling out on a beautiful sandy beach, preferably one with ready access to a cocktail bar staffed by stunning bikini-clad waitresses. A clear case, you might say, of hot spots winning out over hotspots every time.

During the sixties and seventies, much to the players' delight no doubt, Chelsea made a good number of post-season tours to the sort of glamorous, palm-fringed locations you used to see in *Bounty* chocolate bar ads. Australia, Bermuda, Barbados, Jamaica, Trinidad, Venezuela . . . the list goes on. Trips like these – at a time when most ordinary people went on holiday in Britain or, if they were a bit better off, somewhere in France or Spain – represented a substantial perk of the job. No wonder so many of the players stayed so long at the club.

Only the most dogmatic of trade unionists could possibly describe these trips as 'work', as the players readily admit. "It was like a six-week holiday, to be honest," says John Boyle of a 1965 club tour to Australia. "There was a bit of training, we played a few games, but most of the time we were on the beach, relaxing or having parties.

"Coming back from Australia we stopped off in Hawaii for a while. George Graham met this girl on the beach and obviously thought it would be fun to grab her hand and run into the sea like they do in the films. But he tripped as he ran into the water and we could all hear him shouting, 'Help, I can't swim, I'm going to drown!' In a matter of seconds he'd gone from being a big superstar figure to a helpless bloke flapping around in the water in a state of panic." Luckily, Graham's female companion came to his rescue – or, remembering his yawn-inducing reign as Arsenal manager some 25 years later, maybe that should be 'unluckily'. "Usually, though, George was the smoothest operator you could ever hope to see," adds Boyle.

Nine years later Australia was again the Blues' destination, with Dave Sexton's men playing half a dozen matches against State teams. The Chelsea party consisted of a mix of seasoned pros and promising youngsters, among them rookie striker Steve Finnieston.

"It was basically a holiday," he says, echoing Boyle. "Although the games were a big thing for me as I hadn't yet made my debut, I was still out drinking and partying with the rest of the lads. Anyway, before the last game against New South Wales in Sydney, most of us went out till around three in the morning. I was thinking, 'Well, at least we don't have to report for the game until half past one so I'll get eight hours sleep.' Then , at 7am, the phone goes in my bedroom, and it's Dave Sexton. 'Get up, you're coming to church!' he said. I was surprised he even knew I was a Catholic as I was very lapsed. In church with Dave and Peter Bonetti I could hardly keep my eyes open, but I was trying to pretend I wasn't dog-tired. I felt shattered in the afternoon and, to make matters worse, Dave picked me in midfield. We lost 2–1, which was the first time a Chelsea team had been beaten in Australia."

Football may not top the list of popular sports Down Under, but at least the Aussies show some enthusiasm for the game. The same, alas, can't be said of our American cousins who even now still generally view 'soccer' as an unfathomable past-time for 'sissies', girls and Latino immigrants. So, when the Blues headed across the pond on a North American tour in May 1967, they must have been wondering about what sort of reception was awaiting them.

As it turned out, Chelsea went down a storm – not so much with the American public, only a handful of whom actually attended the games, but with the local women. "The team we were playing in New York asked us all along to a party," recalls Tommy Baldwin. "Me, Johnny Boyle and a couple of others went along. We walked into this house, got a drink, sat down and it seemed a bit strange because everyone was watching the television. So I glanced at the screen, and was a bit surprised to see a blue movie.

"Then some skimpily dressed girls came into the room and sat next to us. It was beginning to click that this wasn't quite a normal party, but we all took full advantage. I think maybe the Americans thought this is the sort of thing soccer teams like to do. It seemed that they were laying it all on for us and it was all part of their hospitality. That was pretty much a one-off: I hadn't known anything like it before and nothing similar to that happened afterwards."

John Boyle has an altogether different recollection of the event – for a start, he says, it took place in Los Angeles rather than the Big Apple. "Yes, it was definitely Hollywood, not New York. And the other team didn't invite us to a party, either. What happened was that two wise guys from Glasgow – two jack the lads – were hanging around the team because of the Scottish connection with Tommy Docherty. These two guys told us that there was a party on that evening. A group of about six of us went along and when the door of this big flat opened we saw an old-fashioned cine film showing a blue movie. There were about five or six stunning girls there and within a few minutes one of them said, 'Hey, do you want to come to bed with me?' I was 20 at the time, she was very attractive, so I didn't need any further encouragement. We came back down, had a drink and left. It was a brothel! When we got outside someone was collecting money, and they said, 'Right, all the greedy bastards who went twice owe me 20 dollars!'"

Bizarrely, Boyle ran into one of the girls he'd, er, become acquainted with over a year later when Chelsea played a Fairs Cup match at Morton. "One of the girls in America was Scottish," he says. "My parents were with me in the players' bar at Morton after the match and this girl came over to us and said, 'Oh, Mrs Boyle, your son's a really nice boy!' At first I didn't recognise her but once she'd spoken I remembered her as being the girl from Hollywood. I was in a bit of a panic what with my parents being there, but she didn't give away any details. I think she just wanted to say 'hello'."

'Woh, We're Going to Barbados!' Remember Typically Tropical's one hit wonder? Shame, really, that it didn't hit the charts until 1975 otherwise the Chelsea boys could have belted it out on the plane as they flew off to the sun-kissed Caribbean island in May 1970. On the other hand, maybe they didn't feel much like singing as most of the squad were nursing brain-splitting hangovers.

"We'd won the FA Cup, we were going to take the trophy out with us to Barbados and the night before we left Eric Swayne fixed up a party for us at the Meridiana restaurant," remembers Alan Birchenall. "When we walked down the stairs into the restaurant every other chair was filled with one of his Page Three models – all fully clothed, in case you're wondering. Afterwards we went to a club before finally staggering home. It was a brilliant night. One player, who shall remain nameless, got off with one of the girls and ended up with four false fingernails stuck in his arse. He wandered around for three days out in Barbados without even noticing they were there. It was only when another player drew his attention to the marks in the showers that he realised the nails were still embedded in his bum cheek!"

A salutary lesson, you might have thought. But did this poor player's misadventure have any effect on his team-mates' crumpet-chasing antics in Barbados? In a word, no. "While we were staying at the hotel in Barbados some of the lads made a play for one of the girls behind the bar," continues Birch. "But although she was attractive, she was a stuck-up bird and gave them all the cold shoulder. In an attempt to warm up this ice maiden, Eddie McCreadie told her that I had suffered a terrible acci-dent and was paralysed from the waist down.

"I played along with the scam, telling her that I feared my career was over. At this point, the lads turned up with a wheelchair they'd found in the hotel foyer to ferry me off to the club we'd been to the previous evening, Alexandria's Nightclub in Bridgetown. While the other lads went to check out the action the girl stayed with me in the VIP lounge, telling me that she hoped we would be able to dance together one day.

"After three hours the joke was beginning to run out of control, and I decided to end it when my favourite Rolling Stones record, *Satisfaction*, came on. I told her I could feel some sensation in my legs and, as she screamed with delight, I tottered to my feet. She supported me to the dance floor where I suddenly burst into my best Mick Jagger strut. The look on her face went through all the emotions – from disbelief to anger, to finally seeing the funny side.

"Some people might think it was a bit sick, but you have to have a footballer's mentality to appreciate it. You've got to look at it in the context. You do these things when you're a young bloke. It was a classic. You wouldn't think a woman would fall for a stunt like that, but she did."

For the most part, the games Chelsea played on their various tours were uncompetitive affairs. Even at half pace and after a night spent sampling the local tipple the Blues were usually way too good for their enthusiastic but technically limited opponents. Indeed, some of the scorelines in the history books suggest mismatches of almost David and Goliath proportions: 15–0 v St James Montego Bay in 1964, 12–0 v Tasmania in 1965, 10–0 v Barbados in 1972 and so on. Just occasionally, though, Chelsea would face opposition who were a genuine match for them.

In February 1971 the Blues flew out to Jamaica to play Santos of Brazil in a prestigious friendly. The Brazilians' star player was none other than the legendary Pele, then at the height of his formidable powers. Four other members of Brazil's wonderful 1970 World Cup-winning squad were also in the Santos team – the great Carlos Alberto, defensive midfielder Clodoaldo and reserves Joel and Edu. Little wonder, then, that for the Chelsea players this was a friendly with a difference – and, what's more, it was a game they desperately wanted to win.

"It was a tough match," says Tommy Baldwin. "At one point Pele was playing down the right hand side when Eddie McCreadie came in and brought him down pretty hard. Ten minutes later Pele had the ball in the centre circle and he just made a beeline for Eddie in the left back position. He ran at him, knocked the ball past him and as Eddie tried to get back, Pele knocked him spark out with his elbow. Pele was the most complete player I ever played against. He had everything: pace, control, heading and shooting ability, he scored goals, but he could handle himself physically too as Eddie found out."

On the Chelsea bench, John Boyle saw McCreadie's dazed state as his big chance. "I remember really hoping at the time that Dave would bring me on, just so that I could say that I'd played against Pele," he says. Unfortunately for Boylers, Eddie recovered and Sexton, clearly treating the match very seriously, chose not to use any of his substitutes. Santos won the game 1–0, their late goal sparking a good-natured pitch invasion which held up play for six minutes until the Jamaican police cleared the crowd with a baton charge.

After the game some of the Chelsea players went to a Kingston night-club where they bumped into a familiar face. "When we walked through the door there was Pele with a nice-looking blonde on his arm," recalls Tommy Baldwin. "We went up to him and he seemed pleased to see us. He was drinking gallons of vodka and orange, smoking a few fags and he had this blonde lady with him. I thought, 'Brilliant, this is the greatest player in the world and he can still enjoy himself!'

"We had a good night, and had a few drinks with him. He was a lovely bloke, not big-headed or anything. He wanted to talk about football all the time, about different games, training programmes and the game in England. I'd actually met him once before. In 1966, when I was still at Arsenal, I was living in digs with John Radford in north London. The landlady went on holiday for a while so Arsenal put us both up in a hotel in Finsbury Park. It just so happened that Santos were staying in the same hotel. Some guy came in to our room and introduced us both to Pele. We said 'hello' and Pele signed a card for me which I've still got."

Whether rubbing shoulders with the world's greatest player, relaxing in their own inimitable way in some of the planet's most exotic locations or getting embroiled in some unlikely far-flung adventures, the Chelsea lads had some of their most memorable experiences while on tour. Footballers plus sun plus beer is always likely to be an explosive mixture but Alan Birchenall, for one, has a theory why the Blues' overseas antics were wilder than most.

"We lived all over the place in London and the Home Counties so unless there was a club function you never saw us all out together," he points out. "That's probably why when we got together on tour it was twice as mad."

CHAPTER THIRTEEN

BLUE IS THE COLOUR

CHAPTER THIRTEEN
BLUE IS THE COLOUR

By the summer of 1971 Chelsea were firmly established as London's most glamorous side. The club's location just off the fashionable King's Road, the epicentre of 'Swinging London' throughout the 1960s, had added a sprinkling of stardust during the previous decade. But now, with the FA Cup and European Cup Winners' Cup safely locked away in the Stamford Bridge trophy cabinet, substance had been added to the Blues' hip image. Their triumphs had even led to a subtle change in the team kit, with two gold 'victory' stars proudly sitting either side of the club badge.

Despite their recent achievements, however, Chelsea couldn't claim to be the capital's most successful team. That accolade had to go to Arsenal, winners of the Double in season 1970/71 – only the second time the feat had been accomplished in the twentieth century. The Gunners' triumphs, though, had been based on solid defending, a flair-free midfield and a series of ultra-functional 1–0 victories. Their pragmatic, results-obsessed and, at times, downright dreary football failed to captivate neutrals in the way that Chelsea's free-flowing game did. Only ex-Blue George Graham and Charlie George, the long-haired Islington teenager who had scored Arsenal's winner in the FA Cup Final against Liverpool, possessed a fraction of the charisma which oozed through the Chelsea team. Otherwise, there was simply no comparison in the glamour stakes.

Take the two goalkeepers, for instance. In goal for the Gunners, Bob Wilson's hallmark was his bravery: he specialised in diving at forwards' feet and quite often ended up with a kick in the head for his troubles. Peter Bonetti, on the other hand, was a much more spectacular keeper, probably the most acrobatic in the league at the time. He also had a brilliant nickname, an exotic-sounding surname and was the first keeper to bring out his own gloves – all important factors in the school playground, where the Cat was the role model for countless aspiring young goalies.

In the battle of the destroyers, meanwhile, Ron Harris had a much larger public profile than Arsenal's hatchet man, midfielder Peter Storey. Again, the nickname issue was crucial – every football fan in the country knew who Chopper was and many enjoyed his no-nonsense approach to defending.

With the exception of Charlie George (who, in any case, was often on the bench), Arsenal's attack lacked a genuinely exciting superstar along the lines of an Osgood, Cooke or Hudson. The Gunners' two main strikers, John Radford and Ray Kennedy, were a pair of hard-working performers who complimented each other well and regularly appeared on the scoresheet, but they didn't set pulses racing in the way, say, that an extravagant Cooke dribble or outrageous Osgood dummy could. Of course, Arsenal's highly organised, well-drilled and effective team play couldn't be lightly dismissed but, as far as Blues fans were concerned, there was no question of envious glances being cast towards Highbury.

Moreover, there was a general feeling that Chelsea could build on their Cup triumphs, even perhaps finally emulating the heroes of 1955 by lifting the title. This, after all, was an era when the championship was extremely open, with six different clubs – Arsenal, Everton, Leeds, Manchester City, Manchester United and Liverpool – having won the title in the preceding six seasons. There was no reason at all, it seemed, why Chelsea, who had finished in sixth place the previous season, couldn't add a new name to that list. The talent was undoubtedly there; just a little more consistency and, possibly, application was required.

It was all the more disappointing for Chelsea fans, then, that the Blues got off to such a poor start to the 1971/72 season. A 3-0 defeat at Arsenal on the opening day was bad enough, but worse was to come four days later when the they lost 3-2 at home to Manchester United, who managed to claim the points despite having George Best sent off for swearing at a linesman just before half-time. Immediately after the game Dave Sexton dropped a bombshell by announcing that Peter Osgood was being placed on the transfer list for "lack of effort and doing less and less".

Asked by a reporter how much Chelsea wanted for their star striker, Sexton replied: "Although a firm figure has not been fixed, it will be something around £250,000. If anybody wants to pay that or exchange a player, that is okay. He has done great things for Chelsea and I should be sorry to see him go. I hope it does not come to that."

The fans reacted to this shock news with fury. Outside the Bridge the following day blue-scarfed demonstrators paraded with placards reading 'Ossie must stay', 'Don't leave Ossie' and 'Sexton must relent'. The campaign was successful: Sexton did relent and Osgood was taken off the transfer list. However, the whole episode suggested that the manager was altogether less enamoured of the England forward than were Osgood's adoring fans in the Shed. "It was completely out of the blue," recalls Peter Osgood. "I wasn't happy."

The fact that Ian Hutchinson, in his comeback game after a cartilage operation, had broken his leg in a reserve match at Swindon made it all the more surprising that Sexton was prepared to sell Osgood. If anything, Chelsea needed to buy a striker rather than sell one. Despite his apparent willingness to offload Osgood, Sexton knew that his attack required strengthening and was keen on Chris Garland, Bristol City's poodle-permed centre forward. The Robins, though, weren't prepared to sell their top asset for less than £100,000, a fee the Chelsea board were reluctant to meet unless they could raise some cash from elsewhere.

"I couldn't get any money from the board," Sexton said later, "so the only way of funding a deal was to sell somebody." But who? David Webb, for one, was dismayed when he discovered the identity of the player Sexton was prepared to sacrifice in order to bring Garland to Chelsea.

"Coming out of a League Cup game we'd won 2–0 against Plymouth at the Bridge, I bumped into Jimmy Bloomfield, the Leicester manager," he recalled. "He asked me if I'd seen Keith Weller. I answered in the affirmative and enquired if he wanted me to pass on his regards. When Bloomfield told me that Chelsea had agreed to sell Weller to City, I went numb. I couldn't believe it. Keith was a key player. He gave the team balance. To me, that was the beginning of the end. That made me stop believing in Chelsea as a force that was going onwards and upwards."

Sexton now maintains that selling Weller was "the biggest mistake I ever made", giving credence to Webb's view that the transfer was something of a turning point in the Blues' fortunes. "He was one of my signings and I liked him as a player," Sexton said a few years ago. "But then at the beginning of that season we'd got some injuries to our strikers. In came Chris Garland from Bristol City and out went Keith to Leicester.

But I don't know what else I could have done: my hands were tied. I could hardly have come up with the money myself."

True, but maybe Sexton could have exerted more pressure on the board. Money *was* available for new players as, later that month, the £170,000 purchase of Steve Kember from Crystal Palace proved. On the other hand, Sexton had been tracking Kember for some time so it's possible the board gave him a stark choice: Kember or Garland, but not both without funds being raised through a sale.

An industrious midfielder with three England Under-23 caps to his name, Kember was initially reluctant to leave the club he had supported as a boy. Perhaps, though, he felt he would be safer playing for the Blues rather than against them.

"We played Chelsea in the FA Cup when I was still at Palace in 1971," he recalls. "I went to close Ron Harris down and as he cleared the ball he's gone bosh and he's done me, shattered all my teeth. One tooth came out completely and the other split in two. So they put a peg in and attached the other tooth to it and they were alright. Then playing for Chelsea against Leeds, I went round Paul Madeley one side and Ossie went round him the other. As I've gone to tackle Madeley, Ossie accidentally kicked me in the face and knocked my teeth out again."

The unfortunate Kember was also in the wars on his Chelsea debut, away to Sheffield United. "After about 10 minutes of play, United were awarded a free-kick," he says. "Geoff Salmons, who used to be able to smash a ball in those days, whacked the ball straight into my face. I was seeing double for the rest of the game. I suppose I should have come off but it was my debut and I had this thing in the back of my mind that I had to stay on."

The game at Bramall Lane ended in a 1-0 defeat for the Blues, leaving them with a dismal record of just two wins in their first ten league games. With a championship challenge appearing distinctly unlikely, the season would depend yet again on Chelsea's performances in the cups.

Since winning the trophy in 1965, the League Cup had become a depressing black hole for Chelsea. Not once had the Blues got past the fourth round and on three occasions they had been dumped out of the competition by lower league opposition. A run in the League Cup was very much overdue, especially as the competition now boasted a prestigious Wembley final and a passage to the UEFA Cup for the winners. Having disposed of Plymouth comfortably enough, Chelsea were drawn away to Nottingham Forest. In a tempestuous 1–1 draw at The City Ground, Chris Garland was clattered by Forest defender Barry Lyons and limped off. Lyons didn't know it, but he would very soon be following Garland into the treatment room.

"Chris got done by a bad tackle and there was a big ruck," recalls Peter Osgood. "Suddenly, I felt a tap on my shoulder, so I turned round and it was Ron Harris. He was squinting because the game was under floodlights and Ron's eyesight wasn't good at the best of times. 'Who was it, Os, what number?' he whispered. I told him, 'Number six' and ten minutes later Forest's number six was carried off on a stretcher."

Maybe Chopper was in a generous mood, though, because Lyons was back for the replay a week later – unlike Garland, who was out of action for over a month. Chelsea won the game 2–1, thanks to goals by Baldwin and Osgood, setting up a fourth round tie with Bolton Wanderers, then chasing promotion from the old Third Division.

As he always did in the League Cup, Sexton fielded a strong side against the Trotters. Weak line-ups had never been a factor in the Blues' early exits from the competition and unfamiliar faces could not be blamed for the disappointing 1–1 draw with Bolton, either. Chelsea simply weren't playing well.

By the time of the replay at Burnden Park in early November, confidence in the Blues' camp had been dealt a further shattering blow by their unexpected failure to overcome Swedish part-timers Atvidaberg in the European Cup Winners Cup. Sensing another upset, the press pack headed north to Lancashire with sharpened pencils. The journos didn't get the story they wanted: instead, the back page headlines heaped praise on the Blues as they crushed Bolton 6–0, Tommy Baldwin claiming a hat-trick.

The result seemed to kick-start Chelsea's season. A Peter Osgood goal was enough to clinch victory at Norwich in the fifth round and by the time the Blues lined up at the Bridge for the first leg of the semi-final against Tottenham, the holders of the League Cup, they were undefeated in 14 matches in all competitions.

Despite being played just three days before Christmas, the match against Spurs attracted Chelsea's largest ever crowd for a home League Cup tie, 43,330. The fans were rewarded with a breathtaking London derby, which had more twists and turns than a John Le Carré novel. Osgood's cleverly angled shot gave Chelsea a first-half lead, but two quick-fire second half goals by Terry Naylor and Martin Chivers appeared to have changed the course of the match. Almost immediately, though, Garland levelled with a header from Houseman's corner and then, with just five minutes left, Naylor handled in the box. Hollins blasted the penalty high past Pat Jennings at the Shed end to give Chelsea a slender first-leg lead.

Two weeks later the teams met again at White Hart Lane in front of another enormous crowd. Chivers gave Tottenham the lead with a powerful volley just before half-time, but an equally thunderous shot from Garland deservedly restored Chelsea's aggregate advantage in the second half. With the clock ticking down, Spurs increased the pressure on the Blues' goal in a desperate bid to force extra-time. Like Chelsea, Tottenham had their own long throw expert, centre forward Martin Chivers, and his airborne missiles were causing panic in the Blues' defence.

"Chivers threw the ball in, it came off the ground and hit me on the chest and the upper arm," recalls Alan Hudson. "With the pitch being muddy the ball made a mark on my chest which I tried to show the referee, but he wasn't interested. He gave Spurs a penalty and Martin Peters scored. I was thinking, 'Oh dear, I thought we'd be at Wembley in ten minutes' time'. But with just a minute left we got a free-kick on the left-hand side near the corner flag. Johnny Hollins went after the ball to take it but I got in front of him and pushed him aside. I could see all our big lads running forward and I thought, 'Don't put it in the air, that's what they're expecting.' So I drove it in low instead. It worked. Big Pat Jennings missed it at the near post and it went through Cyril Knowles' legs and bobbled into the far corner. For me, it was a massive relief because I'd given the penalty away a few minutes earlier. Now, I'd got us the goal to take us to a major final. Looking back, I'd say that was my most important goal for Chelsea."

Hudson's slightly fortunate goal, which gave Chelsea a 5-4 aggregate victory over two tumultuous games, sent the Blues fans in the 52,755 crowd into raptures. The players were in celebratory mood, too, and – decent restaurants being thin on the ground around White Hart Lane – headed back en masse to their King's Road 'manor' for something to eat and drink.

"A group of about five of us had a meal in Alexander's," remembers Huddy. "There was me, Ossie, Chris Garland – who'd played terrifically in the two games against Spurs and had scored a great goal at White Hart Lane – and a couple of others. We had some champagne – in fact, we pretty much drank everything that night – and we were laughing and joking all evening; we were in great spirits because one thing is winning, another thing is winning and playing the way we had played that night. We were brilliant, we really played some fantastic football. And it wasn't just me who thought so. I went back to Alexander's the next day for lunch and Terry Venables was there. We sat down and had a chat and Venables said to me, 'I was there last night and that was the best performance I've ever seen from a Chelsea team'."

The Chelsea party finally left Alexander's in the early hours of the morning. Intoxicated by the heady mix of post-victory euphoria and copious amounts of champers, Ossie, Huddy and co couldn't resist breaking into song. "All we were singing was 'We're on our way to Wembley' and 'we shall not be moved' on our way to our cars," says Peter Osgood.

"Suddenly, the Old Bill turned up out of nowhere. There were loads of them, three or four vans. At first I thought there must have been a shooting or something, but they came over to us. 'Have you been drinking?' they asked. I said, 'Yes, we've just got through to the League Cup Final and we've been celebrating. We've just been singing a Chelsea song, that's all, we're not upsetting anybody.'

"One of the policemen said, 'Well, there have been complaints. Get in your car and drive off.' My mate Danny Gillen, a big lad who became Phil Collins' minder, heard this and said, 'That's exactly what you want him to do because you'll nick him for drink-driving.' All of a sudden he was having a ruck with the copper and, when I went over to calm the situation, a policeman put my arm up behind my back and said, 'You're nicked as well, Osgood!' They took us in the meat wagon down to the police station and locked us in the cells. Then, around four o'clock in the morning, a policeman came in and said, 'Hoppit, here are you car keys.'

"When I got to Magistrates' court the next day my brief asked the copper what happened.

'Well,' he said, 'Osgood had to be restrained, and he staggered when he got into the Black Maria'.

So my brief asked him, 'Was he drunk?'

'Oh, yes. He was drunk,' the copper replied.

'And what time was this?'

'About half past one.'

'And what time did you give him back his car keys?'

'Four o'clock.'

'So, you gave a drunk man his car keys back did you?'

The magistrate listened to this exchange and banged his hammer – case dismissed. He just threw the case out. My brief did a brilliant job. I thought he was on their side to begin with, but he just led the copper right into it."

A good day for British justice then and, more importantly, for Ossie, who was now free to concentrate on the build-up to the final with the rest of the team. As now, the League Cup was very much secondary to the FA Cup but, since all Football League clubs had become obliged to enter and a Wembley final had replaced the old two-legged format in 1967, the competition had been growing in stature. Reaching the final was definitely a big deal, and the Blues decided to mark their achievement by cutting a record.

In the early seventies football records were still something of a novelty and, to the music critics' exasperation, occasionally struck a chord with the record-buying public. In 1970, for instance, the England World Cup squad had topped the charts with *Back Home* prior to heading off to Mexico to defend the Jules Rimet trophy. Then, the following year, Arsenal reached Number 16 with their FA Cup Final record, *Good Old Arsenal*, an uninspiring dirge set to the tune of *Rule Britannia* and with lyrics by football pundit Jimmy Hill.

Wisely, Chelsea preferred to commission a couple of professional songwriters, Peter Lee Stirling and Daniel Boone, and they came up with a jaunty little number called *Blue is the Colour*. The idea, as with all football records before and since, was that the players would sing the song themselves. Meanwhile, the Larry Page Orchestra, who specialised in instrumental versions of pop songs and had recently released an album of Kinks covers entitled *Kinky Music*, were signed up to provide the backing music.

"We recorded it at a studio in Islington," remembers Tommy Baldwin. "We knocked it out first or second go and we did an LP at the same time. In the morning we took about 10 cases of lager in and a couple of cases of vodka and by the evening we were pretty drunk. But it came out okay. A lot of the lads did a solo vocal for the album tracks – I remember Ossie did a version of *Chirpy Chirpy Cheep Cheep* – but I just stayed in the chorus. After the amount of vodka I'd drunk that was all I could manage."

The album, perhaps inevitably, quickly found its way into the remainder section but the single did well, rising to number five in the charts. "*Blue is the Colour* was a very catchy tune but I was still surprised it sold so well," says John Dempsey. "It wasn't just Chelsea fans who were buying it, obviously." With the Blues rubbing shoulders in the top five alongside the likes of T Rex's *Telegram Sam*, Nilsson's *Without You* and Chicory Tip's *Son of My Father* the call went out for the squad to appear on *Top of the Pops*.

"When we turned up at the studio at BBC Television centre at White City we were all wearing our ordinary clothes – leather jackets and whatever – and the producer wasn't very impressed," recalls Dempsey. "He said we didn't look like a proper group so somebody had to rush out to Marks and Spencers and come back with 14 identical jumpers. I can't remember what colour they were, they may have been blue. There was a fan with us, a friend of Ian Hutchinson, and for a laugh we sneaked him into the group at the back. People watching at home must have wondered who he was.

"We had a rehearsal which went okay and then we went on stage. Gilbert O'Sullivan was on the other stage and the Sweet were also on that night. It went fine, they were a bit worried we wouldn't remember the words so off screen above the stage they had huge boards with the lyrics on them; I didn't really need them as the words were fairly easy to remember."

John Boyle, though, has a different memory of the event, in which the rehearsal went far from 'okay'. "When we got there, a guy told us to sing along to the music – but we made an awful racket, just terrible," he says. "So, Eddie McCreadie said to him, 'Look, do you want a good song? Well, what we need are four bottles of vodka and a couple of crates of lager – then come back later on.'" So we went back on stage quite a bit later, and suddenly it was like having 16 Frank Sinatras!"

"We were outrageous," adds Alan Hudson. "We were running amok in the BBC studios. We had a lot of beer in our dressing room and we'd been drinking all day by the time we got on. We ended up down at Alexander's that night, and three of the boys had a trio of Pan's People with them. Dee Dee Wilde was with Tommy Baldwin, and a couple of others were there. I think it was someone like John Phillips or Hutch who got lucky."

Despite its crossover appeal and 12–week stay in the charts, *Blue is the Colour* didn't make the players rich. They each made around £300 from the record, the rough equivalent then of a couple of weeks' wages before bonuses. More importantly, though, the song – like *The Liquidator* – was to become an essential and much-loved part of the pre-match build up at Stamford Bridge. Even today, *Blue is the Colour* still gets the crowd going at the Bridge, although it has to be said most fans would benefit from a short refresher course in the lyrics.

Blue is the Colour's climb up the charts mirrored Chelsea's increasingly good form as the League Cup Final with Stoke City approached. Two weeks before Wembley, on February 19th, Dave Sexton was presented with a gallon of Bell's whisky on the Stamford Bridge pitch after being voted Manager of the Month for January. Later that afternoon he saw two goals from Peter Osgood help the Blues to a 2–1 victory over Leicester, a result that extended their impressive recent record to one defeat in 24 games.

Two of those games had come in the FA Cup. In the third round Chelsea had won 1–0 at Blackpool, thanks to a John Dempsey header, and in the fourth round Bolton were seen off with the minimum of fuss; Hollins, Cooke and Houseman netting in a 3–0 victory at the Bridge. A fifth round draw away to Second Division Orient appeared far from daunting and only increased the feeling that the in-form Blues could make a return trip to Wembley later in the season.

On paper, Orient had few players to worry Chelsea. Ian Bowyer, a busy midfielder who would go on to win the league and European Cup with Nottingham Forest, was their most accomplished performer, but otherwise the O's, – who also had future Blues flop Dennis Rofe at left-back – were almost entirely made up of unknown journeymen. At first, the gap in class looked more like a chasm as Chelsea strolled into a two-goal lead through Webb and Osgood. But with a minute left of the first half the course of the match, Chelsea's season and, some might argue, the Blues' future over the next few years was changed by a single dramatic moment.

"We were cruising at Orient and then they scored right before half-time," remembers Alan Hudson. "I was standing near their centre half Phil Hoadley when he shot, he hit this ball from at least 35 yards and it kind of bobbled up just right for him. On another day it would have gone miles wide but this thing flew in the net."

Worse was to follow three minutes into the second half when indecision in the Chelsea defence allowed Micky Bullock to equalise. As the game neared the end with the scores level, a replay at the Bridge – which, surely, would be a formality for the home side – looked on the cards.

But, in the 89th minute, bearded Orient striker Barrie Fairbrother took advantage of some more sloppy Blues play – "a horrendous defensive balls up by us", is Alan Hudson's description – to score the winner.

The mood in the Chelsea camp after the defeat was one of complete deflation, mixed with anger at the basic errors which had cost them the match. "It's disgraceful – leading 2–0 then losing 3–2 to a team like that," Blues full back Paddy Mulligan said afterwards. "If I were running a schoolboy team and they allowed the same thing to happen, I would really murder them." What was all the more galling was that the defence had been playing so well up to the Orient game, conceding just that one goal to Leicester in the previous five matches.

Still, at least there was the League Cup Final to look forward to the following Saturday. Stoke, Chelsea's opponents, were a lower mid-table First Division side who relied heavily on a core of veteran players, including England goalkeeper Gordon Banks, pipe-smoking captain Peter Dobing and former Arsenal and Newcastle star George Eastham. The game with Chelsea would be the Potters' first ever visit to Wembley and they had got there the hard way, needing two replays to get past West Ham in the semi-final.

In the hour before the Final kicked off the 100,000 crowd was entertained by the band of the Royal Artillery and the final of ITV's *On the Ball* Penalty Prize competition, hosted by – who else? – Jimmy Hill. The teams then emerged from the tunnel to a thunderous reception to be presented to the guest of honour, UEFA President Gustav Wiederkehr.

In selecting his team, Dave Sexton had ignored the Brisbane Road debacle and made just one enforced change from the previous week, Chris Garland replacing the cup-tied Steve Kember. Sexton named Tommy Baldwin as substitute, even though the forward had only just returned from an unauthorised holiday in Spain.

"I went AWOL after being dropped so often and I disappeared off to Benidorm," says the Sponge. "But I came back the week before we got beat by Orient in the FA Cup and Dave asked me to come in for training in the week before the final. He fined me again – I think it went up to about £50 that time – and then said I'd be sub."

Baldwin came on for the injured Paddy Mulligan at half-time, with Peter Houseman retreating to left-back. By that time, the score was 1–1, Peter Osgood having cancelled out Terry Conroy's early header. The Blues' goal was an unusual one: lying on the ground after challenging for Cooke's cross, Osgood reacted instantly when the ball rebounded to him and, despite being surrounded by Stoke defenders, hooked his shot past Banks from near the penalty spot. It was an audacious finish, and one a less quick-witted player would probably not even have attempted.

The stage looked set, then, for the Blues to go on and claim a third different cup in three seasons but, to the joy of their fans and most neutrals, it was Stoke who lifted their first ever trophy thanks to a late goal by the oldest of their old stagers, 35-year-old George Eastham.

"Had we won the game against Orient we'd have been flying but I think the defeat had a knock-on effect; we were feeling a little bit flat," says Alan Hudson. "Another factor was that Dave Sexton didn't learn his lesson from the 1970 Final and he played Webby at right back. Terry Conroy tore him apart and Stoke's winning goal came from the left wing. Conroy took it up to Webby, he dived in again and Conroy went by him. He crossed it to John Ritchie, who headed down, Jimmy Greenhoff smashed it and George Eastham knocked in the rebound."

Sexton himself, though, looked for scapegoats elsewhere, notably Ron Harris who was replaced as captain, first by John Hollins then, at the start of the following season, by Eddie McCreadie. Publicly, however, the Chelsea boss remained upbeat, saying afterwards, "Our season is by no means over – there is still much to play for. We have bounced back before. We shall do so again."

Indeed, for a while, the Blues performed a passable imitation of a yo-yo, winning five straight games at the end of March and the beginning of April to give themselves a decent chance of a UEFA Cup place. This sequence was remarkable for a four-goal burst from David Webb in two of the victories, while Sexton employed the defender as a makeshift striker during an injury crisis.

Yet Webb's success as a striker was nothing compared to his most unlikely alter ego as an emergency goalkeeper. Earlier in the season, a few days before the first leg of the League Cup semi-final, Webb had replaced the injured Peter Bonetti in goal after 30 minutes of the Blues' match at Coventry. In those days there were no substitute goalkeepers, so Webb's hour between the sticks – during which he conceded just one goal in a 1-1 draw – was not, in itself, particularly unusual.

Ten days later, though, and it was a different story altogether. "Peter was still out injured," recalls Webby. "Then John Phillips had stayed overnight at John Hollins' house and as he got out of bed in the morning he slipped a disc. The club had already allowed Steve Sherwood to go home to Yorkshire. So they sent a police escort to get him back. In the meantime, we submitted two team sheets, one with Steve Sherwood in goal and another one with me in the net. The referee said he'd give it till quarter to three. Steve Sherwood came running through the door at ten to three, but the ref wouldn't budge."

To the amazement of the crowd, Chelsea took to the field with Webb in the goalkeeper's kit. Ever the showman, the Blues' new custodian knelt down in his penalty area in front of the Shed and pretended to pray. Who knows, maybe he really did appeal for divine intervention. He would certainly need all the help he could get. Not only were Ipswich a useful mid-table team, they also came to the Bridge fired by a sense of injustice from the corresponding fixture the previous season when an Alan Hudson shot which had struck the outside of a stanchion had been incorrectly given as a goal.

John Dempsey, for one, didn't have a great deal of confidence in Webb's goalkeeping abilities. "It was brave of him to volunteer to go in goal but I looked at him and thought, 'Blimey, we could let in five or six today.' Surprisingly, though, he had very little to do. If I'd been Bobby Robson, who was the manager of Ipswich then, I'd have told my players to test him out from all over the pitch but they hardly had a shot. It was nerve-wracking but we got through it without conceding a goal."

"Webb has played so many roles that he has become the Alec Guinness of Stamford Bridge," wrote Laurie Pignon in *The Daily Mail* after the Blues' 2–0 victory. At the end of the season the versatile Webb was voted the club's 'Player of the Year', although nobody was quite sure whether he'd won the award for his resolute defending, his goal-poaching striker's instincts or, indeed, his eye-catching stint as a stand-in keeper. Probably, the recognition was for his whole-hearted approach to whichever role he was asked to perform.

"Webby was 150 per cent every time," says Peter Osgood. "I remember playing against Blackpool once. We were 3–0 down with 20 minutes to go and, all of a sudden, this ball's come over and – boom! – Webby's knocked it in. I said, 'What are you doing up here?' He said, 'Fuck tactics, I'm staying up here with you' and it worked, we won 4–3! The nice thing about Webby was that he'd go for everything. If there was a 60:40 ball in their favour he'd make it 50:50, and he'd get the knock downs so for me it was perfect when he went up front. Like Hutch, he'd play the battering ram role."

Webb was equally committed off the pitch, putting his surplus energies into a variety of business interests. These included, at various times, a wig shop, a Sunday league kit-cleaning scheme and a car lot. "Webby was a romancer," says Ossie. "He used to come in to training and we'd say, 'What have you bought today?' Some of the business interests he had in his playing days weren't so successful but they've put him in good stead for later on. He's done some good deals and he's become a millionaire."

A poor run of just one win in their last six games meant the Blues finished the 1971/72 season in seventh position, a couple of places short of a UEFA Cup slot. Overall, despite the excitement generated by the League Cup run, it had been a disappointing season. The expected title challenge had not materialised, neither of the two expensive new signings, Chris Garland and Steve Kember, had made a great impact and, more worryingly, there were signs of discontent among the established players.

Osgood was still unhappy about being transfer-listed at the start of the season. Alan Hudson, too, was upset after being repositioned from the centre to the right side of midfield to make way for Sexton's new signing, Steve Kember. "That's when it all started to go wrong. That was the writing on the wall. I didn't mind going out wide now and again, but I didn't like being stuck out there. You're only going to get the ball when other people give it to you. If you play in the middle, you can go and get it for yourself. It makes you a better player, because you're always involved. Playing me on the right wing was like asking a marathon runner to become a sprinter, really. It just wasn't me. It wasn't that I was being selfish or anything like that – I thought I wasn't helping the team. Sexton was getting me to play wing back, effectively – to track back and pick up a full back, and then get forward to join in the play."

Another malcontent was Tommy Baldwin, who was becoming increasingly fed up with being left off the team sheet. "Dave played me all the time to start with but later he decided he didn't like my lifestyle and I was often left out," he says. "He played me in the finals, though. Dave was completely different to Tommy Docherty. Much quieter, he was the sort of manager who wanted to organise your lifestyle. He wanted everyone to be an upright citizen, non-smoking, no dirty women sort of guy. Be regular and improve every day on the football pitch. He was fighting a losing battle with that team, though."

For the time being, however, the players' grumblings were only a minor blot on the Bridge landscape. Overall, there was an optimistic mood about the place, no more so than on 5th June 1972 when chairman Brian Mears announced plans for the total redevelopment of the ground, a project which had first been discussed three years earlier.

Mears' vision, he told journalists at a press conference, was to create a new 60,000 capacity stadium, costing around £5.5 million, by the end of the seventies. The first stage of the redevelopment would see a massive three-tier, 12,000 capacity stand built in place of the existing 5,000 capacity East Stand. Once completed, the stand would be the largest in Britain. Quite possibly, the warmest, too, as the design by architects Darbourne and Darke provided an option to pipe hot air through small holes underneath each seat. Other elements in the grandiose scheme included 156 private viewing boxes, bars, restaurants, new offices and leisure facilities. "We will make the home of Chelsea FC second to none in Europe," predicted Mears. "And Dave Sexton will still have all the money he needs to buy new players."

Coming a year after Mears had, apparently, ended speculation about Chelsea's future at the Bridge by announcing the purchase of the ground freehold from the JT Mears estate for £475,000, this latest news seemed to indicate a bright future for the club.

Press reaction was overwhelmingly positive. "It is a breathtaking venture," wrote Danny Blanchflower in *The Sunday Express*. "Brian Mears, you have given Chelsea fans a cause to be proud of. We hope you make it and that we are around at the end of the seventies to help you celebrate the big opening." J.L. Manning in the *Evening Standard* was equally enthusiastic: "Not in my lifetime has a British football club set out to rebuild itself completely. For 70 years there has been sporadic patching up, but nothing to compare with what Chelsea have decided to do."

In the short term, however, the redevelopment of the East Stand was an inconvenience for players and supporters. As bulldozers and wrecking balls piled into the old stand with the force of a Chopper Harris tackle it was, quite literally, a case of having the builders in for the whole season. The home and away dressing rooms had been located in the East Stand; with these no longer operational, the players would have to change in temporary Portakabins which were more Sunday League than First Division. There was change, too, on the North Terrace as the 1,000-capacity North Stand – that bizarre-looking structure on wooden stilts which loomed over the away fans – was demolished following reports that it had rocked alarmingly during a recent match.

For the first game of the 1972/73 season against Leeds, 51,000 fans packed into the three remaining stands while another 9,000 were locked out. The crush was so great hundreds of youngsters spilled over from the terraces and watched the game cross-legged on the grass behind the greyhound track. Leeds, FA Cup winners and runners-up in the league the previous season, and now sporting numbered tags on their socks, promised to be stiff opposition. Yet, thanks in part to an injury to David Harvey which forced Peter Lorimer to go in goal, the Blues thumped their deadly rivals 4–0. The second goal was probably the best: Cooke collecting Hudson's superb defence-splitting long pass and angling a left-foot shot past Leeds' stand-in keeper at the Shed end. Few Blues fans could have imagined a better start to the campaign, although the hyper-critical Brian Glanville remained under-whelmed in *The Sunday Times*. "The immense skill in the [Chelsea] team still does not yet find full expression, while tactically we saw nothing new from either side," he complained.

The news was not all good, though. Eight supporters had been taken to hospital after a crash-barrier had collapsed under the weight of the crowd. As a result, the Stamford Bridge capacity was cut by around 30% to 36,000 for the remainder of the season. A series of pitch invasions by jubilant fans during the Leeds game also led to the club becoming the first in Britain to erect wire fences behind both goals.

As it turned out, there wasn't a great deal for the fans to get excited about after that opening day win as the gaping hole where the East Stand once stood seemed to drain both players and fans of their energies. "There was a morbid atmosphere and it became like two cemeteries in one," says Alan Hudson, referring to the now visible expanse of Brompton Cemetery beyond the cranes and digging machines.

"Without the East Stand there was an eerie feeling about the place," agrees John Dempsey. "Instead of dug-outs on the side of the pitch, there were benches which was very odd. It wasn't the best atmosphere and teams were no longer intimidated about coming to the Bridge."

One fan went further, describing the home support as "a disgrace" in a letter to 'In Off The Post', the programme's letters column. "It's no wonder visiting sides settle in so quickly; they feel as much at home as our lads," wrote Mrs Elaine Walker from Surrey. "Is any other team greeted with such apathy? It's not surprising Chelsea play so well away from home."

In fact, Chelsea's away form wasn't any better, either, and the Blues' final position of 12th was their lowest since they were promoted back to the First Division a decade earlier. Yet again, the fans looked to the cups for some cheer and, for a while at least, another Wembley appearance seemed possible.

In the League Cup, the Blues saw off Southend, Derby, Bury and Notts County on their way to a semi-final with newly-promoted Norwich City. Chelsea, hot favourites to reach the final against Tottenham or Wolves, appeared to have warmed up in the best possible way for the tie when, just four days before the first leg, they crushed the Canaries 3–1 at the Bridge. This game was notable for two goals by Shed hero Ian Hutchinson, in his comeback match after almost two years' absence through injury. This, though, was very much a case of a dress rehearsal being more successful than the first night as, back at the Bridge, Norwich surprisingly won 2–0 in the first leg of the semi. A week later in the return leg at Carrow Road, Norwich led 3–2 on the night when a thick East Anglian mist descended on the stadium, making visibility virtually impossible for players, fans and the referee.

"With six minutes to go one of the Norwich players was running through the centre of the pitch and Eddie McCreadie just punched him," recalls John Phillips. "The referee, Gordon Hill, came running up to see the City player lying on the floor. The fog had obscured his view and he asked what had happened. When the Norwich guy told him he'd been hit, Gordon Hill just said, 'I've had enough of this', and called the match off." The reprieve was short-lived as Norwich won the rescheduled game 1–0 to go through to the final against Tottenham.

Chelsea enjoyed no better luck in the FA Cup. After knocking out Brighton, Ipswich and Sheffield Wednesday the Blues met Double-chasing Arsenal in a sell-out London derby at the Bridge in the quarter-final. The match finished 2–2 with all the goals, including a stunning 20-yard left-foot Osgood volley which went on to win BBC's 'Goal of the Season' competition, coming in the first half. "We should have beaten them," says Steve Kember. "For one of their goals 'Sticks', John Phillips, dived past the post to make a save. The ball wasn't going in but he somehow pushed it into the back of the net."

Three days later a crowd of nearly 63,000 poured into Highbury for the replay, with an estimated 10,000 locked outside. London pride as well as Cup glory was at stake – just as it had been in the Chelsea-Tottenham

League Cup clashes the previous year – and for fans of both teams this was the 'must see' game of the season. With Second Division Sunderland lined up as semi-final opponents whichever side emerged victorious on a mild spring evening would be firm favourites to reach Wembley.

Playing some of their best football of the campaign, Chelsea took the lead when John Hollins crossed for Peter Houseman to score with a rare header. The Blues were still on top when, right on half-time, Arsenal were awarded a controversial penalty after Steve Kember brought down George Armstrong.

"It was just inside the box," admits Steve. "What annoyed me about it was that I'd chased George Armstrong all the way back from their 18-yard box. I was convinced I'd made the tackle but at the last moment he toed the ball on and I caught him. It wasn't intentional. The ref gave it outside. Then Frank McLintock and Alan Ball virtually manhandled him over to the lino and the lino said it was inside."

Ball scored from the spot and, in the second half, Ray Kennedy scored the winner for the Gunners. The only consolation for Blues fans was that Arsenal surprisingly lost to Sunderland in the semi-final.

In terms of playing staff, Sexton had stayed broadly loyal to his double Cup winners throughout the 1972/73 season. The one exception was Charlie Cooke who, to the disappointment of his many fans on the Shed, was sold in a job-lot with Paddy Mulligan to Crystal Palace in September 1972. New faces, meanwhile, included Bill Garner, a powerful centre forward whose heading ability had impressed when the Blues met his previous club, Southend, in the League Cup; Gary Locke, an athletic, pacy right-back who had come through the youth system; and Ian Britton, a tiny, Scottish terrier of a midfielder who had a run in the side in the second half of the season. The fresh faces were welcome as a number of the established players were starting to look stale, jaded and unmotivated. In his autobiography Alan Hudson admits, "I stopped caring around then", and he was far from alone in appearing a listless shadow of his former self.

Chelsea were beginning to look like a side in transition. But transition to what? A dismal run of three league wins in 25 games between late October and April clearly suggested that the road ahead could be rocky. Three straight home victories at the very end of the season, including one over Manchester United in Bobby Charlton's last match for the Reds, raised spirits slightly but by then the fans had voted with their feet. Attendances at the Bridge had dropped to below 20,000 for some run-of-the-mill fixtures, although more than 40,000 crammed in for Charlton's emotional farewell.

For the bean-counters at the club, declining gates had come at the worst possible time. Building costs for the new East Stand were increasing by the day thanks to roaring inflation and the 1973 oil crisis. Meanwhile, pay strikes on the site and the Conservative government's imposition of a national three-day working week to conserve fuel usage had combined to put the scheduled completion date of the stand back a full year, to the summer of 1974.

You didn't need to be a latter-day Nostradamus to sense that storm clouds were forming above the Bridge. Very soon those clouds would open with drastic consequences.

CHAPTER FOURTEEN

END OF THE DREAM

CHAPTER FOURTEEN
END OF THE DREAM

Chelsea went into the 1973/74 season, a campaign which was to be remembered as one of the most troubled in the club's history, in reasonable shape. Two pre-season tours, the first to Germany and Holland and the second to Spain, had proved successful exercises, with the Blues emerging unbeaten from five matches against tough local opposition, including Werder Bremen and Celta Vigo. Even the fact that three Chelsea players – Peter Osgood, Eddie McCreadie and Steve Kember – had been sent off in two matches in Spain was open to a positive interpretation, suggesting that the trio's competitive instincts were well and truly intact.

For the first game of the season away to Derby County, Dave Sexton was able to call on eight of the players who had won the FA Cup three years earlier. The exceptions were Charlie Cooke, who was no longer at the club; John Dempsey, who was to miss the whole season with Achilles tendon and ankle injuries; and Tommy Baldwin, who, once again, had not been selected. Steve Kember, Chris Garland and John Boyle, playing his last ever game for Chelsea before moving to Orient via a loan spell at Brighton, took their places. Alan Hudson, annoyed at being played on the right of midfield, had seen his pre-season request for a transfer turned down by Dave Sexton and was relegated to the substitute's bench.

The trip to the Baseball Ground did not turn out to be a happy one. Chelsea lost the match 1–0, while clashes between rival groups of fans on the pitch resulted in eight arrests. Following further defeats at newly-promoted Burnley and at home to Sheffield United, the Blues found themselves planted firmly at the bottom of the First Division after three games.

The pre-season optimism had already evaporated before August was out.

In the summer, inspired by the 'Magical Magyars' who had thrashed England at Wembley in 1953, Dave Sexton had requested a new change kit in Hungary's colours of red, white and green. The team looked great, but their performances on the road remained largely disappointing.

The picture appeared a little rosier by mid-December when, after better results in the late autumn, the Blues had risen to the heady heights of 13th. The chief factor in the steady improvement was the rich goalscoring vein struck by Peter Osgood, now back in the England squad after a gap of three years, and the recalled Tommy Baldwin – 17 goals between them in 14 matches. If the duo could keep up that sort of return maybe something could be salvaged from the season after all.

In the event, they weren't given much chance to add to their combined tally. Shortly before Christmas 1974, Chelsea's revival came to a shuddering halt as they lost 2–1 at the Bridge to unbeaten leaders Leeds and 2–0 away to Wolves the following week. Still, a Boxing Day encounter at home to struggling West Ham looked to be the ideal fixture to launch another good run.

"The West Ham game was the catalyst of everything that happened next," says Alan Hudson. "I scored a goal and we were 2–0 up at half-time. We were all over them, it should have been a few a more. Then, all of a sudden, they seemed to score every time they attacked in the second half. It wasn't as though they outplayed us. There was no build up to their goals. They came from goal kicks from their keeper and mess ups by our centre halves, that sort of thing." Nonetheless, the 4–2 final score to the Hammers – for whom Frank Lampard (senior) got the all-important first goal – represented a stunning turnaround and left Dave Sexton fuming.

"We came in after the game and Dave gave me and Peter Osgood hell," continues Huddy. "We had a meeting the next day and Dave said, 'It's you two, you're letting down the team.' It was an unbelievable thing to say, but I think it had been boiling up inside him." Hudson had good reason to be bewildered by Sexton's outburst as he had been Chelsea's best player against West Ham, setting up the Blues' first goal with a pass to Ian Britton, then scoring a superb second himself after beating three defenders.

Sexton's scathing criticism of Osgood, meanwhile, was nothing new. Earlier in the season, after a League Cup defeat at Stoke, the Blues' boss had blamed his star striker for the loss. The row which ensued ended with Osgood swearing at Sexton and storming off to a Stoke nightclub. Yet, despite these run ins, Sexton was seriously considering making Osgood the new Chelsea captain.

"Dave came to see me and said, 'How do you fancy being captain?' says Ossie. "I told him I'd think about it, although I wasn't that keen on the idea because Chopper was our skipper." In fact, at the time John Hollins was wearing the armband, having taken over the captaincy from Eddie McCreadie in September.

Three days after the West Ham debacle Chelsea lost for the fourth consecutive game, going down 1–0 at home to second-placed Liverpool. The result saw the Blues drop to 18th in the league table, just two places clear of the relegation zone. Losing to the high-flying Scousers was no disgrace in itself, but for Sexton it was the last straw. For the next match, away to Sheffield United on New Year's Day, he decided to drop four senior players: Peter Bonetti, Peter Osgood, Alan Hudson and Tommy Baldwin, although the Sponge did make the bench. "I have no comment to make on why they were dropped," Sexton told the press, "but they are all fit."

The dropped players were stunned by Sexton's shake up of the team. "Dave called me in on the Monday morning after the Liverpool game," remembers Ossie. "He said, 'There are going to be some changes for the next game: I'm dropping you, Alan Hudson and Peter Bonetti.' So I went from being captain to being dropped!"

Tommy Baldwin was equally surprised to find himself out of the team. "I was on a great run," he says. "I'd scored something like nine goals in eleven games and Dave Sexton was praising the fuck out of me. 'Look at Tommy,' he'd say, 'that's the effort I want to see from all of you.' Then suddenly he decided to drop me. I couldn't believe it. 'I've dropped Ossie, so I've got to drop you as well,' he said. Huddy and Peter Bonetti were out of the team as well. I was so pissed off I just hopped on a plane to Benidorm, where I had a place I shared with John Boyle just outside Alicante. When I got back I went on loan to Millwall and Manchester United and that was me pretty much finished at Chelsea."

By the time the Sponge returned from his impromptu holiday on the Costa Blanca he found a club in full-scale crisis. Peter Bonetti, obviously, wasn't happy about being replaced by John Phillips but had accepted his demotion in a professional manner. However, Sexton's decision to drop both Osgood and Hudson at the same time had brought the simmering tensions between the manager and his two star players to a head. The row that ensued would have far-reaching consequences for the club and the individuals concerned and, even now, remains one of the most controversial episodes in Chelsea history. As you might expect, the three protagonists have slightly different versions of events.

"Sexton said, 'You two won't be playing on Tuesday against Sheffield United,'" recalls Hudson, "The following day we came out for training and we were knocking balls about before the session on the reserves' side of the ground. Dario Gradi, the reserve team manager, asked us what we were doing and we said, 'Well, we're going to play in the reserves tomorrow so we're training with you.' He got the raving hump with us, and then Dave sent someone across to get us. We were walking over there and Dave left the group of players and came over to us, saying, 'What's it all about?' How Dave and Osgood never had a fight I don't know. It ended up with Ossie saying, 'Fuck this, if you don't want us you can get rid of me, I can't go on like this!' and Dave said, 'Well, I will get rid of you!' I said, 'Well, what's good enough for him is good enough for me.'"

Peter Osgood has a similar recollection of the training ground bust up, although he maintains that Hudson rather than himself asked for a transfer initially. This was an important distinction as, under FA rules, only players who had not asked for a move were entitled to five per cent of the transfer fee when they eventually switched clubs. Dave Sexton, though, has no doubt that both players demanded a move.

"I dropped Bonetti, Osgood, Hudson and Baldwin for a game away to Sheffield United, and we won," he said later. "When I got back the next day, the problems started. Osgood and Hudson took umbrage and asked for a transfer. They were the two heroes, so it weakened my popularity. Nevertheless, I wouldn't handle it any differently today. They couldn't tell me who to pick for the team – that was my prerogative. If they were not happy, they could go. Neither Osgood or Hudson was playing particularly well. The manager has to make the decisions, leave people out, put others in, whatever. You have to do that over years and years. And nine times out of ten it's okay. People will accept it. But on the odd occasions, they won't accept it – and you'll have to get over it."

At the time, the club quickly upped the ante, releasing the following statement to the press within hours of the training ground argument:

"Hudson and Osgood both refused to train with the first team squad this morning and have been suspended by the club for one week. Both have expressed a wish to move and Chelsea are making them available for transfer immediately."

For the media the announcement was a sensation and the tabloids, in particular, needed little encouragement to go into overdrive. "Showdown!" shrieked *The Sun's* back page, above the sub-heading "Sexton to sell rebels". The list of clubs supposedly interested in Osgood and Hudson pretty much filled up the rest of the page with Arsenal, Spurs, Manchester United, Leicester, QPR, Southampton and Norwich all getting a name check.

"We are interested in both players because men of that calibre become available very rarely," Southampton boss Lawrie McMenemy told reporters. Norwich manager John Bond echoed those comments, saying, "No manager in his right mind can say he is not interested in two players of their quality. We would like them both but whether they would like to come here remains to be seen."

A few days later the chase for Osgood took a continental twist as *The Sun* reported that Real Madrid were prepared to sell their German midfield star Gunter Netzer to fund a £600,000 bid for the Chelsea centre forward. "We enquired about Osgood six weeks ago and now we hear he is on the transfer list we shall try again," Real President Santiago Bernabeu said. The news of the Spanish giants' interest prompted *The Sun's* Alex Montgomery to write: "Real see Osgood as a carbon copy of the legendary Alfredo di Stefano and their answer to Johann Cruyff's pulling power at Barcelona."

But 'El Os' was not to be. Nothing came of Real's enquiry and on January 10th, during a six-hour board meeting called to discuss the crisis, Chelsea accepted a £175,000 offer from Derby for Osgood with Rams striker Roger Davies moving in the opposite direction in part-exchange. Ossie, however, told Derby boss Dave Mackay he needed more time to consider the move and ultimately decided against it because he didn't fancy moving up north.

The speculation surrounding Osgood's likely destination continued on a daily basis. According to some reports both Arsenal and Spurs were now targeting the England striker, although Chelsea were said to be reluctant to sell their prize asset to either of their main London rivals. "The worry for Chelsea is that Osgood could do a Pied Piper and drag hundreds of his young fans with him to the new club," reported *The Sun*.

While the double transfer saga dragged on, Chelsea had to get on with playing football matches. An FA Cup third round home tie against west London neighbours QPR, now back in the First Division after a four-year gap, revived memories of the classic quarter-final in 1970 at Loftus Road. This time, though, there would be no Osgood hat-trick or words of praise for Hudson from the watching England manager as, to no one's surprise, neither player was recalled to the Chelsea team.

Under manager Gordon Jago, Rangers were already showing signs of the exciting, adventurous football which would soon see them eclipse Chelsea as both the most successful and most entertaining side in west London, if not the whole of the capital. Their team had a good balance between old pros, such as Terry Venables and former Arsenal Double-winning captain Frank McLintock, and promising younger players, including nippy winger Dave Thomas and future England captain Gerry Francis, a skilful and energetic midfielder. The jewel in Rangers' crown, though, was Stan Bowles, a hugely talented but occasionally wayward striker in the Osgood mould.

Without their own two most skilful performers, Chelsea looked pedestrian by comparison. Rangers had the best of the game at the Bridge and seemed set to go through when Francis stepped up to take a second-half penalty. However Phillips, enjoying one of his best games for Chelsea, dived to his right to save the spot-kick and earn the Blues a replay. Not that it mattered much, as a Stan Bowles goal at Loftus Road settled the tie. Chelsea, with David Webb playing the entire match at centre forward, never remotely looked like equalising in a match Rangers dominated throughout.

"Absurdly, it was as though Wellington had carried Waterloo by the margin of a single musket ball," one newspaper informed its readers. "The rout was that complete, that absolute in Rangers' command of all football's most exciting skills."

For Chelsea supporters this Cup defeat against local neighbours, who until recently had been very much in the shadow of the Blues, was hard to stomach. To many fans, the absence of Hudson and Osgood from the line-up at Loftus Road felt like a needless self-inflicted injury. Why weren't the two stars in the team? Were they going to be sold? Couldn't the rift with Sexton be resolved? These questions were asked over and over again in the pubs around the ground and on the tube ride home. Perhaps sensing that the fans were becoming increasingly disgruntled, the club addressed the crisis head on in the home programme against Derby, four days after the defeat at Loftus Road.

After admitting that recent events had caused "anxiety and great distress" and pointing out that a good relationship between manager and playing staff was "an absolute prerequisite for the ultimate success and happiness of a club", the programme notes spoke of "a clash of personalities [which] has existed at Stamford Bridge between manager and one or two players."

For the benefit of any fans who hadn't been avidly following the news on the back pages, the unnamed writer (probably programme editor Albert Sewell) went on to name the two players. "Peter Osgood and Alan Hudson were insistent that the situation could not be improved, [so] the board felt they had no alternative but to make them available for transfer." Nor, it seemed, was there much chance of the two stars returning to the team. "We would like to thank them for their services to Chelsea," the programme notes continued, "and wish them success in the future." In the key part of the final paragraph, the column asserted that "the long-term future and good of our club must come above all other considerations. We have backed manager Dave Sexton 100 per cent in this matter . . ."

In fact, the programme article was already out of date. Alan Hudson had been sold to Stoke for £240,000, a new British transfer record, earlier in the week and was due to make his debut for the Potters against Liverpool that afternoon. "Tony Waddington [Stoke's manager] believes in freedom of expression in training and playing, while Dave Sexton was a coach who had set ideas about training routines," was Hudson's parting shot. Still, as far as Osgood was concerned, the club's policy appeared unequivocal – there was simply no way back for the Shed idol.

There was some better news for Chelsea fans, though. Two days before the Derby game Dave Sexton brought Charlie Cooke back to the Bridge from Crystal Palace, where he had been stagnating in the reserves. The £17,000 fee represented great business for the Blues as they had sold the Scottish international to the Eagles for five times that amount just 16 months earlier. More importantly, Cooke's return gave the team and the crowd a much-needed lift at time when the Bridge was enveloped in a thick cloud of gloom and despondency. The player himself seemed to sense that the fans were fed up and, above all, craved the sort of thrilling spectacle they had become accustomed to in the glory years.

"All I ask of Chelsea fans is that they are patient with me and I shall try to turn on the old magic in return," Cookie promised.

Before the Derby match Cooke was given a rapturous reception by all three sides of the ground. And once the game kicked off he demonstrated that he had lost none of his dazzling array of skills during his brief sojourn in south London. However, despite Cooke's wizardry, Chelsea could only manage a 1–1 draw. Bill Garner scored the Blues' goal but, along with strike partner Chris Garland, struggled to make much of an impression against the Rams' England international central defensive pairing of Roy McFarland and Colin Todd. Garner and Garland were tireless workers for the cause but, without Osgood, it was apparent that the Blues' attack lacked the necessary craft, cunning and invention to break down the division's most organised defence. The supporters wanted Osgood back and so too did a section of the media.

"Chelsea without Peter Osgood are like Samson with a crewcut," wrote Peter Batt in *The Sun*. "His is not a capricious talent that can be blown away like froth from a pint of Guinness. Whatever the cost to Sexton's pride, however many dents are inflicted on the club's image, Ossie should be wooed back to Stamford Bridge."

The Blues, though, still seemed determined to sell Osgood. Stoke manager Tony Waddington put in a bid, hoping to reunite Ossie with his old mate Alan Hudson, only to be told that Chelsea were now solely interested in a player-exchange package. Ideally, any deal that could be struck would involve a striker arriving at the Bridge. The Blues were in dire need of another forward, especially now that Tommy Baldwin, after years of seeing his requests for a move rejected, had finally joined Osgood on the transfer list.

A week after the draw with Derby, Chelsea travelled to Stoke for the first ever First Division match to be played on a Sunday. The sell-out 32,000 crowd suggested that Sunday football had a bright future and, from a Stoke viewpoint, the day couldn't have gone better as the home side recorded a 1–0 win. Inevitably, Hudson played a blinder against his old club, winning the Man of the Match award and, more importantly, the late penalty which Geoff Hurst smashed past Phillips.

Two weeks later even a hard-fought 1–0 Chelsea win at home to Manchester City couldn't stem the constant crowd chants for Osgood. Yet, if the fans thought they could influence the manager, they were very much mistaken. "Dave was a man of set views and Ossie was a fiery character, so there was always going to be a clash," says John Dempsey. "There was no chance of the other players intervening or saying anything that could possibly change Dave's mind once he had decided what he was going to do."

The supporters could chant all they liked, but it wouldn't make any difference. In fact, if anything, a reconciliation between manager and player seemed even more unlikely than before, especially after Sexton fined both Osgood and Ian Hutchinson for taking an unauthorised holiday in Spain in February.

The last chance of a rapprochement came when Osgood approached Sexton with a view to signing a new contract. "I was training with the reserves," says Ossie, "but eventually I went to see Dave and said, 'Look, this is ridiculous. I'm due a new contract.' He said, 'Okay, let's resolve it. I'll see the chairman for you.' So about two weeks later I went to see the chairman and said, 'Mr Brian, about my new contract?' He looked blank and said, 'Nobody's mentioned it to me, son.' So that was me finished with Dave, and basically I was gone."

Meanwhile, on the pitch, there was little for the fans to cheer. At the beginning of the season the FA had introduced a new 'three up, three down' rule to all divisions of the Football League, and the effect of the change was to spread alarm throughout the lower half of the First Division. Chelsea were still in deep trouble and although two of the relegation places looked destined to be filled by Norwich and Manchester United, it was anybody's guess who would be joining them. For a long while, Birmingham had appeared certainties for the drop but a recent run of good form had given the Brummies cause for hope, producing worried expressions among fans up and down the country. Aside from Leeds and Liverpool at the top and the two stragglers at the bottom there was very little between the rest of the teams; incredibly, towards the end of February, only seven points separated third-placed Derby from Chelsea and West Ham, joint fourth bottom.

At the beginning of March the Blues' relegation worries intensified when they crashed 3–0 at Upton Park, Hammers midfielder Billy Bonds hitting all three goals. In the days after this latest reverse press reports appeared suggesting that Dave Sexton had left the club after refusing to take Osgood off the transfer list. Brian Mears moved swiftly to quash the rumours, following a meeting with his manager.

"Dave Sexton is still the manager of the club," he said. "There is no question of his being sacked or resigning. The club from the chairman right down to the players has 100 per cent confidence in Dave Sexton. At today's meeting we discussed the problems that have faced the club over the past few weeks. They were both personal and internal."

Soon afterwards, the long-running Osgood transfer epic, which was threatening to spill over into the summer thanks to the impending transfer deadline date, finally came to an end when Chelsea accepted Southampton's offer of £275,000 for the player. The fee was a record for both clubs and, added to the transfer fee received for Hudson, meant the Bridge coffers had swelled by over half a million since the New Year.

If Dave Sexton had hoped to use some of this money to bolster his squad for the relegation run-in he was to be disappointed. With the East Stand continuing to eat up money like a bank cash dispenser in reverse, no funds would be released for new signings.

"We were told the new East Stand was going to take a year to build, but that was a massive underestimate," Sexton complained later. "It wasn't only a drain on resources – it's like if you've got the builders in at your house and they're doing something in the kitchen for a month. It's inconvenient. We had this for over two years. It was like living on a building site."

Meanwhile, two consecutive home wins in March, against Burnley and Newcastle, eased the Blues' relegation fears a little. The headlines after the Burnley game, though, were all about the size of the crowd – a pitiful 8,171, Chelsea's lowest post-war league attendance at that point. The fans were back at the end of the month for the visit of Tommy Docherty's Manchester United but the Blues lost 3–1, a result which did little for United's survival prospects but put Chelsea back in trouble. Much would depend on the Blues' two Easter fixtures, away to Tottenham and Southampton.

For the vital game at White Hart Lane on Easter Saturday, Sexton surprised Chelsea's travelling support by selecting three young, virtually unknown players: left-back John Sparrow, making just his second first-team appearance; highly-rated midfielder Ray Wilkins, in his first start for the team; and, also making his first start, striker Kenny Swain, who had been spotted by Dario Gradi playing for non-league Wycombe Wanderers. It was a bold gamble by Sexton, but at half-time it appeared to have back-fired as the Blues trailed 1–0. The trapdoor to the Second Division was beckoning. In the second half, though, Chelsea hit back with goals from two unlikely sources, defenders Ron Harris and Micky Droy, to take the two points.

A 0–0 draw at The Dell two days later virtually guaranteed Chelsea's survival. All the same, a meagre total of one point from their last four games left the Blues just a single point clear of the unlucky team who claimed the third relegation place above Norwich and Manchester United, Peter Osgood's Southampton. A last day defeat at home to Stoke, the eighth time the Blues had lost in front of their fans that season, was particularly galling. Another poor crowd of just over 17,000 turned up to watch Alan Hudson dominate midfield again and score the only goal of the game.

Revitalised and rejuvenated, Huddy had been an inspiration since arriving in the Potteries and had helped guide his new club from the nether regions to fifth place in the league. Unlike Peter Osgood, who was now contemplating life in the Second Division, leaving Chelsea had worked out well for Hudson. Even now he has no regrets about the move.

"I wanted to go in a way because I wasn't enjoying my football," he says. "I was being messed about. I went to Stoke, they were fifth from bottom and finished up fifth from top. It was all down to me going there. Tony Waddington got the other players to give me the ball all the time; it was the complete opposite of what was happening at Chelsea.

"My relationship with Dave was strained by the end. I think his problem was that he was frustrated. He was a clean living chap: he never drank, he never smoked, he was football mad. He was a strong Catholic and wherever we went on tour or in Europe he would go to church. You can understand why he may not have liked what we were getting up to. After all, our mob were professional drinkers.

"It was just a life he didn't like and I think jealousy came into it. He would have liked to have been us, he wanted to be a player. I don't know what he was like as a player because his career had been finished by a knee injury. I think he looked at me, Ossie and Charlie Cooke and thought, 'If I had their ability there's no way I'd live my life like they do', and I think that was his hang up, I really do.

"He was alright as a coach but I trained with Don Howe at Arsenal and I found Don was far superior and he would have an occasional laugh with you, too. The problem with Dave was he should have been a coach. If he'd just have been a coach he would have been alright because then he wouldn't have had any say about the things the manager does at a club. The same with Don Howe; he took over as manager of Arsenal and he was useless so he went back to coaching where he was brilliant. Had Tommy Docherty stayed and Dave been the coach around that time I'm quite sure we'd have won the championship. I'm quite certain about that, because we'd have been able to say to Dave, 'Look, fuck off, just coach', but you can't say that to the manager."

Despite this critique of Sexton, Huddy believes the ultimate responsibility for the partial dismantling of the early seventies team lies with the directors. "Personally, I blame the board," he says. "The directors near enough demanded Sexton to sell Osgood and myself. I can just hear their reasoning: 'We'll get rid of Hudson because young Ray Wilkins can play like him. And Osgood, who needs a troublemaker?' But Peter Osgood has never been replaced since the day Chelsea sold him."

Whichever way you looked at it, the 1973/74 season had been little short of a disaster for Chelsea. Nearly relegated, out of both Cups in the first round, two star players sold and no replacements bought, an unfinished new stand haemorrhaging money, falling gate receipts, a growing hooligan minority among their fans . . . still, on the plus side, at least Chelsea had more to smile about than Manchester United.

The close season should have provided some relief, but it didn't. First David Webb, disillusioned by recent developments at the club, asked for a transfer and left for QPR for £100,000. Then Eddie McCreadie, whose career had been blighted by injury in the past three years, announced his retirement. Their departures represented two more broken links with the FA Cup-winning era. Finally, a petty dispute erupted over the players' daily expenses for the summer tour to Australia.

Clearly it would take more than the forced removal of a couple of so-called malcontents before peace and harmony reigned at the Bridge.

CHAPTER FIFTEEN
DOWN AND OUT

CHAPTER FIFTEEN
DOWN AND OUT

he best thing that could be said about the 1973/74 season from Chelsea's point of view was that it was over. Many supporters were dismayed by the departures of Alan Hudson and Peter Osgood, and to a lesser extent, that of David Webb, but the arrival of a new campaign encouraged fans to look forward rather than back. Whatever the problems of the previous months and whichever unknown difficulties lay ahead, the August sunshine brought a renewed sense of optimism to the Bridge.

The news that the East Stand, minus the much-vaunted heating system which had proved too costly to install, had finally been completed should have added to the prevailing positive mood. However, the champagne toast to the colossal structure had a distinctly bitter aftertaste. The final bill, around £2 million, was double the original estimate and left the club in severe debt. What's more, huge corners had been cut in the building of the stand, which in years to come would cost Chelsea many more millions to fix. "Everything about that design was appalling," complained Ken Bates in 1999. "If you could think of a mistake in a building contract, the Chelsea board made it. They even had an architect who had never worked on a stadium. Since I took over the club, we've spent about £10 million on it trying to make a silk purse out of a pig's ear."

The architectural critics, though, loved the stand. "As a shelter for a crowd of British football fans, the East Stand is in a class of its own," enthused *Design* magazine in March 1975. The huge structure was even the subject of a short film in the BBC2 series 'Building Sites', presented by the Chelsea-supporting architect Nigel Coates. "The stand is expectant even when it's empty," he noted. "The roof is just flying straight out – it's leaping out like a panther towards the pitch." Er, if you say so, Nige.

The East Stand opened to the paying public on 17th August 1974, with ticket prices ranging from 80p in the lower tier to £2.50 in the middle tier. Fittingly, the new look to the ground was matched by a couple of fresh faces in the Chelsea squad: David Hay, a dynamic midfielder who had just put in some eye-catching performances for Scotland at the 1974 World Cup signed from Celtic for a club record £225,000; and left-winger John Sissons, a veteran of West Ham's 1964 FA Cup-winning side, arrived from Norwich. Both made the starting line-up for the first match of the season, an undemanding looking fixture at home to newly-promoted Carlisle.

On a hot summer afternoon in front of 31,268 fans and the *Match of the Day* cameras Chelsea had the bulk of possession but still went down to a dismal 2–0 defeat against the Cumbrians. To say the result didn't augur well for the rest of the season was a massive understatement: Carlisle had been widely tipped to go straight back down and even their one famous name, Chris Balderstone, was much better known as a cricketer than a footballer.

The poor start continued. Just two wins in the first ten league games suggested another season of struggle was looming. At least Chelsea had Tottenham for company in the relegation zone while Arsenal, just four years after winning the Double, had begun the season in abysmal form and were rock bottom. The pressure was mounting on all three London managers: Sexton, Arsenal's Bertie Mee and Tottenham's recently installed boss Terry Neill.

On October 3rd, five days after a 1–0 home defeat by Wolves, Dave Sexton was sacked as Chelsea manager. Officially, Sexton had "resigned", but few fans doubted that the Chelsea board had done little, or nothing, to persuade him to stay.

"I could see my sacking coming," Sexton said. "I wasn't the most popular bloke – managers never are. It's the players who are the crowd's favourites, quite rightly. Still, it wasn't a very pleasant period for me. The fact I had four children and they could all read the papers wasn't nice."

The board's decision to let Sexton go represented a stunning volte-face. Only a few months previously the board had backed their manager in the bitter stand-off with the club's two biggest stars, now they were showing him the door too.

"The only thing I would criticise the board at Chelsea for is that they backed Dave Sexton over Peter Osgood and Alan Hudson but within a matter of months they sacked Dave," says Ron Harris. "I found that strange. I don't think he deserved to get the sack."

Other players, though, were not especially saddened by Sexton's departure. A common view was that while he had great qualities as a coach, Sexton was a remote and uncommunicative manager.

"His man-management of players let him down," argues Steve Kember. "Dave didn't talk to anybody. He rarely used to talk to you or encourage you. Dave took the training and on matchdays he said his bit. After the game, he shot off. Some say managers should be aloof. I think to get the best out of the players you've got to be with them and have them with you. You need to win their respect.

"Dave would have been fantastic in today's modern football where you just coach and don't worry about players' contracts or get involved in discussions with them," adds Ron Harris. "I think he found it a little bit difficult if it got a bit heated, with a contract dispute or something like that."

Even Sexton himself has admitted that he found some aspects of management trying. "I can't say I enjoyed looking after the contracts and being in charge of discipline, particularly," he said. "But it's something that needed to be done, so I did it. It's been suggested that I would have been happier having someone else taking care of it, but that would have undermined my authority."

Leaving Stamford Bridge for the last time, Sexton said: "Perhaps someone can come and do better things towards the success that Chelsea deserve." He would, though, be a hard act to follow. Whatever his faults as a man manager, the two major trophies he had won made him Chelsea's most successful boss ever – a title, incidentally, he would hold until the Vialli era 25 years later.

Sexton's transfer policy, too, had been generally good, especially in the early years. Nobody would quibble over the signings of the likes of David Webb, John Dempsey, Ian Hutchinson and Keith Weller, all of whom made huge contributions to Chelsea's cup triumphs. The later signings – Steve Kember, Chris Garland and Bill Garner, for example – were not quite in the same category, and certainly compared unfavourably with the players Sexton let go such as Osgood, Hudson and Weller.

The loss of these players left new boss Ron Suart, formerly Sexton's assistant, with a squad which was short on quality, particularly in attacking positions. Nonetheless, Suart got on with the job with the minimum of fuss, enjoying an obligatory honeymoon period of five games without defeat. Sticking faithfully to the old guard, Suart gave few opportunities to the young players who had featured at the end of the previous season. Even Ray Wilkins, who had already shown signs of the visionary passing that was to become his forte at Chelsea, had to settle at first for a place on the bench at best.

The limitations of this policy were soon shown up, however. In a League Cup replay against bogey side Stoke the Blues were hammered 6–2, the briefly recalled Tommy Baldwin scoring his last ever goal for Chelsea. The following month Chelsea lost 5–0 at Newcastle, all the goals coming in the second half as the pace of Gallowgate hero Malcolm 'Supermac' Macdonald left Micky Droy and John Dempsey floundering.

Wilkins eventually returned to the side in December, when his intelligent distribution of the ball helped Chelsea put together their best run of the season, three wins and a draw in four games. Even the Blues' most ardent fans, though, had to admit the team wasn't playing well, while the press reports were scathing. The 2–0 home win over Luton on December 7th, Chelsea's first victory for two months, was described by one journalist as "a game which would find a place on any short-list of the worst First Division matches", while another complained of "a bumbling apology of a match".

There was no shortage of entertainment, however, when a group of Chelsea players, led by goalkeeper John Phillips, put on a spoof pantomime at the club's Christmas dinner a couple of weeks later. "I was the compere and firstly I introduced the chairman, Brian Mears, as a clown and his brother as an alcoholic," recalled Phillips. "Next I introduced Martin Spencer, the club's financial advisor, holding an abacus. Then I made apologies for Viscount Chelsea who was away at a horse race and Richard Attenborough who was absent filming.

"We proceeded to re-enact a meeting, bringing up all the things that had been said during the course of the season including the night we got beat at Stoke when one of the directors remarked to us that we were grossly overpaid. Players are not known for their intellect, but they do have good memories. We also sacked the manager, Ron Suart, who was sitting in the audience at the time. Everyone who was involved with the club was there, from the cleaning lady upwards.

"At the end of the evening the chairman approached and we expected the inevitable, 'You five are on the transfer list. We don't want you. You're bad influences.' Instead, he praised our performance, saying it showed the spirit of the club. And I thought, 'You stupid prat, can't you see what we're saying? Can't you see it?'

"I had sleepless nights at the time because I was so worried about the state the club was in. I'd go in the next day and see the manager and I'd tell him what was wrong with the club. He'd invariably agree with me and tell me what he was going to do. So you'd wait for changes to come and you'd wait and wait. They never came. The club had cancer, which needed cutting out. There should have been an enormous purge. Chelsea didn't have any money to replace what it had, so invariably they got the youngsters in. In a good side you can bring in two or three young players from time to time. But to bring them in *en bloc* – it was never going to come off."

In fact, Suart remained reluctant to play the younger players until after a fourth round FA Cup defeat at home to fellow strugglers Birmingham. John Sparrow, Ian Britton and striker Steve Finnieston all had extended runs along with Wilkins and, for a short while at least, results improved.

The mini-revival, though, came to an end with a 2–1 defeat at home to champions-to-be Derby and, the following week, Chelsea suffered a humiliating 7–1 reverse at Wolves. With their confidence in tatters, the Blues' form continued to dip worryingly. Once again, relegation was on the agenda. In a late bid to avoid the drop Eddie McCreadie, who had been working as Ron Suart's coach, was promoted to team manager with Suart taking on a new role as general manager.

"I want to give the fans something to believe in," McCreadie announced, "they have suffered enough. My policy will be to bring a great team back to a great club."

With three games to go Chelsea were just outside the drop-zone, a point clear of Tottenham and Luton who both had a game in hand. Carlisle, as expected, were adrift at the bottom and all but relegated. Arsenal, though, had recovered after their dreadful start and were safely ensconced in mid-table. The Blues' next fixture, away to Spurs, would go a long way to determining their fate.

In the build up to one of the most important games in Chelsea's history, Eddie McCreadie made the bold decision of selecting 18-year-old Ray Wilkins as his new skipper. "Wilkins will be the future captain of the club," he told reporters. "He captained the reserves on several occasions when I played with them and he is a very capable young man. He has the quality of leadership and is well respected."

Youthful faces also figured prominently in McCreadie's team selection for the game at White Hart Lane. Out went Hollins, Kember and Houseman from the team which had lost 1–0 at home to Manchester City the previous week and in came Sparrow, Britton and, making his Chelsea debut, striker Teddy Maybank. A future *Blind Date* contestant, the blond-haired Maybank had impressed McCreadie in a friendly match against Fulham earlier in the week, but it seemed a reckless gamble to thrust the untried youngster into what promised to be a vicious north London relegation dog fight.

More than 51,000 fans packed into White Hart Lane for what was, in effect, a cup final. Defeat for either side would mean almost certain relegation, while a draw would only please Luton. On the other hand, a win would all but guarantee survival and send the losers spiralling towards the Second Division. No wonder, then, that the supporters of both teams were fired up. The raucous, passionate atmosphere didn't take long to spill over into outright violence as fans decked out in the fashions of the day – multi-coloured tank tops, flared trousers and tottering platform soles – traded blows on the pitch before the game.

Unsurprisingly, the match itself was a tense, nervous, tetchy affair. Chelsea held out until ten minutes into the second half, when Steve Perryman scored for Spurs from close range. Tottenham's frizzy-haired Scottish international striker Alfie Conn added a second 15 mins from time to leave Chelsea staring into the abyss.

The Blues' only hope was to win their final two matches at home to Sheffield United and Everton – a tall order considering that both teams were in the top six and chasing European qualification. In the event, Chelsea could only manage two 1–1 draws and finished second bottom, above Carlisle but behind Luton on goal average. Tottenham survived by a single point – so, as it turned out, a draw at White Hart Lane would have saved Chelsea and relegated Spurs instead.

"I honestly believe if the senior players had played at Tottenham we'd have got a result and stayed up," says Steve Kember, pointing the finger at McCreadie's team selection for the game at White Hart Lane. Certainly, the decision to pitch the totally inexperienced Maybank into a game of such magnitude was hard to fathom. On the other hand, the senior players had performed disappointingly for much of the season. Was there any reason to suppose they would have played any better at Spurs? In any case, there were many more factors behind Chelsea's relegation than a misguided team selection for one match. As the old saying goes, the league table doesn't lie. And, at the end of the 1974/75 season, the table suggested that Chelsea's squad simply wasn't good enough to stay in the First Division. Like Kember and John Phillips, John Dempsey argues that too many young players were rushed into the first team too quickly.

"The young players who came into the side, with the exception of Ray Wilkins who was clearly a fine player, perhaps weren't quite ready for first team football," says Dempsey, "especially as they were being thrown into a relegation battle. Having said that, players like Ian Britton, Steve Finnieston, Tommy Langley and Ray Lewington all did very well under Eddie McCreadie later. It was asking a lot of them, though, to replace the likes of Osgood, Webb and Hudson."

An alternative view came from former manager Tommy Docherty. "Chelsea have kept their senior players too long," he said, shortly after the Blues' relegation was confirmed. "I feel sorry for Eddie McCreadie who will be tagged as the manager who took them down. He only had three games and Ron Suart should have stayed."

If relegation was a shock, it wasn't a complete surprise. Chelsea had been steadily declining for some years. David Webb dates the turnaround in fortunes as early as September 1971 when Dave Sexton sold Keith Weller. Other players point to the morale-sapping loss of two major cup ties in a week in the spring of 1972 as another important turning point. "It all went a bit sour after that," says Dempsey. Clearly, the acrimonious departures of Peter Osgood and Alan Hudson, allied to the lack of funds made available for adequate replacements, were also key moments in Chelsea's subsequent slump.

Maybe, too, the wild lifestyle of some of the players caught up with them a little towards the end. "It was probably part of our downfall that there were too many good nights out," admits Charlie Cooke. "It all seemed kind of innocent at the time, but in the long term it wasn't all that good for the team. We had a couple of moments when we were disciplined for our stupidity, but it was never anything to do with the actual playing of the game. I think there was a kind of self-destruction in there, too. Probably we were all a bit immature. It was hard for Dave Sexton – we were just a bunch of maniacs."

Faced with the prospect of managing the Blues in only their second post-war season outside the top flight, Eddie McCreadie made all the right noises. "Next season? No sweat. We will win the Second Division," he confidently asserted. Despite the mounting financial problems afflicting the club, chairman Brian Mears remained equally bullish: "Any cuts in our playing staff will not be for economy reasons," he insisted. "It is a question of streamlining the staff. If we are successful, the crowds will support us."

As part of the 'streamlining' process five senior players were placed on the transfer list: Steve Kember, Peter Houseman, Tommy Baldwin, Bill Garner and John Hollins, while Peter Bonetti was amongst those given a 'free'. All except Garner would leave in the summer, although Bonetti, to the delight of the Chelsea crowd, soon returned from exile in the North American Soccer League, joining five other grizzled survivors of the 1970 squad: Ron Harris, John Dempsey, Charlie Cooke, Ian Hutchinson and Marvin Hinton.

But the glory days were well and truly over. Despite a brief resurgence under Eddie McCreadie, who led his young side to promotion in 1977, the Blues would spend seven of the next nine seasons in the Second Division. The period became known among fans as 'the gloomy years' as financial crises, hooliganism, falling crowds, a crumbling stadium and poor football culminating in a close flirtation with relegation to the Third Division combined to make Stamford Bridge one of the English game's more depressing venues. "The whole place became a rancid meat pie crawling with maggots," is Alan Hudson's succinct summary.

The joyous nights in Manchester and Athens soon seemed to belong to a different, far-off era, even while Peter Bonetti, Ron Harris and Peter Osgood, returning to the Bridge for a brief and unproductive spell in the late seventies, played out the last games of their long Chelsea careers. And the more the team struggled in the years that followed, the more fans and the media would hark back to the great days of Ossie, Huddy, Cookie, Hutch and the Cat.

It wasn't simply that those players had enjoyed genuine success while the next two decades only produced a couple of Second Division titles and two triumphs in the much-mocked Full Members Cup. Just as important as the silverware was the team's compelling mix of qualities at the height of its powers. Flair, inspiration and flamboyance in attack, allied to grit, determination and steely resilience in defence. Add to that a commitment to entertainment, which frequently produced football of a breathtaking standard and a healthy dollop of unpredictability which left the fans never quite knowing what to expect.

Above all, the Blues side of the early seventies had more characters than a Russian novel. Virtually all the players stood out from the crowd for one reason or another. Peter Osgood, for his all-round showmanship, spectacular goals and equally spectacular hairstyle. Ian Hutchinson for his gangling gait, incredible long throws and lion-heated bravery. David Webb for his never-say-die spirit and extraordinary ability to turn his hand (or foot) to any role, from goalkeeper to striker. Ron Harris, arguably the most feared hardman of his time and an inspirational captain. Charlie Cooke and Alan Hudson, two of the most naturally gifted players ever to pull on a Chelsea shirt . . . the list goes on.

Idolised and revered by their thousands of fans, these Chelsea boys truly were the kings of the King's Road. And, even if the Abramovich era turns the Stamford Bridge trophy cabinet into an Aladdin's Cave of silverware, their legend will live on.

CHAPTER SIXTEEN

THEN AND NOW

CHAPTER SIXTEEN
THEN AND NOW

Shortly before the end of the 2003/04 season Ron Harris was at Stamford Bridge one evening being interviewed for Chelsea TV. As he was about to leave the studio he was asked to wait in an office. Somebody wanted to see him.

"Within a couple of minutes Roman Abramovich came in with an interpreter, one of the Chelsea directors," recalls Ron. "I don't really know why he wanted to see me but I sat there talking to him for about an hour and half."

The meeting between the two men, embodiments of Chelsea past and present, was mentioned in the matchday programme for the dreary 0–0 draw with Middlesbrough. "It was fascinating, I believe, for everyone there," wrote editor Neil Barnett, before adding rather coyly, "this is not the place to discuss what was said." Now, for the first time, the details of what was discussed at that meeting can be revealed – and Barnett is right, what was said was fascinating, especially in light of later developments at the Bridge.

"First of all, he asked me what I thought Chelsea's best current team was," says Ron. "So I told him the eleven players I'd pick. Then, he asked me quite a lot about what it was like in my day. He was interested to hear that we never chopped and changed the side like recent Chelsea managers have with the rotation system. I've never been a great believer in that – if I'm playing alongside somebody I want to get to know their good habits and bad habits, and vice versa. So I didn't agree with Claudio Ranieri's tinkering around because if you keep the same team you build up partnerships and understanding.

"I asked Abramovich who he thought was the best team in the Premiership was and he told me 'Arsenal'. I said to him if you name their side which started off at Chelsea when they drew 1–1 in the Champions League only Keown, Reyes, Parlour and Clichy of their recognised first-team squad didn't play. So they've got about 18 players to pick from; under Ranieri, Chelsea had 30-odd. He did say to me that he thought the squad was too heavy and would be coming down to 24 players. I was very impressed with the fellow. He gave me the impression that Chelsea supporters can only look ahead to good times."

Roman Abramovich is a busy man. His time is precious. It seems unlikely, then, that he chatted to Ron Harris for 90 minutes simply for want of something better to do. The nature of the conversation suggests that the Chelsea owner was picking Harris' brains – and why not? As the club's all-time record appearance maker, Chopper has a wealth of experience and his passion for the club is unquestionable – as he says, "I'd run through a brick wall for Chelsea."

In recent years a popular pre-match pastime in the pubs around Stamford Bridge has been 'guess the team'. Anyone who got eight or nine starters right was doing well; getting ten or all eleven correct was virtually impossible, thanks to Claudio Ranieri's frequently baffling 'pick 'n' mix' team selection policy.

Under the Chelsea regime of Jose Mourinho things promise to be different. More like the Ron Harris era, in fact. *Senhor* Mourinho may be interested to learn that when the Blues won the FA Cup in 1970 they used just 13 players during their eight match campaign and one of those, Marvin Hinton, only featured as a substitute in the Final. Just another six players were used in the season as a whole and of those only Alan Birchenall played more than ten games. Success was based on a settled team and a small, close-knit squad.

Winning the FA Cup for the first time in the club's history was a momentous event for the Blues and their fans in 1970. That unforgettable night at Old Trafford when Ron Harris raised the Cup remains embedded in the club's psyche, as even Roman Abramovich may appreciate after his long chat with Chopper. However, times have changed, and doing well in the domestic cup competitions is no longer a top priority for leading English clubs. Chelsea's main focus, like that of Arsenal and Manchester United, is now on the Champions League and the Premiership.

Of those two competitions the Premiership has become something of a Holy Grail for the Blues. As most supporters know only too well, Chelsea

have won just one league title in a hundred years of trying. Even that
sole triumph was 50 years ago, as opposition fans like to remind the
Bridge faithful every so often: "Black-and-white, you won the league in
black-and-white," they sing. Very droll.

The sixties and seventies teams failed to emulate Ted Drake's title-winning
heroes of 1955, although Tommy Docherty's 'Diamonds' came close in
1965. Otherwise, despite consistently finishing in the top six, the Blues
of Ossie, Chopper and co never really mounted a genuine championship
challenge. Considering the talent that the squad possessed, the lack of a
convincing title tilt requires some explaining.

"On our day, when we played the football we were capable of, we could
beat anybody," says Peter Osgood, keen to downplay any suggestion that
the seventies side's failure to lift the title somehow invalidates its claim
to greatness. "Leeds were one of the best club sides in the world at the
time and we could match them or anybody else on our day, but we just
weren't consistent enough. Sometimes we didn't gee ourselves up for the
lesser games and that's why we never won the title. But, in full flow,
we were an awesome side's. We were bloody good. We had guys who
could kill teams off, sometimes in just a ten-minute spell."

And Ron Harris adds: "With the players we had we were always a
better bet to win the Cup than the league. We had players who the
bigger the game, the bigger the crowd, the better they would perform.
Players like Ossie, Huddy and Charlie Cooke. When it came to grinding
results out week in week out they weren't consistent at doing it. Oz,
who was 'the King', he played like he felt. If he went up to Manchester
United, for example, and felt like doing the business he would do it. On
the other hand, sometimes in the dressing room he'd go, 'Huh, I don't
think I'll be running around much today' and he wouldn't. He wouldn't
run from here to there, but he'd be honest enough to tell you. Then,
come the big games in Europe or in the cup, he put in some brilliant
performances. I always think he was like a matador in the bullring, the
way he responded to the occasion and the crowd."

John Dempsey agrees with Harris that Chelsea's main failing was that, unlike
the Leeds or Arsenal sides of the time, the team struggled to notch up those
ugly 1–0 wins which often form the bedrock of a championship-winning
season.

"I think the reason why we never won the championship is that we
weren't the sort of team that could grind out the narrow wins when we

weren't playing well," he says. "We could win 5–0 one week and then lose 1–0 or 2–1 the next. I think the problem was that we relied so much on our flair players – Ossie, Alan Hudson and Charlie Cooke – that when their form dipped a bit we couldn't dig out results like some other teams."

Typically, Alan Birchenall has a slightly leftfield take on the topic. "I know it sounds daft but we had too many brilliant players to win the championship," he says. "We had great individuals who could always win us a cup because on our day, when we were really flowing, we were as good as any team, not just in this country but in the world. We could be that good. But you couldn't guarantee it. Great teams win championships, but we had great players rather than a great team. Individually, yes, we had some fantastic players, but it wasn't like when we played crap we got a result, a scrappy 1–0. When we played crap we got beat. We had to play well to win, but when we did play well it was unbelievable at times."

That makes the Chelsea team of the early 1970s sound a little like the under-achieving galacticos who have flattered to deceive at Real Madrid in the last couple of years. Certainly, the Blues were unpredictable, but in many ways that only added to the excitement of following Chelsea at the time. One week the fans would be shaking their heads as the team played a collective stinker; the next they'd be roaring their heads off after a five-star virtuoso display. Yet for skipper Ron Harris, this tendency towards inconsistency should not overshadow the underlying cohesion, balance and unity which underpinned the Blues' success.

"We had a terrific blend," he says. "We had three fantastic players – Ossie, Huddy, Charlie Cooke – and then we had a back four who could hold their own. We needed them as much as they needed us. We had Johnny Hollins who was a fantastic competitor, and a fitness freak who could run from the first minute to the last minute. Peter Houseman did a good job. He got a lot of criticism, but I don't think people realised the work he did for the team. Peter Bonetti was second to none in goal. I think we were one of the sides that never feared going up to Leeds and getting rolled over because of their reputation. We had fellows who could look after themselves."

Assessing the team's strengths, Peter Osgood also points to a complex mix of qualities, a delicate interweaving of skill, steel and stamina running through the Blues' core. "Centre forwards who score goals and win you games will always get more accolades than the defence or the goalkeeper and the midfield," he points out. "But I always think that the back four and the midfield makes a team. If you've got a solid back four and a great keeper, which we did have, and geniuses like Charlie Cooke and Alan Hudson in midfield – and I mean real geniuses, because they were world-class and they would be worth fortunes today – as well as a work-house like Johnny Hollins, then you've got the makings of a side. Even today, I wouldn't swap any of our midfield for any current midfielder, even Patrick Vieira or Frank Lampard."

Of course, Ossie is bound to be biased towards his old team-mates. Yet that doesn't necessarily mean his judgement is wrong, and he is certainly not alone in ranking the stars of the 1970s above those of a more recent vintage. In 2002 the official *Chelsea Magazine* sparked many a pub debate along the King's Road by asking former Blues from the 1950s onwards to nominate their greatest ever Chelsea players. Peter Osgood himself topped the list, while Alan Hudson won the midfielder's section, Peter Bonetti was voted the club's greatest goalkeeper and Ron Harris ran Marcel Desailly very close for the title of best ever defender. Charlie Cooke, Eddie McCreadie and John Hollins also figured in the top 15, cementing the seventies side dominance of the poll.

This wasn't a case of old mates voting for each other, either. Ron Harris, for example, got the nod from both Roy Bentley, the Blues' legendary title-winning skipper *and* Frank Sinclair, goalscoring hero in the 1998 League Cup Final. Alan Hudson, meanwhile, was nominated by his old youth team coach Frank Blunstone *and* Brazilian-born defender Emerson Thome, who clearly didn't neglect his Chelsea history studies during his brief spell at the club in 2000. The two Peters, Osgood and Bonetti, also received votes from across the generations.

Who knows, in years to come a similar list may well feature more players from the Abramovich era and rather fewer from the glory days of the 1970s. Certainly the likes of John Terry, Frank Lampard and Eidur Gudjohnsen have made a few footsteps along the ladder which ends at the pedestal marked 'Chelsea legend'. But to be certain of a place on the plinth they'll need some medals to show for their efforts. All Chelsea fans will be hoping that those honours include the one that eluded Tommy Docherty and Dave Sexton's men in the sixties and seventies – the league title. Win the Premiership, and the Blues of today will rightly join Ossie, Huddy, Chopper and the Cat in the all-time Chelsea pantheon.

WHERE ARE THEY NOW?

WHERE ARE THEY NOW?

TOMMY BALDWIN
Still living on the King's Road around the corner from his local, The Imperial, the Sponge does PR work for the Wildwood golf course in Surrey.

ALAN BIRCHENALL
Leicester City's 'club co-ordinator', the Birch is an ebullient figure behind the mic at the Walkers Stadium on matchdays. In 2000 he brought out his hugely entertaining autobiography, *Bring Back the Birch* (Polar Publishing) and in 2002 he was awarded the MBE for his fund-raising efforts for various charities. "It came out on the local radio," he says, "'Alan Birchenall has got an MBE in the New Year's Honours List . . . , but not for football.' I thought, 'You bastards!'"

PETER BONETTI
After a brief period as a guest house owner on the Isle of Mull, the Cat became a goalkeeping coach, working for Chelsea, England and Fulham among others. He is currently employed by Manchester City.

JOHN BOYLE
Briefly manager of Dartford, Boylers now works as a security guard at the Office of Science and Technology in central London. Given the choice, he says he'd rather watch cricket than football these days.

CHARLIE COOKE
After finishing his career in the USA, Charlie set up a coaching school for children in 1985 and has remained in the States ever since. He lives in Cincinnati.

JOHN DEMPSEY
John managed Dundalk, Maidenhead and Egham after ending his career in the States, where he was voted 'Defender of the Year' in 1979 (ahead of Franz Beckenbauer). He now works as a special needs career in a resource centre in Edgware.

TOMMY DOCHERTY

Following his departure from the Bridge, the Doc managed Rotherham, QPR, Aston Villa, Hull, Scotland, Manchester United, Derby, Preston and Wolves as well as a number of clubs abroad. His ready wit is now employed on the after-dinner circuit.

RON HARRIS

After a spell as manager of Aldershot, Ron branched out into the leisure business owning a golf course and, more recently, a fishing complex. Like Tommy Docherty, Chopper is now a regular after-dinner speaker.

MARVIN HINTON

Marv finally hung up his boots at the age of 46, while with Eastbourne United. Eight years later a car accident left him with two plates in his right leg. Now retired from his job in the removal business, he still watches Chelsea regularly and travelled with his family to Rome for the Blues' stunning 4–0 win over Lazio in October 2003.

JOHN HOLLINS

Chelsea boss for two and a half years until he was sacked by Ken Bates in March 1987, Holly has also managed Swansea, Rochdale and Stockport.

PETER HOUSEMAN

Tragically, Peter and his wife, Sally, and two friends were killed in a car crash in March 1977 two years after the left-winger had moved from Chelsea to Oxford United. A specially arranged game between Chelsea's 1977 side and the 1970 vintage raised nearly £20,000 for the couples' children.

ALAN HUDSON

Huddy spent two months in intensive care after being hit by a car in 1997 and has spent years recovering from his injuries. "I've got to be delighted with how I am now," he says. A year before the accident he brought out his autobiography, *The Working Man's Ballet* (Robson Books), and in August 2004 he produced a new book about Chelsea in the Abramovich era called *The Tinker and the Talisman*.

IAN HUTCHINSON

Hutch died in September 2002 after a long illness. "He was my best mate," says Peter Osgood. "We called each other 'bruv' and that's what we were like, brothers. I wouldn't have swapped him for anyone in the league." The club marked his death with a minute's silence before the Blues' UEFA Cup home game with Viking FK.

STEVE KEMBER

After ending his career back where he started at Crystal Palace, Steve has managed the Eagles on four occasions, most notably saving them from relegation to the Second Division on the last day of the 2000/01 season.

EDDIE McCREADIE

Chelsea manager from 1975 to 1977, Eddie resigned as Blues boss after the board refused to provide him with a club car and a written contract. He emigrated to the USA and now lives in Memphis.

PETER OSGOOD

Like his old mate Chopper, Ossie is much in demand as an after-dinner speaker. In 2002 he brought out his autobiography *Ossie: King of Stamford Bridge* (Mainstream Publishing) to excellent reviews. In the same year he was controversially sacked by then chairman Ken Bates from his position as a matchday host at the Bridge, and now performs a similar role for his local club, Southampton.

DAVE SEXTON

Dave managed QPR, Manchester United and Coventry after leaving the Bridge and, well into his seventies, is still working in the game at the highest level, checking out England's future opponents for Sven Goran Eriksson.

BOBBY TAMBLING

Chelsea's all-time leading scorer, Bobby now lives in Ireland. In 2004 he made an emotional return to the Bridge for a series of events held in his honour.

DAVID WEBB

Manager of Chelsea for three months in 1993, Webby has been boss of Southend on no fewer than four occasions. He has also managed Torquay, Bournemouth and Brentford.

KEITH WELLER

Another player to finish his career in America, Keith now lives in Seattle. Sadly, in 2002 he was diagnosed as suffering from leomysarcoma, a rare form of cancer. An appeal fund set up by his former Leicester team-mate Alan Birchenall has allowed Keith to seek alternative medical treatment for his condition at a clinic in Mexico.

THE
STATS
1961-1975

LEAGUE DIVISION 1

		P	W	D	L	F	A	W	D	L	F	A	Pts
1.	Ipswich Town	42	17	2	2	58	28	7	6	8	35	39	56
2.	Burnley	42	14	4	3	57	26	7	7	7	44	41	53
3.	Tottenham Hotspur	42	14	4	3	59	34	7	6	8	29	35	52
4.	Everton	42	17	2	2	64	21	3	9	9	24	33	51
5.	Sheffield United	42	13	5	3	37	23	6	4	11	24	46	47
6.	Sheffield Wednesday	42	14	4	3	47	23	6	2	13	25	35	46
7.	Aston Villa	42	13	5	3	45	20	5	3	13	20	36	44
8.	West Ham United	42	11	6	4	49	37	6	4	11	27	45	44
9.	West Bromwich Albion	42	10	7	4	50	23	5	6	10	33	44	43
10.	Arsenal	42	9	6	6	39	31	7	5	9	32	41	43
11.	Bolton Wanderers	42	11	7	3	35	22	5	3	13	27	44	42
12.	Manchester City	42	11	3	7	46	38	6	4	11	32	43	41
13.	Blackpool	42	10	4	7	41	30	5	7	9	29	45	41
14.	Leicester City	42	12	2	7	38	27	5	4	12	34	44	40
15.	Manchester United	42	10	3	8	44	31	5	6	10	28	44	39
16.	Blackburn Rovers	42	10	6	5	33	22	4	5	12	17	36	39
17.	Birmingham City	42	9	6	6	37	35	5	4	12	28	46	38
18.	Wolverhampton Wanderers	42	8	7	6	38	34	5	3	13	35	52	36
19.	Nottingham Forest	42	12	4	5	39	23	1	6	14	24	56	36
20.	Fulham	42	8	3	10	38	34	5	4	12	28	40	33
21.	Cardiff City	42	6	9	6	30	33	3	5	13	20	48	32
22.	**CHELSEA**	42	7	7	7	34	29	2	3	16	29	65	28

Top league scorer: Bobby Tambling, 20 goals
Average home attendance: 27,013

FA CUP
(3) Liverpool (A)   L3–4

LEAGUE CUP
Did not enter

LEAGUE DIVISION 2

		P	W	D	L	F	A	W	D	L	F	A	Pts
1.	Stoke City	42	15	3	3	49	20	5	10	6	24	30	53
2.	**CHELSEA**	42	15	3	3	54	16	9	1	11	27	26	52
3.	Sunderland	42	14	5	2	46	13	6	7	8	38	42	52
4.	Middlesbrough	42	12	4	5	48	35	8	5	8	38	50	49
5.	Leeds United	42	15	2	4	55	19	4	8	9	24	34	48
6.	Huddersfield Town	42	11	6	4	34	21	6	8	7	29	29	48
7.	Newcastle United	42	11	8	2	48	23	7	3	11	31	36	47
8.	Bury	42	11	6	4	28	20	7	5	9	23	27	47
9.	Scunthorpe United	42	12	7	2	35	18	4	5	12	22	41	44
10.	Cardiff City	42	12	5	4	50	29	6	2	13	33	44	43
11.	Southampton	42	15	3	3	52	23	2	5	14	20	44	42
12.	Plymouth Argyle	42	13	4	4	48	24	2	8	11	28	49	42
13.	Norwich City	42	11	6	4	53	33	6	2	13	27	46	42
14.	Rotherham United	42	11	3	7	34	30	6	3	12	33	44	40
15.	Swansea Town	42	13	5	3	33	17	2	4	15	18	55	39
16.	Preston North End	42	11	6	4	43	30	2	5	14	16	44	37
17.	Portsmouth	42	9	5	7	33	27	4	6	11	30	52	37
18.	Derby County	42	10	5	6	40	29	2	7	12	21	43	36
19.	Grimsby Town	42	8	6	7	34	26	3	7	11	21	40	35
20.	Charlton Athletic	42	8	4	9	33	28	5	1	15	29	56	31
21.	Walsall	42	7	7	7	33	37	4	2	15	20	52	31
22.	Luton Town	42	10	4	7	45	40	1	3	17	16	44	29

Top league scorer: Bobby Tambling, 35 goals
Average home attendance: 29,356

FA CUP

(3) Tranmere (A)	D2–2
(Rep) Tranmere (H)	W3–1
(4) Charlton (A)	W3–0
(5) Manchester United (A)	L1–2

LEAGUE CUP

Did not enter

SEASON 1963–64

LEAGUE DIVISION 1

		P	W	D	L	F	A	W	D	L	F	A	Pts
1.	Liverpool	42	16	0	5	60	18	10	5	6	32	27	57
2.	Manchester United	42	15	3	3	54	19	8	4	9	36	43	53
3.	Everton	42	14	4	3	53	26	7	6	8	31	38	52
4.	Tottenham Hotspur	42	13	3	5	54	31	9	4	8	43	50	51
5.	**CHELSEA**	42	12	3	6	36	24	8	7	6	36	32	50
6.	Sheffield Wednesday	42	15	3	3	50	24	4	8	9	34	43	49
7.	Blackburn Rovers	42	10	4	7	44	28	8	6	7	45	37	46
8.	Arsenal	42	10	7	4	56	37	7	4	10	34	45	45
9.	Burnley	42	14	3	4	46	23	3	7	11	25	44	44
10.	West Bromwich Albion	42	9	6	6	43	35	7	5	9	27	26	43
11.	Leicester City	42	9	4	8	33	27	7	7	7	28	31	43
12.	Sheffield United	42	10	6	5	35	22	6	5	10	26	42	43
13.	Nottingham Forest	42	9	5	7	34	24	7	4	10	30	44	41
14.	West Ham United	42	8	7	6	45	38	6	5	10	24	36	40
15.	Fulham	42	11	8	2	45	23	2	5	14	13	42	39
16.	Wolverhampton Wanderers	42	6	9	6	36	34	6	6	9	34	46	39
17.	Stoke City	42	9	6	6	49	33	5	4	12	28	45	38
18.	Blackpool	42	8	6	7	26	29	5	3	13	26	44	35
19.	Aston Villa	42	8	6	7	35	29	3	6	12	27	42	34
20.	Birmingham City	42	7	7	7	33	32	4	0	17	21	60	29
21.	Bolton Wanderers	42	6	5	10	30	35	4	3	14	18	45	28
22.	Ipswich Town	42	9	3	9	38	45	0	4	17	18	76	25

Top league scorer: Bobby Tambling, 27 goals
Average home attendance: 31,347

FA CUP

(3) Tottenham (A)	D1–1	
(Rep) Tottenham (H)	W2–0	
(4) Huddersfield (H)	L1–2	

LEAGUE CUP

(2) Swindon (A)	L0–3

LEAGUE DIVISION 1

		P	W	D	L	F	A	W	D	L	F	A	Pts
1.	Manchester United	42	16	4	1	52	13	10	5	6	37	26	61
2.	Leeds United	42	16	3	2	53	23	10	6	5	30	29	61
3.	**CHELSEA**	42	15	2	4	48	19	9	6	6	41	35	56
4.	Everton	42	9	10	2	37	22	8	5	8	32	38	49
5.	Nottingham Forest	42	10	7	4	45	33	7	6	8	26	34	47
6.	Tottenham Hotspur	42	18	3	0	65	20	1	4	16	22	51	45
7.	Liverpool	42	12	5	4	42	33	5	5	11	25	40	44
8.	Sheffield Wednesday	42	13	5	3	37	15	3	6	12	20	40	43
9.	West Ham United	42	14	2	5	48	25	5	2	14	34	46	42
10.	Blackburn Rovers	42	12	2	7	46	33	4	8	9	37	46	42
11.	Stoke City	42	11	4	6	40	27	5	6	10	27	39	42
12.	Burnley	42	9	9	3	39	26	7	1	13	31	44	42
13.	Arsenal	42	11	5	5	42	31	6	2	13	27	44	41
14.	West Bromwich Albion	42	10	5	6	45	25	3	8	10	25	40	39
15.	Sunderland	42	12	6	3	45	26	2	3	16	19	48	37
16.	Aston Villa	42	14	1	6	36	24	2	4	15	21	58	37
17.	Blackpool	42	9	7	5	41	28	3	4	14	26	50	35
18.	Leicester City	42	9	6	6	43	36	2	7	12	26	49	35
19.	Sheffield United	42	7	5	9	30	29	5	6	10	20	35	35
20.	Fulham	42	10	5	6	44	32	1	7	13	16	46	34
21.	Wolverhampton Wanderers	42	8	2	11	33	36	5	2	14	26	53	30
22.	Birmingham City	42	6	8	7	36	40	2	3	16	28	56	27

Top league scorer: Barry Bridges, 20 goals
Average home attendance: 37,054

FA CUP

(3) Northampton (H)	W4–1
(4) West Ham (A)	W1–0
(5) Tottenham (H)	W1–0
(6) Peterborough (H)	W5–1
(S/F) Liverpool (Villa Park)	L0–2

LEAGUE CUP

(2) Birmingham City (A)	W3–0
(3) Notts Co. (H)	W4–0
(4) Swansea (H)	W3–2
(5) Workington (A)	D2–2
(Rep) Workington (H)	W2–0
(S/F-1) Aston Villa (A)	W3–2
(S/F-2) Aston Villa (H)	D1–1
(Final-1) Leicester City (H)	W3–2
(Final-2) Leicester City (A)	D0–0

LEAGUE CUP FINAL TEAM

Ist leg: *Bonetti, Hinton, Harris R, Hollins, Young, Boyle, Murray, Graham, McCreadie, Venables, Tambling* Scorers: *Tambling, Venables (pen), McCreadie*

2nd leg: *Bonetti, Hinton, McCreadie, Harris R, Mortimore, Upton, Murray, Boyle, Bridges, Venables, Tambling*

LEAGUE DIVISION 1

		P	W	D	L	F	A	W	D	L	F	A	Pts
1.	Liverpool	42	17	2	2	52	15	9	7	5	27	19	61
2.	Leeds United	42	14	4	3	49	15	9	5	7	30	23	55
3.	Burnley	42	15	3	3	45	20	9	4	8	34	27	55
4.	Manchester United	42	12	8	1	50	20	6	7	8	34	39	51
5.	**CHELSEA**	42	11	4	6	30	21	11	3	7	35	32	51
6.	West Bromwich Albion	42	11	6	4	58	34	8	6	7	33	35	50
7.	Leicester City	42	12	4	5	40	28	9	3	9	40	37	49
8.	Tottenham Hotspur	42	11	6	4	55	37	5	6	10	20	29	44
9.	Sheffield United	42	11	6	4	37	25	5	5	11	19	34	43
10.	Stoke City	42	12	6	3	42	22	3	6	12	23	42	42
11.	Everton	42	12	6	3	39	19	3	5	13	17	43	41
12.	West Ham United	42	12	5	4	46	33	3	4	14	24	50	39
13.	Arsenal	42	8	8	5	36	31	4	5	12	26	44	37
14.	Blackpool	42	9	5	7	36	29	5	4	12	19	36	37
15.	Newcastle United	42	10	5	6	26	20	4	4	13	24	43	37
16.	Nottingham Forest	42	11	3	7	32	26	3	5	13	25	46	36
17.	Sheffield Wednesday	42	11	6	4	35	18	3	2	16	21	48	36
18.	Aston Villa	42	10	3	8	39	34	5	3	13	30	46	36
19.	Sunderland	42	13	2	6	36	28	1	6	14	15	44	36
20.	Fulham	42	9	4	8	34	37	5	3	13	33	48	35
21.	Northampton Town	42	8	6	7	31	32	2	7	12	24	60	33
22.	Blackburn Rovers	42	6	1	14	30	36	2	3	16	27	52	20

Top league scorer: George Graham, 17 goals
Average home attendance: 31,344

FA CUP

(3)	Liverpool (A)	W2-1
(4)	Leeds (H)	W1-0
(5)	Shrewsbury (H)	W3-2
(6)	Hull City (H)	D2-2
(Rep)	Hull City (A)	W3-1
(S/F)	Sheffield Weds. (Villa Park)	L0-2

LEAGUE CUP

Did not enter

FAIRS CUP

(1)	AS Roma (Italy) (H)	W 4-1
	AS Roma (A)	D0-0
(2)	Wiener SC (Aust) (A)	L0-1
	Wiener SC (Aust) (H)	W2-0
(3)	AC Milan (Italy) (A)	L1-2
	AC Milan (H)	W2-1
(Play-off)	AC Milan (A)	D1-1 (Won on toss of coin)
(4)	Munich 1860 (A)	D2-2
	Munich 1860 (H)	W1-0
(S/F)	Barcelona (A)	L0-2
	Barcelona (H)	W2-0
(Play-off)	Barcelona (A)	L0-5

LEAGUE DIVISION 1

		P	W	D	L	F	A	W	D	L	F	A	Pts
1.	Manchester United	42	17	4	0	51	13	7	8	6	33	32	60
2.	Nottingham Forest	42	16	4	1	41	13	7	6	8	23	28	56
3.	Tottenham Hotspur	42	15	3	3	44	21	9	5	7	27	27	56
4.	Leeds United	42	15	4	2	41	17	7	7	7	21	25	55
5.	Liverpool	42	12	7	2	36	17	7	6	8	28	30	51
6.	Everton	42	11	4	6	39	22	8	6	7	26	24	48
7.	Arsenal	42	11	6	4	32	20	5	8	8	26	27	46
8.	Leicester City	42	12	4	5	47	28	6	4	11	31	43	44
9.	**CHELSEA**	42	7	9	5	33	29	8	5	8	34	33	44
10.	Sheffield United	42	11	5	5	34	22	5	5	11	18	37	42
11.	Sheffield Wednesday	42	9	7	5	39	19	5	6	10	17	28	41
12.	Stoke City	42	11	5	5	40	21	6	2	13	23	37	41
13.	West Bromwich Albion	42	11	1	9	40	28	5	6	10	37	45	39
14.	Burnley	42	11	4	6	43	28	4	5	12	23	48	39
15.	Manchester City	42	8	9	4	27	25	4	6	11	16	27	39
16.	West Ham United	42	8	6	7	40	31	6	2	13	40	53	36
17.	Sunderland	42	12	3	6	39	26	2	5	14	19	46	36
18.	Fulham	42	8	7	6	49	34	3	5	13	22	49	34
19.	Southampton	42	10	3	8	49	41	4	3	14	25	51	34
20.	Newcastle United	42	9	5	7	24	27	3	4	14	15	54	33
21.	Aston Villa	42	7	5	9	30	33	4	2	15	24	52	29
22.	Blackpool	42	1	5	15	18	36	5	4	12	23	40	21

Top League scorer: Bobby Tambling, 21 goals
Average home attendance: 35,525
Player of the Year: Peter Bonetti (Inaugural season)

FA CUP

(3) Huddersfield (A)	W2–1
(4) Brighton (A)	D1–1
(Rep) Brighton (H)	W4–0
(5) Sheffield Utd (H)	W2–0
(6) Sheffield Weds. (H)	W1–0
(S/F) Leeds (Villa Park)	W1–0
(Final) Tottenham (Wembley)	L1–2

FA Cup Final team: Bonetti, Harris A, McCreadie, Hollins, Hinton, Harris R, Cooke, Baldwin, Hateley, Tambling, Boyle
Scorer: Tambling

LEAGUE CUP

(2) Charlton (H)	W5–2
(3) Blackpool (A)	D1–1
(Rep) Blackpool (H)	L1–3

LEAGUE DIVISION 1

		P	W	D	L	F	A	W	D	L	F	A	Pts
1.	Manchester City	42	17	2	2	52	16	9	4	8	34	27	58
2.	Manchester United	42	15	2	4	49	21	9	6	6	40	34	56
3.	Liverpool	42	17	2	2	51	17	5	9	7	20	23	55
4.	Leeds United	42	17	3	1	49	14	5	6	10	22	27	53
5.	Everton	42	18	1	2	43	13	5	5	11	24	27	52
6.	**CHELSEA**	**42**	**11**	**7**	**3**	**34**	**25**	**7**	**5**	**9**	**28**	**43**	**48**
7.	Tottenham Hotspur	42	11	7	3	44	20	8	2	11	26	39	47
8.	West Bromwich Albion	42	12	4	5	45	25	5	8	8	30	37	46
9.	Arsenal	42	12	6	3	37	23	5	4	12	23	33	44
10.	Newcastle United	42	12	7	2	38	20	1	8	12	16	47	41
11.	Nottingham Forest	42	11	6	4	34	22	3	5	13	18	42	39
12.	West Ham United	42	8	5	8	43	30	6	5	10	30	39	38
13.	Leicester City	42	7	7	7	37	34	6	5	10	27	35	38
14.	Burnley	42	12	7	2	38	16	2	3	16	26	55	38
15.	Sunderland	42	8	7	6	28	28	5	4	12	23	33	37
16.	Southampton	42	9	8	4	37	31	4	3	14	29	52	37
17.	Wolverhampton Wanderers	42	10	4	7	45	36	4	4	13	21	39	36
18.	Stoke City	42	10	3	8	30	29	4	4	13	20	44	35
19.	Sheffield Wednesday	42	6	10	5	32	24	5	2	14	19	39	34
20.	Coventry City	42	8	5	8	32	32	1	10	10	19	39	33
21.	Sheffield United	42	7	4	10	25	31	4	6	11	24	39	32
22.	Fulham	42	6	4	11	27	41	4	3	14	29	57	27

Top league scorer: Peter Osgood, 16 goals
Average home attendance: 35,746
Player of the Year: Charlie Cooke

FA CUP

(3) Ipswich (H)	W3–0
(4) Norwich (H)	W1–0
(5) Sheffield Weds (A)	D2–2
(Rep) Sheffield Weds (H)	W2–0
(6) Birmingham (A)	L0–1

LEAGUE CUP

(2) Middlesbrough (A)	L1–2

LEAGUE DIVISION 1

		P	W	D	L	F	A	W	D	L	F	A	Pts
1.	Leeds United	42	18	3	0	41	9	9	10	2	25	17	67
2.	Liverpool	42	16	4	1	36	10	9	7	5	27	14	61
3.	Everton	42	14	5	2	43	10	7	10	4	34	26	57
4.	Arsenal	42	12	6	3	31	12	10	6	5	25	15	56
5.	**CHELSEA**	42	11	7	3	40	24	9	3	9	33	29	50
6.	Tottenham Hotspur	42	10	8	3	39	22	4	9	8	22	29	45
7.	Southampton	42	13	5	3	41	21	3	8	10	16	27	45
8.	West Ham United	42	10	8	3	47	22	3	10	8	19	28	44
9.	Newcastle United	42	12	7	2	40	20	3	7	11	21	35	44
10.	West Bromwich Albion	42	11	7	3	43	26	5	4	12	21	41	43
11.	Manchester United	42	13	5	3	38	18	2	7	12	19	35	42
12.	Ipswich Town	42	10	4	7	32	26	5	7	9	27	34	41
13.	Manchester City	42	13	6	2	49	20	2	4	15	15	35	40
14.	Burnley	42	11	6	4	36	25	4	3	14	19	57	39
15.	Sheffield Wednesday	42	7	9	5	27	26	3	7	11	14	28	36
16.	Wolverhampton Wanderers	42	7	10	4	26	22	3	5	13	15	36	35
17.	Sunderland	42	10	6	5	28	18	1	6	14	15	49	34
18.	Nottingham Forest	42	6	6	9	17	22	4	7	10	28	35	33
19.	Stoke City	42	9	7	5	24	24	0	8	13	16	39	33
20.	Coventry City	42	8	6	7	32	22	2	5	14	14	42	31
21.	Leicester City	42	8	8	5	27	24	1	4	16	12	44	30
22.	QPR	42	4	7	10	20	33	0	3	18	19	62	18

Top league scorer: Bobby Tambling, 17 goals
Average home attendance: 37,595
Player of the Year: David Webb

FA CUP

(3) Carlisle (H)	W2–0
(4) Preston (A)	D0–0
(Rep) Preston (H)	2–0 (Abandoned – floodlight failure)
(Rep) Preston (H)	W2–1
(5) Stoke (H)	W3–2
(6) WBA (H)	L1–2

LEAGUE CUP

(2) Birmingham City (A)	W1–0
(3) Derby Co. (H)	D0–0
(Rep) Derby Co. (A)	L1–3

FAIRS CUP

(1) Morton (Scot) (H)	W5–0
Morton (A)	W4–3
(2) DWS Amsterdam (Holl) (A)	D0–0
DWS Amsterdam (H)	D0–0 (Lost on toss of coin)

LEAGUE DIVISION 1

		P	W	D	L	F	A	W	D	L	F	A	Pts
1.	Everton	42	17	3	1	46	19	12	5	4	26	15	66
2.	Leeds United	42	15	4	2	50	19	6	11	4	34	30	57
3.	**CHELSEA**	**42**	**13**	**7**	**1**	**36**	**18**	**8**	**6**	**7**	**34**	**32**	**55**
4.	Derby County	42	15	3	3	45	14	7	6	8	19	23	53
5.	Liverpool	42	10	7	4	34	20	10	4	7	31	22	51
6.	Coventry City	42	9	6	6	35	28	10	5	6	23	20	49
7.	Newcastle United	42	14	2	5	42	16	3	11	7	15	19	47
8.	Manchester United	42	8	9	4	37	27	6	8	7	29	34	45
9.	Stoke City	42	10	7	4	31	23	5	8	8	25	29	45
10.	Manchester City	42	8	6	7	25	22	8	5	8	30	26	43
11.	Tottenham Hotspur	42	11	2	8	27	21	6	7	8	27	34	43
12.	Arsenal	42	7	10	4	29	23	5	8	8	22	26	42
13.	Wolverhampton Wanderers	42	8	8	5	30	23	4	8	9	25	34	40
14.	Burnley	42	7	7	7	33	29	5	8	8	23	32	39
15.	Nottingham Forest	42	8	9	4	28	28	2	9	10	22	43	38
16.	West Bromwich Albion	42	10	6	5	39	25	4	3	14	19	41	37
17.	West Ham United	42	8	8	5	28	21	4	4	13	23	39	36
18.	Ipswich Town	42	9	5	7	23	20	1	6	14	17	43	31
19.	Southampton	42	3	12	6	24	27	3	5	13	22	40	29
20.	Crystal Palace	42	5	5	10	20	36	1	9	11	14	32	27
21.	Sunderland	42	4	11	6	17	24	2	3	16	13	44	26
22.	Sheffield Wednesday	42	6	5	10	23	27	2	4	15	17	44	25

Top league scorer: Peter Osgood, 23 goals
Average home attendance: 40,341
Player of the Year: John Hollins

FA CUP

(3) Birmingham (H)	W3–0
(4) Burnley (H)	D2–2
(Rep) Burnley (A)	W3–1 (aet)
(5) Crystal Palace (A)	W4–1
(6) QPR (A)	W4–2
(S/F) Watford (White Hart Lane)	W5–1
(Final) Leeds (Wembley)	D2–2 (aet)
(Rep) Leeds (Old Trafford)	W2–1 (aet)

FA Cup Final Team (both games)
Bonetti, Webb, McCreadie, Hollins, Dempsey, Harris R, Baldwin, Cooke, Osgood, Hutchinaon, Houseman Sub: Hinton
Scorers (Wembley): Houseman, Hutchinson
Scorers (Old Trafford): Osgood, Webb

LEAGUE CUP

(2) Coventry City (A)	W1–0
(3) Leeds (A)	D1–1
(Rep) Leeds (H)	W2–0
(4) Carlisle (A)	L0–1

LEAGUE DIVISION 1

		P	W	D	L	F	A	W	D	L	F	A	Pts
1.	Arsenal	42	18	3	0	41	6	11	4	6	30	23	65
2.	Leeds United	42	16	2	3	40	12	11	8	2	32	18	64
3.	Tottenham Hotspur	42	11	5	5	33	19	8	9	4	21	14	52
4.	Wolverhampton Wanderers	42	13	3	5	33	22	9	5	7	31	32	52
5.	Liverpool	42	11	10	0	30	10	6	7	8	12	14	51
6.	**CHELSEA**	**42**	**12**	**6**	**3**	**34**	**21**	**6**	**9**	**6**	**18**	**21**	**51**
7.	Southampton	42	12	5	4	35	15	5	7	9	21	29	46
8.	Manchester United	42	9	6	6	29	24	7	5	9	36	42	43
9.	Derby County	42	9	5	7	32	26	7	5	9	24	28	42
10.	Coventry City	42	12	4	5	24	12	4	6	11	13	26	42
11.	Manchester City	42	7	9	5	30	22	5	8	8	17	20	41
12.	Newcastle United	42	9	9	3	27	16	5	4	12	17	30	41
13.	Stoke City	42	10	7	4	28	11	2	6	13	16	37	37
14.	Everton	42	10	7	4	32	16	2	6	13	22	44	37
15.	Huddersfield Town	42	7	8	6	19	16	4	6	11	21	33	36
16.	Nottingham Forest	42	9	4	8	29	26	5	4	12	13	35	36
17.	West Bromwich Albion	42	9	8	4	34	25	1	7	13	24	50	35
18.	Crystal Palace	42	9	5	7	24	24	3	6	12	15	33	35
19.	Ipswich Town	42	9	4	8	28	22	3	6	12	14	26	34
20.	West Ham United	42	6	8	7	28	30	4	6	11	19	30	34
21.	Burnley	42	4	8	9	20	31	3	5	13	9	32	27
22.	Blackpool	42	3	9	9	22	31	1	6	14	12	35	23

Top league scorer: Keith Weller, 13 goals
Average home attendance: 39,546
Player of the Year: John Hollins

FA CUP

(3) Crystal Palace (A)	D2–2	
(Rep) Crystal Palace (H)	W2–0	
(4) Manchester City (H)	Lo–3	

LEAGUE CUP

(2) Sheffield Weds. (A)	D1–1	
(Rep) Sheffield Weds. (H)	W2–1	
(3) Middlesbrough (H)	W3–2	
(4) Manchester Utd (A)	L1–2	

EUROPEAN CUP WINNERS CUP

(1) Aris Salonika (Greece) (A)	D1–1	
Aris Salonika (H)	W5–1	
(2) CSKA Sofia (Bulg) (A)	W1–0	
CSKA Sofia (H)	W1–0	
(3) Bruges (Belg) (A)	Lo–2	
Bruges (H)	W4–0 (aet)	
(S/F) Manchester City (H)	W1–0	
Manchester City (A)	W1–0	
(Final) Real Madrid (Athens)	D1–1 (aet)	
(Rep) Real Madrid (Athens)	W2–1	

European Cup Winners Final; Cup Team
Bonetti, Boyle, Harris R, Hollins, Dempsey, Webb, Weller, Hudson, Osgood, Cooke, Houseman
Subs: Mulligan, Baldwin
Scorer: Osgood

Replay: As above, except Baldwin for Hollins. Sub: Smethurst
Scorers: Dempsey, Osgood

LEAGUE DIVISION 1

		P	W	D	L	F	A	W	D	L	F	A	Pts
1.	Derby County	42	16	4	1	43	10	8	6	7	26	28	58
2.	Leeds United	42	17	4	0	54	10	7	5	9	19	21	57
3.	Liverpool	42	17	3	1	48	16	7	6	8	16	14	57
4.	Manchester City	42	16	3	2	48	15	7	8	6	29	30	57
5.	Arsenal	42	15	2	4	36	13	7	6	8	22	27	52
6.	Tottenham Hotspur	42	16	3	2	45	13	3	10	8	18	29	51
7.	**CHELSEA**	**42**	**12**	**7**	**2**	**41**	**20**	**6**	**5**	**10**	**17**	**29**	**48**
8.	Manchester United	42	13	4	4	39	26	6	8	7	30	35	48
9.	Wolverhampton Wanderers	42	10	7	4	35	23	8	4	9	30	34	47
10.	Sheffield United	42	10	8	3	39	26	7	4	10	22	34	46
11.	Newcastle United	42	10	6	5	30	18	5	5	11	19	34	41
12.	Leicester City	42	9	6	6	18	11	4	7	10	23	35	39
13.	Ipswich Town	42	7	8	6	19	19	4	8	9	20	34	38
14.	West Ham United	42	10	6	5	31	19	2	6	13	16	32	36
15.	Everton	42	8	9	4	28	17	1	9	11	9	31	36
16.	West Bromwich Albion	42	6	7	8	22	23	6	4	11	20	31	35
17.	Stoke City	42	6	10	5	26	25	4	5	12	13	31	35
18.	Coventry City	42	7	10	4	27	23	2	5	14	17	44	33
19.	Southampton	42	8	5	8	31	28	4	2	15	21	52	31
20.	Crystal Palace	42	4	8	9	26	31	4	5	12	13	34	29
21.	Nottingham Forest	42	6	4	11	25	29	2	5	14	22	52	25
22.	Huddersfield Town	42	4	7	10	12	22	2	6	13	15	37	25

Top league scorer: Peter Osgood, 18 goals
Average home attendance: 38,787
Player of the Year: David Webb

FA CUP

(3) Blackpool (A)	W1–0
(4) Bolton (H)	W3–0
(5) Orient (A)	L2–3

LEAGUE CUP

(2) Plymouth (H)	W2–0
(3) Nottingham Forest (A)	D1–1
(Rep) Nottingham Forest (H)	W2–1
(4) Bolton (H)	D1–1
(Rep) Bolton (A)	W6–0
(5) Norwich (A)	W1–0
(S/F-1) Tottenham (H)	W3–2
(S/F-2) Tottenham (A)	D2–2
(Final) Stoke (Wembley)	L1–2

League Cup Final Team
Bonetti, Mulligan, Harris R, Hollins, Dempsey, Webb, Cooke, Garland, Osgood, Hudson, Houseman
Sub: Baldwin
Scorer: Osgood

EUROPEAN CUP WINNERS CUP

(1) Jeunesse Haut. (Lux) (A)	W8–0
Jeunesse Haut. (Lux) (H)	W13–0
(2) Atvidaberg (Swed) (A)	0–0
Atvidaberg (H)	1–1 (Lost on away goals)

LEAGUE DIVISION 1

		P	W	D	L	F	A	W	D	L	F	A	Pts
1.	Liverpool	42	17	3	1	45	19	8	7	6	27	23	60
2.	Arsenal	42	14	5	2	31	14	9	6	6	26	29	57
3.	Leeds United	42	15	4	2	45	13	6	7	8	26	32	53
4.	Ipswich Town	42	10	7	4	34	20	7	7	7	21	25	48
5.	Wolverhampton Wanderers	42	13	3	5	43	23	5	8	8	23	31	47
6.	West Ham United	42	12	5	4	45	25	5	7	9	22	28	46
7.	Derby County	42	15	3	3	43	18	4	5	12	13	36	46
8.	Tottenham Hotspur	42	10	5	6	33	23	6	8	7	25	25	45
9.	Newcastle United	42	12	6	3	35	19	4	7	10	25	32	45
10.	Birmingham City	42	11	7	3	39	22	4	5	12	14	32	42
11.	Manchester City	42	12	4	5	36	20	3	7	11	21	40	41
12.	**CHELSEA**	**42**	**9**	**6**	**6**	**30**	**22**	**4**	**8**	**9**	**19**	**29**	**40**
13.	Southampton	42	8	11	2	26	17	3	7	11	21	35	40
14.	Sheffield United	42	11	4	6	28	18	4	6	11	23	41	40
15.	Stoke City	42	11	8	2	38	17	3	2	16	23	39	38
16.	Leicester City	42	7	9	5	23	18	3	8	10	17	28	37
17.	Everton	42	9	5	7	27	21	4	6	11	14	28	37
18.	Manchester United	42	9	7	5	24	19	3	6	12	20	41	35
19.	Coventry City	42	9	5	7	27	24	4	4	13	13	31	37
20.	Norwich City	42	7	9	5	22	19	4	1	16	14	44	32
21.	Crystal Palace	42	7	7	7	25	21	2	5	14	16	37	30
22.	West Bromwich Albion	42	8	7	6	25	24	1	3	17	13	38	28

Top League scorer: Chris Garland and Peter Osgood, 11 goals
Average home attendance: 29,739
Player of the Year: Peter Osgood

FA CUP

(3) Brighton (A)	W2–0
(4) Ipswich (H)	W2–0
(5) Sheffield Weds. (A)	W2–1
(6) Arsenal (H)	D2–2
(Rep) Arsenal (A)	L1–2

LEAGUE CUP

(2) Southend (A)	W1–0
(3) Derby Co. (A)	D0–0
(Rep) Derby Co. (H)	W3–2
(4) Bury (A)	W1–0
(5) Notts Co. (H)	W3–1
(S/F-1) Norwich (H)	L0–2
(S/F-2) Norwich (A)	2–3 (Abandoned – fog)
(S/F-2) Norwich (A)	L0–1

LEAGUE DIVISION 1

		P	W	D	L	F	A	W	D	L	F	A	Pts
1.	Leeds United	42	12	8	1	38	18	12	6	3	28	13	62
2.	Liverpool	42	18	2	1	34	11	4	11	6	18	20	57
3.	Derby County	42	13	7	1	40	16	4	7	10	12	26	48
4.	Ipswich Town	42	10	7	4	38	21	8	4	9	29	37	47
5.	Stoke City	42	13	6	2	39	15	2	10	9	15	27	46
6.	Burnley	42	10	9	2	29	16	6	5	10	27	37	46
7.	Everton	42	12	7	2	29	14	4	5	12	21	34	44
8.	QPR	42	8	10	3	30	17	5	7	9	26	35	43
9.	Leicester City	42	10	7	4	35	17	3	9	9	16	24	42
10.	Arsenal	42	9	7	5	23	16	5	7	9	26	35	42
11.	Tottenham Hotspur	42	9	4	8	26	27	5	10	6	19	23	42
12.	Wolverhampton Wanderers	42	11	6	4	30	18	2	9	10	19	31	41
13.	Sheffield United	42	7	7	7	25	22	7	5	9	19	27	40
14.	Manchester City	42	10	7	4	25	17	4	5	12	14	29	40
15.	Newcastle United	42	9	6	6	28	21	4	6	11	21	27	38
16.	Coventry City	42	10	5	6	25	18	4	5	12	18	36	38
17.	**CHELSEA**	**42**	**9**	**4**	**8**	**36**	**29**	**3**	**9**	**9**	**20**	**31**	**37**
18.	West Ham United	42	7	7	7	36	32	4	8	9	19	28	37
19.	Birmingham City	42	10	7	4	30	21	2	6	13	22	43	37
20.	Southampton	42	8	10	3	30	20	3	4	14	17	48	36
21.	Manchester United	42	7	7	7	23	20	3	5	13	15	28	32
22.	Norwich City	42	6	9	6	25	27	1	6	14	12	35	29

Top league scorer: Tommy Baldwin, 9 goals
Average home attendance: 25,983
Player of the Year: Gary Locke

FA CUP

(3) QPR (H)	D0–0
(Rep) QPR (A)	L0–1

LEAGUE CUP

(2) Stoke (A)	L0–1

LEAGUE DIVISION 1

		P	W	D	L	F	A	W	D	L	F	A	Pts
1.	Derby County	42	14	4	3	41	18	7	7	7	26	31	53
2.	Liverpool	42	14	5	2	44	17	6	6	9	16	22	51
3.	Ipswich Town	42	17	2	2	47	14	6	3	12	19	30	51
4.	Everton	42	10	9	2	33	19	6	9	6	23	23	50
5.	Stoke City	42	12	7	2	40	18	5	8	8	24	30	49
6.	Sheffield United	42	12	7	2	35	20	6	6	9	23	31	49
7.	Middlesbrough	42	11	7	3	33	14	7	5	9	21	26	48
8.	Manchester City	42	16	3	2	40	15	2	7	12	14	39	46
9.	Leeds United	42	10	8	3	34	20	6	5	10	23	29	45
10.	Burnley	42	11	6	4	40	29	6	5	10	28	38	45
11.	QPR	42	10	4	7	25	17	6	6	9	29	37	42
12.	Wolverhampton Wanderers	42	12	5	4	43	21	2	6	13	14	33	39
13.	West Ham United	42	10	6	5	38	22	3	7	11	20	37	39
14.	Coventry City	42	8	9	4	31	27	4	6	11	20	35	39
15.	Newcastle United	42	12	4	5	39	23	3	5	13	20	49	39
16.	Arsenal	42	10	6	5	31	16	3	5	13	16	33	37
17.	Birmingham City	42	10	4	7	34	28	4	5	12	19	33	37
18.	Leicester City	42	8	7	6	25	17	4	5	12	21	43	36
19.	Tottenham Hotspur	42	8	4	9	29	27	5	4	12	23	36	34
20.	Luton Town	42	8	6	7	27	26	3	5	13	20	39	33
21.	**CHELSEA**	**42**	**4**	**9**	**8**	**22**	**31**	**5**	**6**	**10**	**20**	**41**	**33**
22.	Carlisle United	42	8	2	11	22	21	4	3	14	21	38	29

Top league scorer: Ian Hutchinson, 7 goals
Average home attendance: 27,396
Player of the Year: Charlie Cooke

FA CUP

(3) Sheffield Weds.	(H) W3–2
(4) Birmingham City (H)	L0–1

LEAGUE CUP

(2) Newport Co. (H)	W4–2
(3) Stoke City (H)	D2–2
(Rep) Stoke City (A)	D1–1
(Rep) Stoke City (A)	L2–6